Poet-Chief

James Nolan

Poet-
Chief

The Native American Poetics of
Walt Whitman and
Pablo Neruda

University of New Mexico Press

Albuquerque

Library of Congress Cataloging-in-Publication Data
Nolan, James, 1947–
Poet-chief : the Native American poetics of Walt Whitman
and Pablo Neruda / James Nolan. — 1st ed.
p.   cm.
Includes bibliographical references and index.
ISBN 0–8263–1484–8 (cl)
1. Whitman, Walt, 1819–1892—Aesthetics.   2. Literature, Comparative—
American and Chilean.   3. Literature, Comparative—Chilean and
American.   4. Neruda, Pablo, 1904–1973—Aesthetics.   5. Literature and
anthropology—America.   6. Oral tradition—America.   7. Indians in
literature.   8. Indians—Aesthetics.   9. Poetics.   I. Title.
PS3242.A34N64   1994
861—dc20   93–2379
CIP

In memory of another group of vanishing Americans,
the "disappeared" and disappearing poets and idealists
of my generation
cut down by Pinochet and by AIDS:

"I stop somewhere waiting for you."

Contents

Acknowledgments

I acknowledge with gratitude the Jacob K. Javits Fellowship in the Humanities, which provided the time both to research and write this book, and I am particularly indebted to Jack Schmitt for generously sending me the in-progress manuscripts of his translation of *Canto general*.

For the discerning readings, encouragement, and advice offered at various stages in completing this book, I am grateful to Gwen Kirkpatrick and Richard Bridgman of the Spanish and English departments, respectively, at the University of California, Berkeley, and to Marta Morello-Frosch and Michael Cowan of the Literature Board at the University of California, Santa Cruz.

I am especially thankful to Ulysses D'Aquila for his enthusiasm and for his careful readings of the manuscript, and to Duane Niatum, Philip Lamantia, and Francesca Taylor for inspiring and insightful conversations about American Indian cultures. I also thank my fellow New Orleans-expatriate West Coast cousins: Melissa Viator, for her patient introduction to the baffling miracles of computers; Melinda McGee, for her assistance at the Stanford University library; and Aimée and Randall Nelson, for their hospitality in Santa Cruz. Barbara Guth, my editor at the University of New Mexico Press, has remained thoughtful and supportive throughout the project, and I appreciate her efforts in helping this book to reach print.

Poet-Chief

Introduction
Ancestor-Continents:
American and *Americano*

The whole continent is
obsessed by the question:
what is it to be an American?
—*Octavio Paz*

Anthologies of North American poetry often begin on the sadly perfunctory note of including a selection of American Indian poems to preface a presentation of "the American tradition." Seldom is any attempt made to relate these translations of native oral literature to the poetry that follows. Those few pages are intended to represent, in its entirety, a dark, unknowable *before,* the millennia of "primitive" prehistory preceding the advance of European "civilization." In his popular anthology of the 1940s, Oscar Williams ventures further than most editors in explaining his introductory American Indian material: "I have included these translations because I am sure that the originals were important poetry and because it would be arrogant to call this book 'American' while omitting poetry that existed in America for long centuries before the short few hundred years of the white man's occupation." Williams insists, however, on the lack of any connection between native and later American forms, that "the peculiar handicap of American poetry has been that it has not had just this indigenous epic material as its foundation. Other major literatures can show organic growth from savage and barbaric folklore, warrior songs and ballads, common to a people long in their habitat."[1] What North American poetry lacks, Williams implies, is an aboriginal *Beowulf* to serve as a bridge between continental origins and the culture of European settlers, which is why anthologies such as his leap from the Cherokee to Anne Bradstreet in one disquieting page. This jarring jump prefigures another in North American poetry, the break between Walt Whitman and all North American poets who wrote before him. Certainly, the distance between Whitman's poetry and that of his predecessors and contemporaries is as great as the one between an American Indian incantation and the derivative iambics of colonial verse. These discontinuities, on the one hand, demonstrate the fragmentation of the North American poetic voice; yet, on the other hand, they point toward a uniquely American synthesis that occurs in the final pages of recent anthologies.

This curious synthesis is evident in the contributions of several contemporary poets who seem to represent a closing of this twice-broken circle. The influences of Whitman and of American Indian poetry seem to blend indetectably into each other, as if they sprang from an almost identical poetics. These three brief passages of contemporary North American poetry, for example, are from a non-Indian poet who has adopted an indigenous source of inspiration, a contemporary American Indian poet, and a disciple of Whitman:

> I'm a holy clown woman
> I'm a whirling dervish woman
> I'm a whirling foam woman
> I'm a playful light woman
> I'm a tidal pool woman
> I'm a fast speaking woman[2]

> I am a flame of four colors.
> I am a deer standing away in the dusk.
> I am a field of sumac and the pomme blanche.
> I am an angle of geese upon the winter sky.
> I am the hunger of the young wolf.
> I am the whole dream of these things.[3]

> While the infinite epic of each second in infinity
>   touched me—
> From the birth of the sun,

> From the birth of the earth,
> From the birth of all life
>   to the earliest men,
> From the discovery of fire,
> From the invention of tools. . . .[4]

The first excerpt is from Anne Waldman's *Fast Speaking Woman,* modeled after the chants of the Mazatec shaman María Sabina. The second is from *Angle of Geese and Other Poems* by the Kiowa writer N. Scott Momaday, whose poetry follows traditional forms native to his people. The final passage, by a poet who calls himself Antler, is from "Factory," a poem that Allen Ginsberg has praised as "a definitely powerful epic by one of Whitman's 'poets and orators to come.'" One could profitably compare lines from *Leaves of Grass* to the poetry of any of these three poets, studying Whitman's poetics, as he intended, in the works of his successors. Yet the difficulty in deciphering which, in fact, proceeded from Whitman and which from his aboriginal predecessors indicates perhaps a common source or model shaped by the singular nature of the American experience itself.

The perspective given this national experience while living outside of it can be invaluable, and the way I chose to explain the uniqueness of Whitman to a group of European readers served as the genesis of this book. Not far from the plazas in Barcelona where conquistadors paraded their menageries of American exotica —wild parrots, alligator skins, native peoples—before the unbelieving eyes of sixteenth-century Catalans, I encountered a similar confused disbelief among their descendants when I assigned "Song of Myself" from *The Norton Anthology of American Literature* to an American literature class at the Universidad Central. Before Whitman, the students' interest in North American poetry was less than enthusiastic, yet for those schooled in Wordsworth and Tennyson, at least nineteenth-century American poems sounded and functioned in a somewhat duller fashion as poetry in English should: metaphor, simile, scansion, rhyme scheme, irony, conceit, romanticism, and neoclassicism. Whitman's "barbaric yawp," on the other hand, constituted a genuinely foreign poetics for which these readers were unprepared. It was at this point that I first realized the significance of what at first seemed the unintegrated sampling of American

Indian poetry that introduces "the American tradition" in the *Norton Anthology*. We returned to the notes on repetition, apostrophe, parallel structure, compound elements, animism, tribalism, and shamanism that I had presented to explain the American Indian section, and used them to interpret the seemingly jumbled, egotistical redundancies of the Whitman poem. Compared to the British poetics with which the students were familiar, American Indian poetics provided a surprisingly accurate and useful map to the unchartered terrain of Whitman. As we continued in our reading of twentieth-century North American poetry, from Lindsay and Williams to Ginsberg and Snyder, the oral, tribal poetics of the American Indian, as filtered through a reading of Whitman, seemed to bear a much more definitive relevance to the American voice than any of the recognizably British elements. The two gaping discontinuities in anthologies of North American poetry seemed to coincide in the most unexpected manner: Whitman had not "invented" modern American poetry any more than Columbus had "discovered" the Americas. What was reinvented and rediscovered by Europeans was already here: "The friendly and flowing savage, who is he?" Whitman asks in "Song of Myself." "Is he waiting for civilization, or past it and mastering it?" (39:73).

Just as American Indian poetics served as a model for the poetry of Walt Whitman that baffled my Spanish students, Whitman's poetry has provided me with an approximate map for the equally mysterious mosaic of myths and chants in Pablo Neruda's *Canto general* (1950). Although *Canto general* did not appear in English translation until 1991, beginning in the 1960s Robert Bly had begun to convince North American readers that it "is the greatest long poem written on the American continent since *Leaves of Grass*. It is a geological, biological, and political history of South America. The book contains 340 poems arranged in fifteen sections. The fertility of imagination is astounding."[5] Bly's comparison of Neruda's major book with *Leaves of Grass* is not only complimentary but demonstrates his understanding of the parallel nature of these two monumental American works, which seem to define not only the American experience, from north to south, but the American voice in poetry as well. *Canto general* is the most Whitmanesque work of a poet whom many acknowledge as Latin America's greatest, one whose prolific and influential voice, throughout the various stages of its expression, is greatly indebted to *Leaves of Grass*. In James E. Miller's phrase, both books "create a myth for the mythless American,"[6] and might be considered examples of what he calls the "personal epic." Yet if the epic as a European form must, as Miller explains, be thoroughly revised within the context of the American experience in order to maintain its relevance as a term, one hopes for a more native basis of comparison for the works of the two poets who defined that experience quite deliberately *against* European forms. In establishing a comparative basis for the two greatest nativist poets of the Americas, one could do worse, I am convinced, than to return to that native oral tradition routinely included as merely a preliminary to the poetic canon.

For various historical reasons, Latin Americans have always been considerably more conscious of the native origins of their culture and literature than North Americans. Those several pages dedicated to American Indian literature in North American literary histories are matched twentyfold by similar considerations in accounts of Latin American literary histories.[7] The American Indian as a theme of Latin American writers is a subject perennially discussed, yet there have been few extended considerations of the American Indian poetics of a major Latin American poet. As the basis for a comparative study of Whitman and Neruda, the analogy of American Indian poetics provides a culturally relevant model that relates the North and Latin American experiences on a level most essentially common to them both. Chapters of this book focus on this model in regard to Whitman and Neruda's nativist perspectives and Indianist backgrounds, their oral poetics, shamanic personae, and, in the final chapter, their initiatory journeys in a comparative reading of "The Sleepers" and "Alturas de Macchu Picchu." I have resisted subjecting this uniquely American subject to the obfuscating orthodoxies of recent European theorists, whose terminology clanks like suits of armor to my ears, and so my approach has generated much of its own critical vocabulary. This eclectic perspective, based on borrowings from anthropology, ethnopoetics, linguistics, and comparative mythology, addresses the poetry of Whitman and Neruda in terms of the "maternal and paternal traditions," "illocution," "oral emphatics," "essential detail," "tribal grouping," the "shamanic voice," and the "vertical voyage,"—an interdisciplinary collage of terms adopted to align the sprawling mosaics of the poets' works with the American Indian models they so closely resemble.

Such a consideration of Whitman is long overdue, and provides a necessary key for understanding the various gaps and convergences in the development of the North American poetic voice. Only one major study, George Hutchinson's book on Whitman and shamanism, has moved in the promising direction of relating the poet's persona to a tribal role, yet it hesitates to take the next step, linking this shamanism to Whitman's oral poetics or more specifically to American Indian culture. Several of Neruda's readers, on the other hand, such as Emir Rodríguez Monegal and Manuel Durán, have commented on the poet's pronounced Indianist sympathies as a dominant aspect of *Canto general,* yet without relating this theme to the poetics and persona at work in the book. No writer has previously attempted an extended comparison of these two American poets, although both Fernando Alegría and Rodríguez Monegal have contributed perceptive commentaries on this subject in the contexts of other works. In short, various signs point to the parallel nature of these three paths—of Whitman, of Neruda, and of American Indian poetics—and this book attempts to mark the crossroads where they have converged into the broader common road long identified as the American poetic voice.

This study represents both a geographically horizontal as well as an anthropologically vertical exploration of a poetics that has come to be known, appropriately, as nativist or Americanist. I shall attempt to establish that this poetics is, in several aspects, also Native Americanist; that like many other American arts, our poetry—or an important strain of it—has entered the Americas through the front door of their original cultures, and has therefore been able to make itself at home on these continents. This book coincides with a growing recognition of the "mixed" roots of the hemispheric character and of the overlooked contributions of the American Indian, and adds the American poetic voice to the long list of cultural expressions with uniquely indigenous features. The ambitious scope of such a triangular comparison by analogy has necessarily limited its completeness, and this book is intended as much to suggest a direction in inter-American and cross-cultural readings as to establish its own particular interpretations. In sympathy with its subject, this effort is offered as a healing of the differences that divide us, already exaggerated by the obvious and unalterable contrasts imposed by history and geography. Looking toward the future, it is dedicated to breaking through certain partitions—often made only of Bible-tissue anthology pages—that separate the native, English- and Spanish-language poetic responses to the hemisphere.

What is this many-headed creature, American poetry? "Whatever it is," Louis Simpson writes, "it must have / A stomach that can digest / Rubber, coal, uranium, moon, poems."[8] These digestive powers essential to the continuity of an American poetics are called for in Whitman's "programme of chants," in which he first articulates, perhaps anticipating his own impact on Latin American poetry, the inclusive concept of "Americanos," one triumphantly carried forth by Neruda in *Canto general* with his invocation to an "amor americano" atop the ruins of Macchu Picchu. In "Starting from Paumanok," Whitman recognizes the magnetic unity and continuity that his poetry will represent for future generations of poets on these "ancestor-continents . . . north and south, with the isthmus between":

Successions of men, Americanos, a hundred millions,
One generation playing its part and passing on,
Another generation playing its part and passing on in its turn,
With faces turn'd sideways or backward toward me to listen,
With eyes retrospective towards me.

(2:16–17)

II

Yet a fundamental question persists: American or *Americano?* One of the practical considerations involved in beginning a comparative study of this kind carries us directly to the heart of what this one is about: What do we, the peoples of the New World, call ourselves? The act of naming is essential to the poetry of both Whitman and Neruda. Each attempted to name into unity the physical, cultural, and spiritual qualities of their continents. Originally named by explorers, conquistadors, and mapmakers, the Americas were finally christened by their poetry. A pivotal section of Neruda's *Canto general* is titled "América, no invoco tu nombre en vano." In *An American Primer,* Whitman also insists that "all greatness of any land, at any time, lies folded in its names" (AP:31). Yet as we leave behind the five-hundredth anniversary of the arrival of Columbus, the residents of the northern, central, and southern continents still cannot agree, in any of our languages, about what we are called. Names are also political. They convey complex cultural histories and the relationships of power, and in doing so, contain the seeds of national identities. The uncertainty of our names reflects, to a large degree, the unfinished natures of our hemispheric identities. Do we define ourselves in terms of our geographical locations, as in North, Central, and South American, or in terms of our European backgrounds, as in Latin and Anglo-Saxon American? Do we define ourselves in terms of our language groups, as in Anglo- and Hispanic-American, or in terms of our varying degrees of industrialization, as in First and Third World? And what, in our European-derived languages, do we call the original inhabitants of these continents, the descendants of the mythic Aztlan and Turtle Island?

The New World was born misnamed. Emerson considered it a shame "that broad America must wear the name of a thief. Amerigo Vespucci, the pickle-dealer at Seville . . . whose highest naval rank was a boatswain's mate in an expedition that never sailed, managed to supplant Columbus and baptize half the world with his own dishonest name."[9] "America," that name held sacred by both Whitman and Neruda, was arbitrarily assigned to the new territories by a cosmographer in Saint-Dié, France, Martin Waldseemüller, who reasoned in his *New Introduction to Cosmography* (1504) that "I do not know of any law that would forbid that the land discovered by Amerigo . . . be given his name; since Europe, Asia and Africa have feminine names, let Amerigo's land be called America."[10] Yet this chance designation forms the cornerstone of the mutual identity of three continents. Although there is still little agreement about the exact meanings of the words "America" and "American" in any of their variations, we must choose our identities from among the contradictory forms of the first name of a Florentine pickle-dealer. As Americans, we were named with the same offhanded disregard with which African slaves and the indigenous peoples were given their new names, and in the same manner in which the unpronounceable syllables of immigrant names have always been recast. In wrestling with the issue of slave names, black North American writers such as Toni Morrison have emphasized misnaming as an essential part of the national experience and, underlying it, the anguish of the unfinished American identity.

"American" and "Americano," for instance, possess contradictory and therefore often politically explosive meanings. The English word, particularly within the United States, is the ordinary adjective form used to refer to this country. The Spanish word, on the other hand, especially as used by South Americans, includes the entire American hemisphere. Whitman was the first writer from the United States to employ "Americano" in this broader sense, the same meaning consistently granted it by Neruda and most other Latin American writers. Latin Americans often notice a presumed cultural arrogance on the part of those from the north who use a word exclusively to identify themselves that is necessarily hemispheric. How can any hemispheric consciousness develop, they argue, if the United States has appropriated the very names on which it must be based? Although we fumble with terms such as *pan-* and *inter-American* to denote the hemispheric, the fact remains that if the United States is the only "America" and its citizens the only "Americans," its neighbors are relegated to what connotatively seems the subsidiary continents of Central and South America, as if they were branches of the main office or, as we too often hear, were located in "America's backyard."

The roots of this confusion extend deeply into the piecemeal, state-by-state history of the expansion of what is now the United States. It was not until after the Civil War, in fact, that the United States took the singular rather than the plural verb. During this history, no adjective developed in English for the United States of America, as a whole, other than "American." The United States of Mexico, on the other hand, became popularly known as Mexico and its people as Mexicans. Yet unique among the other American nations, the name of the United States contains no proper noun other than "America" because it represents the union of fifty proper nouns, the names of what Whitman grandly called, as an entity, "these States." If its citizens are not Americans, or rather, if we are not the only ones, what can we be called to establish hemispheric perspective? The choices are limited and vague. Unfortunately, there is no equivalent in English for the accurate but rarely used Spanish word *estadounidense*. One of the reasons that many Latin Americans routinely and often innocently refer to those from the United States as *gringos* and *yanquis* is that, despite the political origins of these terms, no other word in common usage has presented itself, other than the offensively inaccurate *Americano*. Several British writers have attempted to standardize a grammatically awkward solution to this problem, which is to employ the initials U.S. or U.S.A. as an adjective, as in U.S. literature or U.S.A. culture. On the whole, the most widely accepted and least ambiguous variation is the term *North American;* unfortunately, however, it evicts Canadians, Mexicans, and Caribbeans from their continent.

For this reason, it is understandable that Mexican writers such as Carlos Fuentes do not use the term *North American* to refer to the United States, but rather *Anglo-American*. As used by these writers, the parallel Spanish terms *Angloamericano* and *Hispanoamericano* offer clear and convenient geographical as well as cultural distinctions. Yet in English, in the context of the United States, this polarity loses its shape. Within this country, the terms *Anglo* and *Hispanic* are currently used to define ethnic origins: Hispanic-American literature might well refer to works by national authors of Hispanic background. In addition, Anglo-American usually suggests a certain degree of cultural borrowing between Britain and the United States. We speak of T. S. Eliot as an Anglo-American poet in much the same sense as we use the terms *Anglo-Irish* and *Anglo-Indian*. Furthermore, the terms *Hispanic-* or *Spanish-American* exclude the Brazilians and Francophone Caribbeans. A more inclusive term is needed to unify the cultures of the non-English-speaking Americas. In 1900, the Uruguayan José Enrique Rodó published an essay entitled *Ariel,* an address to the youth of the Americas, in which he defines the culture of the American countries of Mediterranean origin as *Latin,* as opposed to the more utilitarian culture of Anglo-Saxon North America. Following the final defeat of Spain during the Spanish-American War, together with the growing threat of the United States, this essay was greeted enthusiastically and became a rallying point for the unity of a *Latin* America. Even beyond Rodó's polemic, *Latin America* is a term both inclusive and appropriate enough to be widely used now in all of the American languages. This term is often paired with *North American,* creating a dichotomy that is neither precise nor parallel, with *Latin* indicating cultural origin, on the one hand, and *North* geographical location, on the other. Yet considering the confusion inherent in the non-hemispheric use of *American,* the ambiguity of *Anglo* and *Hispanic,* and the ungainly grammar of the adjective *U.S.,* the terms *Latin American, North American,* and the hemispheric use of *American* seem like the most defensible choices for a comparative study of this kind.[11]

"Indians! I suppose we are never to get rid of that word," Whitman complained to a biographer, Thomas Donaldson. "It's all wrong. . . . It is as much a misnomer as the word 'American.' These people deserved a higher, a more distinct and a more meaning[ful] name, one relating to their aboriginal or pre-Colombian times."[12] Yet the original inhabitants of the Americas had no collective name for themselves as a people in their hundreds of languages. Even today, in spite of the *de facto* unity presumed by their colonizers, there is little agreement among themselves concerning the name of their race or cultures as a whole. One must choose between equally inappropriate misnomers: red man, Native American, Indian, American Indian, aborigine, *indio,* and *indígena.* In much of Latin America, *indio* has become a racist slur while the broadly acceptable *indígena* has no noun form in English that refers to humans. *Aborigine,* a term used widely in the nineteenth century, especially by Whitman, has fallen out of usage, perhaps because of its exclusive association with the Australian aborigines. *Native American,* the closest English equivalent to *indígena,* could prove confusing in the present context, in which both what is native and what is American will be key terms used to describe various aspects of post-Columbian, European-derived culture. To speak of Native American poetry as a model for a native American poetics is a revealing but perhaps entangling play of words. The term *American Indian* seems like the clearest English misnomer for the autochthonous peoples of the Americas. Although the abbreviated coinage *Amerindian* popularized during the 1930s—together with an English translation of *estadounidense,* United Statesian—tempt with the fresh solutions they offer to old problems, the purpose of this book is not to rename the Americas, but rather to compare the baptisms of language given it by two of its greatest poets.

Both Whitman and Neruda were aware that the only real names belonging to what Whitman called the "unnamed lands" were those that grew there from American Indian place-names. Whitman consistently called himself a son of Mannahatta, as did Neruda a son of his native Arauco, the American Indian name of the province where he was raised. "At the bottom of America without name," he writes in *Canto general,* "was Arauco. . . ." (I:6:26). Considering the European-derived names of many North American cities, Whitman wanted to "chase them away and substitute aboriginal names. What is the fitness—What the strange charms of aboriginal names?—Monongahela—it rolls with venison richness upon the palate" (AP:30). Both poets recognized the ancient race of poets that preceded them in naming the American landscape. Like the names of the great North American and Chilean rivers, the Mississippi and the Bío Bío, these are the native names that unify, rather than divide, the American lands, much as American rivers do. The other American names—the thicket of approximate national misnomers we have traversed—are imposed, in conflict and still seeking their true forms. To collaborate with their American Indian predecessors in naming the unnamed, from a native rather than a European perspective, was one of the common tasks of both Whitman and Neruda, and their use of American vocabularies rich in indigenous words has made their works cornerstones of their national languages. Certainly one of the greatest challenges facing the hemisphere is that all Americans find a common set of references with which to speak to each other not only about where we live but about who we are. Whitman and Neruda began this discourse, which is still plagued at the onset with the difficult but necessary decisions such as those made here. The naming of the Americas is as yet incomplete and awaits, from the north or south, its "poets to come."

1
Influence and Inheritance

Whitman a mountain too vast to be seen.
—*Allen Ginsberg*

One photograph of Pablo Neruda's house in Isla Negra shows the small student desk at which the poet, as a child, sat to write his first poem, in approximately 1914, and on this desk is now placed a framed portrait of Walt Whitman. A larger likeness of the elderly Whitman decorated the walls at Isla Negra, and the carpenter who helped Neruda to hang it innocently asked if this were a picture of the poet's grandfather. Neruda replied that indeed it was.[1] In 1972, several months after he was awarded the Nobel Prize, Neruda arrived in Whitman's Manhattan during the last of his rare visits to the United States, to deliver an address before the PEN Club, and there he appropriately acknowledged the debt to his North American "grandfather": "I was barely fifteen when I discovered Walt Whitman, my primary creditor. I stand here among you today owing this marvelous debt that has helped me to live. . . . I, a poet who writes in Spanish, learned more from Walt Whitman than from Cervantes."[2] Far from exhibiting what Harold Bloom calls an "anxiety of influence,"[3] of the type that resulted in Ezra Pound's brusque truce with Whitman in his poem "A Pact," Neruda freely paid tribute to Whitman throughout his prolific career. As one form of tribute, Neruda translated three sections of "Song of Myself,"[4] together with his Spanish versions of Blake and Shakespeare, and as another, he introduced the North American poet several times as a theme, a voice, or a narrative character in his poetry. In book IX of *Canto general*, "Qué despierte el leñador," he proudly presents to his companion Whitman, a poet whom he calls "innumerable as grain," the heroic productivity of the Soviet people in the rebuilding of Stalingrad, which he asks the North American bard to help him celebrate:

> *Walt Whitman, levanta tu barba de hierba,*
> *mira conmigo desde el bosque,*
> *desde estas magnitudes perfumadas.*
> *Qué ves allí, Walt Whitman?*
>
> . . . .
>
> *Dame tu voz y el peso de tu pecho enterrado,*
> *Walt Whitman, y las graves*
> *raíces de tu rostro*
> *para cantar estas reconstrucciones!*
> *Cantemos juntos lo que se levanta*
> *de todos los dolores, lo que surge*
> *del gran silencio, de la grave*
> *victoria.* . . . .
>
> (3:579–80)

> Walt Whitman, raise your beard of grass,
> look with me from the forest,
> from these perfumed magnitudes.
> What do you see there, Walt Whitman?
>
> . . . .
>
> Give me your voice and the weight of your buried breast,
> Walt Whitman, and the solemn
> roots of your face
> to sing these reconstructions!
> Let's sing together whatever arises
> from all the sorrows, whatever surges
> from the great silence, from the solemn
> victory. . . .
>
> (262)

Neruda considered Whitman to be the first and greatest poet of the Americas, and in the myth of Whitman, largely exaggerated and long pervasive among Latin American writers, Neruda found a symbol, along with that of Lincoln, of all that he admired about his principal political adversary, the United States.

For Neruda, Whitman represented the breadth, honesty, and sheer exuberance of the nineteenth-century United States, a native innocence he saw sadly corrupted in his own century, as reflected in these lines from "Por qué Señor?" in *Fin del mundo* (1969):

> *A los cinco años de este siglo*
> *Estados Unidos cantaba*
> *como una máquina de plata,*
> *susurraba con el sonido*
> *de un granero que se desgrana,*
> *tenía las manos de Lincoln*
> *y la abundancia de Walt Whitman*
>
> . . . .
>
> *Y aquella nación qué se hizo?*
> *Lincoln y Whitman qué se hicieron?*
>   (OC III:383)

> Five years into this century
> the United States sang
> like a silver machine,
> rustled with the sound
> of a granary threshing,
> had Lincoln's hands
> and Walt Whitman's abundance
>
> . . . .
>
> And what happened to that country?
> What became of Whitman and Lincoln?

Another photograph of Neruda's house in Isla Negra shows an antique locomotive he kept in the garden, a preposterous contraption of rusted wheels, gaskets, and nozzles, of which he wrote in *Una casa en la arena* (1966):

*Tan poderoso, tan triguero, tan procreador y silbador y rugidor y
tronador! Trilló cereales, aventó aserrín, taló bosques, aserró dur-
mientes, cortó tablones, echó humo, grasa, chispas, fuego, dando pitazos
que estremecían las praderas.*
  Lo quiero porque se parece a Walt Whitman.

(OC III:82–83)

So powerful, such a wheat-grower, such a procreator and
whistler and roarer and thunderer. It threshed grain, belched
sawdust, felled forests, sawed cross-ties, cut planks, threw off
smoke, grease, sparks, fire, its whistle blowing to make the prai-
ries tremble.
  I love it because it reminds me of Walt Whitman.[5]

Although the enumerative energy of this prose-poem is itself perhaps a
conscious tribute to Whitman, one does not find in the various phases
of Neruda's poetry an identifiably Whitmanian style. "I haven't been
much of a Whitmanian in my style of writing," Neruda has explained,
"but I am profoundly Whitmanian as regards his vital message, his acceptance, his embracing of the world, life, human beings, nature."[6] A
line-by-line or image-by-image exegesis of Neruda's work would not
necessarily yield the type of results that critics expect when they in-
vestigate influences. As is sometimes the case among Whitman's more
deliberate disciples, Allen Ginsberg, for instance, there is no sense in
Neruda's poetry that Whitman himself—to quote one of his more
famous dicta—exists as an "effect or originality to hang in the way . . .
like curtains" between the poet and the reader ("Preface 1855," 717).
Influence is never present on the level of a derivative stylistics.

  On the surface, several obvious differences between the two poets
are immediately evident. Neruda's style, in his middle (1947–57) and
later work (1958–73), is sleek rather than aggrandized, resembling
a wooden sailboat more than a nineteenth-century locomotive. His
lines are considerably shorter than the expansive Whitman's; or, rather,
Neruda's expansive energy is directed vertically rather than horizon-
tally, with the enumerations stretched down the page instead of across
it, as if each poet were curiously following the shape of his country in
the design of his free verse. In general approach, Neruda begins with
the specific and mounts toward the universal, with the same momen-

tum in which Whitman proclaims the cosmic and then incarnates the particulars. Neruda's central metaphors tend to unfold outward, layer after layer, bursting open like seed pods toward the end of the poem; he often uses the mid-line or end-line colon to this advantage. Whitman, on the other hand, constructs his metaphors by the cumulative juxta-position of seemingly unrelated specifics, clusters of which are set apart by semicolons. Neruda's declamatory register, even in his more public poetry, is substantially reduced from the exclamatory platform style of his teacher. On the whole, Neruda's presentation is markedly material, seldom made in terms of the bald nineteenth-century abstractions we encounter in Whitman. Although rarely employing irony, Neruda's voice is more subtle and varied, with a range that leaves latitude for the flattened ironic sensibilities of the twentieth century. Whitman and Neruda, in short, are separated by over half a century of literary ex-perimentation and scientific change, by the differences in the languages in which they wrote, the countries they celebrated, and the times they represented.

Neruda is, in this sense, as much a twentieth-century Chilean poet as Whitman is a nineteenth-century North American poet. Unlike Whit-man, Neruda progressed through a series of dramatically distinct voices and styles, each of which contains much of Whitman and all of which, when considered as a whole, approximate Whitman to a greater degree than any other of his "poets to come." Their identities run parallel, re-markably so at times, yet the voice, vision, and language they often seem to share are no more borrowed or transplanted on the part of Neruda than they were on the part of his predecessor. According to Fernando Alegría in his *Walt Whitman en Hispanoamérica* (1954), in which he de-votes twenty pages to one of the few comparative considerations ever published of the two poets, Neruda, "more than a disciple of Whitman, is his continuer, or better put, his inheritor, as original and profound in range as his own teacher."[7] "I had to be myself," Neruda emphasizes, "striving to branch out like the land where I was born. Another poet of the same hemisphere helped me along this road, Walt Whitman, my comrade from Manhattan."[8] In his "Oda a Walt Whitman," Neruda ex-plains the basis of their relationship: "You / taught me how / to be an American. . . . / Older first cousin / of my roots" (OC II:364–65).

The profound bond between the two poets is, as this ode emphasizes, their Americanness, a form and identity that the elder poet first fashioned in *Leaves of Grass* (1855), almost seventy years before Neruda published his first volume, *Crepusculario* (1923). It is no doubt due to their definitive Americanness that many have regarded Whitman and Neruda as the most influential poets of their national literatures and perhaps the greatest American poets of the nineteenth and twentieth centuries. Yet neither poet, in his greatness nor in his Americanness, stands alone. There has been little awareness that for some time now, looking beyond national borders, North and Latin American poets have been jointly involved in the same process of reinventing a European art form in terms of the American experience, and of using this new form to define the American identity. The dialogue has been opened in both directions, and the influence exerted by Whitman—and by what Fernando Alegría calls the myth of Whitman[9]—upon Latin American poets from the 1890s until the present, has been returned in the growing influence of Neruda—and, appropriately, of a myth of Neruda—upon contemporary North American poetry. Rather than merely tracing influences, however, the intertwining of these two literatures might be more profitably and generously approached in an attempt to understand the mutual project on which the poets of both hemispheres have been collaborating, often in great isolation yet with surprisingly similar results.

This exchange began relatively late, a little more than a century ago, when Latin American *modernismo* was just gaining momentum and Whitman was already advanced to an old age during the prelude to the Gilded Age and the Spanish-American War, which was to establish the economic and political relationship between the two hemispheres well into the future. On April 19, 1887, the exiled Cuban poet José Martí was among the audience that heard Whitman deliver his Lincoln Lecture in New York City. Martí then published an eloquent, lyric testimonial to "The Poet Walt Whitman," which first appeared in Buenos Aires' *La Nación* and was later circulated widely throughout Latin America. Martí was carried away by the "apocalyptic phrases" of Whitman's revolutionary free verse. "Rhymes, stresses?" he writes, "Oh no! His rhythm lives in the stanzas which, in the midst of an apparent chaos of overlying and convulsed sentences, are nevertheless linked by a wise method of composition that distributes the ideas in large musical groups, as the natural poetic forms of a people who do not build stone by stone but by huge masses of stones."[10] Martí recognized this "natural poetic form" as distinctly American, for Martí had dedicated much of his poetry and public rhetoric to a struggle not only for a cultural independence from the Old World, as Whitman did, but also for the colonial liberation of Cuba from Spain. In Whitman, Martí encountered a grand, American-speaking public poet much in the tradition of Spanish public poetry, at a time when a private, English-derived romanticism still haunted most of North American verse. While Martí's *modernista* contemporaries were discovering the French Symbolist poets so deeply affected by the rarefied estheticism of Edgar Allan Poe, another line of North American influence was opening into Latin America that was anti-esthetic, democratic, and in the Spanish tradition, epic and declamatory.

What counted most for Martí was that Whitman's voice defined a New World spirit strongly differentiated from the Old World. Martí insists that Whitman is unlike "the spiritless poets and philosophers—philosophers of a detail or of a single aspect—Sweetness-and-light poets, patterned poets, bookish poets, philosophical and literary figurines."[11] This characterization of an Old World poetics, initiated by Whitman with the claim "No dainty dolce affectuoso I" ("Paumanok": 15:26), announces a strongly consistent theme that would take root in Americanist poetry, prefiguring Neruda's caricature of the cosmopolitan, apolitical "poetas celestiales" in *Canto general* as

> . . . *gidistas,*
> *intelectualistas, rilkistas,*
> *misterizantes, falsos brujos*
> *existenciales, amapolas*
> *surrealistas encendidas*
> *en una tumba, europeizados*
> *cadáveres de la moda.* . . .
> (V:2:478–79)

> . . . Gidists,
> intellectualists, Rilkists,
> mistificators, fake existentialist

sorcerers, surrealist
butterflies burning
in a tomb, Europeanized
cadavers of fashion. . . .
(166–67)

For Neruda, these poets represented the contemporary strain of a "pure" Old World poetry based on European Romanticism, whose "tea drinking" practitioners Whitman called, in his day, "rhymsters, melancholy and swallow-tailed . . . confectioners and upholsterers of verse,"[12] as opposed to himself, "A rude child of the people!—no imitation—no foreigner—but a growth and idiom of America."[13] Thus Martí, through Whitman, was among the first to define a polarity that has sharply divided American poetry throughout this century. In contrast to the elegant Alexandrines of his epoch, Martí recognized in Whitman a form that fit the rough magnitude of the American continents, and his final book of poems, *Versos libres,* is a tribute in title and spirit, if not exactly in style, to the freedom of that voice he admired so late in his career. Much more so than this posthumous volume, however, it was Martí's essay about Whitman that was to serve as what Fernando Alegría calls Whitman's "letter of introduction to the world of Spanish letters."[14]

This letter of introduction was also the origin of a myth of Whitman in Latin America that has often surpassed the actual work of the poet in exerting influence and in attracting adherents. Martí writes, for instance, that "only the books of antiquity, with their prophetic language and sturdy poetry, afford a doctrine comparable to that which is given out in grand, sacerdotal apothegms, like bursts of light, by this elderly poet, whose amazing book has been banned."[15] Although the sixth edition of *Leaves of Grass* was, in fact, temporarily withdrawn because of threatened litigation concerning two of its poems, one can imagine how the mythic proportions of Martí's portrait of a biblical bard uttering lightning bolts from his banned book might stimulate more of a cultish fascination rather than any real understanding of Whitman's work. In truth, much of what was first written about Whitman in Latin America sounds embarrassingly like the self-reviews the poet had placed anonymously in various newspapers, or like the biographies on which Whitman and several of his friends later collaborated. The poetry itself was obscured by an obsessive glorification of the poet's image, which impeded the development of an authentic Whitmanian influence. Instead, Whitman was adopted in name only as the nationalist platform-poet that a decolonialized Latin America then needed, yet this Whitman was not the earthy younger man his poetry actually had celebrated but the august, patriarchal graybeard of his later publicity. Whitman's role as prophetic father figure in the relatively young Latin American republics is understandable in terms of Alegría's contention that "in the Hispanic world the figure of a prophet-bard is not only not in the least strange, but might be described as traditional and common. Therefore, neither the public nor the critics wonder at a canonized image of Whitman, nor submit it to pertinent doubts and investigations."[16] Two other factors contributing to the early mythic misperception of Whitman in Latin America were the broad circulation there of Leon Bazalgette's highly idealized biography, *Walt Whitman, l'homme et son oeuvre* (1908), and the fact that the first translation of his work into Spanish did not appear until Armando Vasseur's volume in 1912, well toward the end of the *modernista* era, during which modern Latin America poetry had already begun.

The most famous poet of this era, the Nicaraguan Rubén Darío, first learned of his fellow American Whitman in a characteristic manner, through a Parisian magazine, the May 1, 1888, issue of the *Nouvelle Revue*. His response was to pay tribute to the inventor of free verse with a sonnet, "Walt Whitman," published in the second edition of *Azul* in 1890. On many levels, Darío's sonnet epitomizes not only the early Latin American misunderstanding of Whitman, but its significance. To Darío it seemed that "the Yankee prophet Whitman imitates Hebrew versification in English."[17] Like most nineteenth-century American poets, Darío's impetus was to translate the New World back into the terms of the Old, the undefined American experience back into European classical definitions. Darío, for instance, envisions a Whitman in "Olympic splendor," carrying "a lyre chiseled from an ancient oak." The American bard is recast as a Greek god speaking in Hebrew, telling "the robust worker to keep on working. / Thus, the poet passes along his trail, / with the splendid countenance of a king."[18] In this sonnet, Whitman's democratic intent, certainly in regard to the "robust worker" with whom he so closely identified, is subverted into the traditional aristocratic distance of the European Romantic. Darío was explicitly anti-democratic; "The rest is yours, democrat Walt Whitman," as he proclaimed in the introduction to *Prosas profanas,* claiming for himself the regal, distant, ancient realm of the imagination, as opposed to the detestable "time and life into which I happened to be born." [19] Much like the North American Modernism of poets such as Stevens and Eliot, *modernismo* as typified by Darío was a form of urban romanticism that carried the interiority of the English Romantics, who projected their emotions onto landscapes, indoors into the modern city, decorating psychological "interiors" with the trappings of French Symbolism. In Ortega y Gasset's term, theirs was a "pure" poetry of the closed imagination, an isolated language experience removed from the impurity of perceived realities. Although many of these poets, such as Darío and Stevens, paid homage to Whitman in their poetry, it was directed to a national fetish of archetypal proportions rather than to the man or his work. During the era of their influence, and of their avant-gardist inheritors—from 1890 until 1930, approximately—the voice of Whitman was relegated to a secondary, almost folkloric importance in the Americas, if it was heard at all.

Just as the influence of Whitman's "impure" poetry disappeared at the beginning of the modernist era, the Americanist voice of Neruda emerged toward the end of it, after he had produced several avant-gardist and hermetic works, such as the first two books of the *Residencias.* Historically bracketed by Whitman and Neruda, this era represents a curious detour in the development of the American voice. Although the dates of North American Modernism and Latin American *modernismo* are not precisely synchronized, both movements duplicate the same perennial American phenomenon: As soon as a new economic class rises to power and seeks cultural validation, its writers or critics turn to Europe. [20] For most of Latin America, independence meant the birth of a new class of free-trade capitalists who replaced the creole oligarchies. By the same token, the rapid industrialization of the post-Civil War United States ushered in the Gilded Age, during which the political and economic power passed from the hands of the Gentlemen Farmers into those of the Robber Barons, whose families Henry James observed trying to "acquire" Europe. Free of any encumbering political attachments to Europe, these new American classes sought their social identities in its tradition and hierarchy, not in the more democratic,

American "folk" forms from which they intended to distinguish themselves. Although Modernist and *modernista* poets did not consciously represent the interests of these classes, whose philistine vulgarities they enjoyed satirizing, the parallel poetic movements of this era sought a self-definition in terms of Europe, introducing a new chapter in the often discussed history of American cultural dependency.

What Randall Jarrell writes about the North American Modernists is also a particularly apt description of the *modernistas:* "To have reached, in 1900, in the United States, the age of twenty-one, or fifteen or twelve—as Stevens and Pound and Eliot did—this was so hard a thing for poets, went so thoroughly against the grain, that they emigrated as soon as they could, or stayed home and wrote poems in which foreignness, pastness, is itself a final good."[21] In the introduction to *Prosas profanas* (1896), Darío makes clear that his true land is not America but the "foreignness" and "pastness" of the imagination. As most of the American poets from this period discovered, the imagination was located in Paris and London, not in Nicaragua or Missouri. French Symbolism, Parnassianism, and the later schools of the avant-garde fueled the poetry of Pound, Eliot, Stevens, H. D., Darío, Lugones, Huidobro, and Borges, among others, and even marked certain stages of the two great Americanists, Vallejo and Neruda. With the exception of Stevens, who traveled abroad only in verse, all of these poets were where American poets during this era were expected to be, in Europe, with their audiences at home awaiting the latest word in American culture from the centers of foreign tradition. Rather than proving themselves in Europe, as it was said that an American artist must, what these poets were proving was the "good taste" of the native classes that read them. This period of American modernism and avant-gardism ended with the crash of 1929. The ensuing world depression, together with the Spanish Civil War, inspired an era of American regionalism and political engagement during which a European-educated "good taste" was as out of fashion as its former audience was bankrupt.

During the modernist era, Whitman's invitation to the muse to migrate to America was seemingly ignored:

> Come Muse migrate from Greece and Ionia,
> Cross out please those immensely overpaid accounts,

. . . .

For know a better, fresher, busier sphere, a wide,
untried domain awaits you, demands you.

("Exposition":2:196)

One of the North American poets of this era, however, who most
readily accepted this challenge to give the muse a home in America was
William Carlos Williams, who claimed that the canonization of Eliot's
The Waste Land in the 1920s set back American poetry by fifty years.
By that, he meant poetry written in the vernacular American language,
in Whitman's voice. American English has continued to grow, Williams
asserts, "by the power of those Whitmans among us who were driven
to take a chance by their fellows and the pride of an emerging race, its
own."[22] Williams' opposition to North American Modernism was not
merely the result of a parochial literary rivalry. Modernism was a natural outgrowth of the European tradition and, as such, was revitalizing
in that context. In the vocabulary of the Russian formalists, European
Modernism employed an "unfamiliarized" language in order to "de-
automatize" a long established, homogenic culture: Mallarmé insisted
on the difference between the language of a newspaper and of poetry.
Williams realized, however, that the object of poetry in the Americas
should be quite the opposite, to give poetic life to familiar language
in order to unify and automatize a new heterogenic culture. Much like
Shakespeare, Whitman utilized colloquial language during a formative
period in the life of the national language and thereby helped to shape
and preserve it. As he writes in *An American Primer,* "These States
are rapidly supplying themselves with new words, called for by new
occasions, new facts, new politics, new combinations" (AP:5). An ex-
journalist, Whitman quite literally made a national poetry out of the
vulgate hodgepodge of a growing language used in American newspapers, turning Mallarmé's dictum on its head. The American modernists ignored this challenge. Just as the expatriate Pound only wrote the
American idiom in dialect, Darío announced that he could not address
the muse in the same language with which he spoke to a countryman.[23]
Stevens also viewed American English as an immigrant dialect containing little poetry: "Ach, Mutter, / This old, black dress, / I have been

embroidering / French flowers on it."[24] The Anglophile Borges, an admirer of Whitman's metaphysics but immune to the influence of his American idiom, confessed to once thinking that since it was too late to begin writing in English, he would have to "make the best of a second-rate literature."[25] The grand departure of the modernist American poets was not to leave behind the American hemisphere but the American languages, which were struggling for form and acceptance.

Yet a second tradition was developing parallel to the modernist one during this era. In the United States, this manifested itself in a nascent regionalism articulated by Vachel Lindsay, Edgar Lee Masters, Edwin Arlington Robinson, Carl Sandburg, Robert Frost, and Langston Hughes, as well as William Carlos Williams. During the modernist era, these poets stayed home and discovered, as Sandburg certainly did in *Smoke and Steel* (1920), the same determined muse that Whitman portrayed in "Song of the Exposition" as a sanguine émigrée

> Making directly for this rendezvous, vigorously clearing
>   a path for herself, striding through the confusion,
> By thud of machinery and shrill steam-whistle undismay'd,
> Bluff'd not by drain-pipe, gasometers, artificial
>   fertilizers,
> Smiling and pleas'd with palpable intent to stay,
> She's here, install'd amid the kitchen ware!
>
>   (3:198)

In Latin America, this other tradition of a Whitman-inspired nativism also began to take root during the *modernista-vanguardista* era with the poetry of the Uruguayans Armando Vasseur and Carlos Sabat Ercasty, of the Peruvian José Santos Chocano and of the Chilean Gabriela Mistral. Each seemed to appropriate a piece of Whitman, often at the expense of the whole, be it his politics or nationalism, his mysticism or simplicity. It was Vasseur, a basically neoclassical poet with advanced social ideas, who published the first translation of Whitman's poetry, as mentioned, in 1912. As a writer, Vasseur was noticeably more interested in Whitman's ideas concerning nationalism, democracy, and urbanism than in his voice, style, or pantheist vision; yet in the introduction to his seminal translation, he identifies that quality in Whitman's poetry that was to have the greatest impact on his Latin American inheritors, namely, "his images and coupling of adjectives, which preserves a primitive design."[26] Although not a primitivist, Vasseur was, according to Alegría, "the initiator in his own country of an ideological, social and positivistic poetry inspired by Marx, Nietzsche and Whitman, poetry that assumes the traits of a literary movement parallel to that other, the decadent-symbolist one led by Herrera y Reissig."[27] The *modernista* poet José Santos Chocano declared himself, in *Alma América* (1906), a "singer of savage and autochthonous America,"[28] generously dividing in half the American territories, the North for Whitman and the South for himself. In the artificial stylistics of the *modernistas,* Santos Chocano cataloged the topographies and peoples of the New World, including American Indians, *charros, llaneros,* and *gauchos,* creating Parnassian dioramas of native life, yet missing everything but the regionalism and, some might argue, the egotism of the poet he considered to be his North American counterpart.

The *posmodernista* poets Carlos Sabat Ercasty and Gabriela Mistral, both of whom were early influences upon Neruda, were already writing in a Whitmanian vein when he first encountered them. Sabat Ercasty's poetry was deeply marked by Whitman's style as well as by his cosmology, especially by the ocean-mother and tree-of-life imagery that would later resurface in Neruda. In these lines from his *Libro del mar* (1922), we see as much of Whitman as of Neruda:

> *Sal de los besos y onda de las cópulas.*
> *Pecho de los deseos y vientre de las maternidades.*
> *Cuello de las caricias y cintura de los abrazos.*
> *Hombro de los descansos y muslo de los comienzos.*
> *Mar inmenso, eléctrico, genitivo.*
> *Mar sensual, voluptuoso, terrible.*
> *Lecho del sol.*
> *Sexo desesperado de la tierra.*
> *Matriz de la vida.*[29]

> Salt of kisses and wave of couplings.
> Breast of desires and womb of motherings.

Neck of caresses and waist of embraces.
Shoulder of repose and thigh of beginnings.
Immense sea, electric and procreative.
Sensual sea, voluptuous and horrible.
Bed of the sun.
Earth's desperate sex.
Life's matrix.

In *Claridad,* a literary journal for which the young Neruda wrote during his student days in Santiago, he reviewed Sabat Ercasty's *Poemas del hombre,* which included this *Libro del mar,* claiming the book as a great inspirer of his early work, according to his biographer Volodia Teitelboim.[30] Later, Neruda did experience a certain anxiety about the influence of Sabat Ercasty, for he sent the elder poet a copy of his *El hondero entusiasta* (unpublished until 1933), asking him if he observed his own imprint in the verses. The young poet was greatly disappointed when Sabat Ercasty responded that, as Neruda recounts in his memoirs, "Yes, there are echoes of Sabat Ercasty in your lines," inspiring him to change direction toward the less rhetorical, unpretentious style of his most popular book, *Veinte poemas de amor y una canción desesperada* (1924).[31]

Another of Whitman's early inheritors who exerted a direct influence on the young Neruda was the other Chilean Nobel Prize winner (1945), Gabriela Mistral, who worked as a country schoolteacher for a time in the frontier town of Temuco, where Neruda was raised. Mistral's persona is that of one of Whitman's earth mothers: She was a poet dedicated to the simplicity of a vernacular American, to the lives of the working class, to the maternal, and to the relationship between the ordinary and the transcendent. She wrote of her work, in words again reflecting as much of Whitman as of Neruda: "I represent the reaction against the purist form of a metropolitan Spanish language. I have tried to create with native modifications. There should be no obstacles to blending in the respective vocabularies of the Spanish American countries, where native words are used to designate things unknown in Europe."[32] As early as 1910, with Enrique González Martínez's call to "wring the neck of the swan,"[33] the movement toward a nativist poetics was gathering momentum, growing quietly alongside of *modernismo* and *vanguardismo,* as did a similar tendency in the United States. By the 1930s, Whitman's influence had become so much a part of the fabric of what is called *posmodernismo* that it is difficult to unravel the lines of direct or indirect, primary or secondary effect. In trying to do so, we are reminded of Gabriel García Márquez's comment that when judging a recent fiction contest in Latin America, not one in a hundred manuscripts failed to show evidence of Faulkner's influence, not because all of the younger writers had firsthand knowledge of Faulkner but because his impact had been so great on the previous generation of Latin American novelists.[34] In a similar manner, in considering Neruda as an inheritor of Whitman, it must be emphasized that inheritance, as opposed to influence, assumes a line of direct descent, a familial relationship.

In the case of American poetry, as in most families, there have been two lines of familial descent, the nativist and the European, or the maternal and paternal. In his introduction to *Latin American Poetry,* Gordon Brotherston mentions that "this modern respect for another, 'maternal' tradition . . . was, then, purposefully awakened with Independence, when the father-fixation of the Colonial period was challenged politically."[35] In view of the common American mythology of the white father/ravager and the Indian mother/ bride, to discuss American poetry in terms of its maternal and paternal traditions is neither arbitrary nor figurative. Both Whitman and Neruda, for instance, identified their poetry, on several levels, with the maternal and native rather than with the paternal and cosmopolitan. Although seldom developed consciously, this polarity informs most discussions of the tendencies in American poetry, as we have observed in the conflict between the modernist and Americanist perspectives in considering the influence of Whitman. The dichotomous qualities that characterize these two traditions might be summarized in this way:

maternal tradition:	*paternal tradition:*
regional in scope	cosmopolitan in scope
oral tradition	European literary tradition
colloquial language	unfamiliarized language
transparent style	self-reflective style

open forms: circular	closed forms: linear
populist persona	detached, romantic persona
incarnates personal geography	incarnates the imagination
anti-esthetic, unlearned	esthetic, learned
tribal, public voice	individual, private voice
leftist politics	rightist politics
science and pantheism	religious symbology
"impure" (Ortega y Gasset)	"pure"
"naive" (Schiller): passion	"sentimental": irony

Just as Whitman defined the maternal tradition in North American poetry, Neruda ultimately did so in the Latin hemisphere. Many notable poets, in various stages of their careers, have mixed the two traditions to a large degree and are children of both parents. Rather than representing a precise technique for classification, this polarity suggests more of a continuum along which most American poets may be located. Certainly, a North American tradition that includes Whitman, Sandburg, Lindsay, Williams, Hughes, and their contemporary followers is significantly distinct from one that includes Longfellow, Poe, Eliot, Pound, Stevens, and their disciples. Likewise, in Latin America the poetry of Neruda, Vallejo, Mistral, Guillén, and Cardenal is clearly defined against a tradition that consists of Darío, Lugones, Huidobro, Borges, and Lezama Lima. In interesting ways, much of American poetry falls in between, such as the avant-garde work with vernacular language of e.e. cummings and Vallejo's *Trilce,* or the enumerative hermeticism of Neruda's first two *Residencias* and of Olivero Girondo, or the public, colloquial presentation of the private romantic agony in Alfonsina Storni and Sylvia Plath.

All American poetry is, to some extent, the product of both traditions. Whitman and Neruda certainly fit within, yet are not contained or defined by, the European perspectives in which most critics place them. Many aspects of Whitman are, without doubt, in the tradition of German Romantic philosophy as absorbed by the English Romantics and later by the North American Transcendentalists: the rediscovery of nature, the primitive, and the language of common speech, as well as a pantheistic spirituality with origins in Hindu Vedanticism. Although these qualities of Whitman do fit into the historical-literary puzzle of European Romanticism, those qualities that cannot be accommodated in this tradition are precisely the ones that mark his power, complexity, and originality. Emerson, for example, the closest thematically to Whitman in his century, wrote convincingly of nature, Americanness, and the primitive power of words, yet he did not write in a manner recognizably natural, American, or primitive. In the same manner, many aspects of Neruda's work are continuations of Spanish and French literature, from Quevedo and Gongora through Hugo and Ponge. Certainly the baroque blend in the earlier poetry of sensuality and morbidity, the addresses to the absent beloved, the Christlike identification with "the people," the mythic quest, and the early fascination with the displacement—and later the simplicity—of objects all contain their obvious correlations in European Romanticism. As with Whitman, however, the elements of Neruda that do not rest comfortably in this tradition are those that best define his Americanness and his power. Even though both Emerson and Darío spoke passionately at times of America, the nativist themes of Transcendentalism and *modernismo* were less the American responses they proposed to be than European responses to the *idea* of America. Even in the earlier, more self-conscious nativist attempts such as Joel Barlow's *The Columbiad* or Andrés Bello's *América,* we hear a distinctly European voice speaking of a New World. In Whitman and Neruda, we hear a voice recognizably belonging to that world. This represents a qualitative leap that cannot be accounted for, even by meticulously reexamining the literary backgrounds of the European languages they employ. It is at this point that Whitman and Neruda depart from the European tradition and begin to have more in common with each other than with their European antecedents.

It should be no surprise that in the past three decades the cycle begun one hundred years ago with Martí's tribute to Whitman has been completed, and many North American poets have turned to Neruda in the same spirit that Neruda and his own poetic ancestors turned to Whitman, in search of the culturally eclipsed other half of their own maternal American tradition. June Jordan has stated that Neruda's "work profoundly affects many North American poets who do not realize, because they have never been shown, the North American/the Walt

Whitman origins of so much that is singular and worthy in the poetry of Neruda."[36] It is significant that Neruda's work went virtually unknown in the United States until the 1960s, when the influence of Whitman finally resurfaced after decades of a dominant canonization of Modernism, Eliot, New Criticism, and the "well wrought" poetry of the 1950s. Much of the reason for Whitman's "rediscovery" may have been due to the regenerative energy and wide notoriety of the Beat writers for whom the poet served as a populist model for their brand of urban Transcendentalism. Prior to this time, Neruda suffered a similar silent disregard in English, considering that the bulk of his most important work had been published prior to 1958. Only one of his volumes appeared in English translation during the 1940s, the Angel Flores version of *Residencia en la tierra*. During the 1950s only two poems appeared in English. Appropriately, "Let the Railsplitter Awake" from *Canto general* was published by the Masses and Mainstream Press of the Communist party in 1951, and William Carlos Williams's translation of "Ode to Laziness" came out in the 1958 edition of *New World Writing*. Neither the McCarthyism, the capitalist optimism, nor the self-enclosed New Critical mentality of this era provided fertile ground for Neruda in the United States. Yet we might say that the translation of William Carlos Williams, one of the few Whitmanian poets of major stature writing at this time, served as Neruda's modest but productive letter of introduction to the world of North American letters.

Esperanza Figueroa has located, however, in her article on Neruda in English, a great amount of interest in the poet during this time in small literary magazines: "hundreds of references to Neruda hidden in English magazines and newspapers. A kind of underground fame, behind the backs of the intentional disregard of the academic world."[37] Interestingly enough, she discovered in her research that many of the translations of the time, such as the one published in *Masses and Mainstream,* attempted to force Neruda in English into the style of Whitman. As if by popular ground swell, eight volumes of Neruda's poetry appeared in translation during the 1960s, when poets such as Robert Bly and James Wright actively campaigned to bring his work to the attention of North American readers. The names of Whitman and Neruda became linked during this time in discussions of American poetry, to the extent that it remains difficult to discern which poet popularized the other. James Wright believes that Whitman returned to North America through Neruda: "The true spirit of Poe was absorbed into contemporary American literature only after Poe had been truly understood by the French. Perhaps the true Whitman may return to the U.S. from . . . South America."[38]

In many ways, Whitman was more "affectionately absorbed" by Latin America than he has been by the country that he celebrated, although his acceptance there has been in somewhat mythic terms. Yet the Latin American Whitman is no more mythic a creature than the North American Neruda has become. Despite Neruda's breadth and fecundity, the myth of Neruda persists in limiting him to a surrealist poet of political protest, no doubt due to the cultural mood during which he became known in the United States. Echoing Fernando Alegría's question "which Whitman?"—the Latin American version claimed by the populist Neruda or by the hermetic Borges[39]—we might well ask "which Neruda?" concerning the radically diverse readings he has received in the United States. Just as the early myth of Whitman in Latin America focused upon an image of the older poet as a prophetic Moses figure of an often narrow nationalism, the initial myth of Neruda in the United States concentrated on his early surrealist period, during which he was associated with García Lorca, and on his later involvement with Allende's socialist coalition government in Chile, as though the poet were no more than a colorful cross between André Breton and Che Guevara. Yet as Neruda confessed in *Estravagario* (1958) about his own poetic personae, "We are many" (OC:II:631), and there are indeed as many Nerudas as there are Whitmans: the nature, the erotic, the nationalist, the spiritual, the political, and the personal poets, all poets of both magnitude and precision, at once universal and enormously detailed. What Neruda accomplished in the many volumes that marked the stages of his prolific career, Whitman accumulated more simultaneously throughout the various editions of the same book: the unity of these poetic voices, a unity threatened by the dramatic yet partial myths that have provided both poets their access across the borders of the hemisphere.

Great poets are mythologized by their audiences for a reason, perhaps so that they might easily extract what they most immediately need. Yet as North and Latin American readers, our needs have surely changed

since the 1960s and the 1890s, the eras during which these poetic exchanges were begun. The familial bond between the two poets points
not only to a much-needed reckoning of the affinity between the two
American hemispheres, but to a deeper need to establish a basis for
an American identity: "roots," as Neruda referred to his fundamental
link with Whitman. As in any relationship between inheritors, these
two poets direct us toward a common ancestor as well as to a mutual
genesis and a primal poetic model that stands outside of the Western
literary tradition. Neruda begins *Canto general* "Before the wig and the
dress coat" (I:1:13), returning to the point of American origins that
Whitman stressed when he rejected the "old forms, old poems" of a
European literature characterized in his letter to Emerson in 1856 as
"dressed up, a fine gentleman, distasteful to our instincts, foreign to our
soil" (734). Whitman complained of "the influence of European literature over us," which he denounced as an "evil" weakening the American
character because "we receive with a blind homage whatever comes to
us stamped with the approbation of foreign critics—merely because it
is so stamped. We have not enough confidence in our own judgment."[40]
Neruda raised the same objections when he protested that in Chile,
"when the mistress of the house shows you something, like china plates
perhaps, she says with a little smile of satisfaction, 'It's imported.' . . .
Cultural colonialism, the derivation of our values from Europe, is typical of us and of our sad cultural situation."[41] It was Whitman who,
above all else, infused Neruda with the courage and direction to dispel
the dominant European cultural models of his own era and to look to
his own American landscape and language as a source for the music,
voice and persona of his poetry. "In fact it was he, Walt Whitman,"
Neruda has claimed, "in the persona of a specific geography, who for
the first time in history brought honor to the American name. The
colonialism of the most brilliant nations created centuries of silence;
colonialism seems to stultify creativity."[42]

  Neruda's relationship with Whitman, as the perfect embodiment of
what Whitman hoped would be his "poets to come," suggests that in
such hemispheric comparisons we might locate a truer perspective on
American writers than in attempting to place them back in the contexts
of the English or Spanish traditions from which many have abruptly de-
parted. The motivating myths of the American experience have always

been those of the future, not of the past, yet the traditional European literary approach has always been to consider writers in terms of their antecedents, not those who follow in similar directions. In this sense, although a consideration of Whitman certainly can help elucidate Neruda, perhaps a reading of Neruda may encourage an even clearer understanding of Whitman. In examining the conscious choices of Whitman's inheritors, we might learn a good deal about Whitman's own unconscious assumptions, and Neruda's American origins may lead us back to a new perspective on Whitman's. As he modestly announced, Whitman wrote only "one or two indicative words for the future," insisting that those who followed him "must justify me." As the first truly American poet, Whitman expected his work to be understood by flipping pages forward, not backward, in anthologies, and with his inheritance also came an obligation to his future poets: "Leaving it to you to prove and define it, / Expecting the main things from you" ("Poets to Come":14).

2

Foreign Words
and Indian Corn

Wordsworth is too tame for the Chippewa.
—*Thoreau*

"*T*he similarity between the evolution of Anglo-American and Spanish American literatures," writes Octavio Paz, "results from the fact that both are written in transplanted languages. Between ourselves and the American soil a void opened up which we had to fill with strange words."[1] These "strange words" represent the radical transformation of European into American forms in response to the New World. Yet the American origins of these new forms, often defined as no more than native extensions of European genres, remain uncertain. The maternal tradition in American poetry, for example, in which we would centrally place both Whitman and Neruda, seems at the onset to lack any clear literary antecedents or culturally appropriate models, as if it were invented Robinson Crusoe-like in this enormous gulf between imported languages and inchoate American nature. Although Neruda can be claimed as an inheritor of Whitman, Whitman's own sources and models have been voluminously examined by critics unable to relate his work to any tradition other than either the imported one with which he broke or the maverick one that he seemed to create *ex nihilo*. Much of the impetus to ferret out both poets' sources is due not so much to an impatience to discover where their poetry originated as much as to the insecurity of not knowing in which tradition it stands.

The maternal tradition appears to lack reference to other established poetics or to any parallel contexts with which it might be compared. It is non-European and, therefore, American by default. Yet like many other distinctly native artistic forms, it bears a significant relationship in its essential qualities to the ancient cultures indigenous to these continents, a model so obvious that it has been consistently overlooked, despite the indispensable way in which the American Indian bridges the void Paz describes between transplanted words and the American soil.

In his letter to Emerson in 1856, Whitman challenged North American culture with the question: "Where are any mental expressions from you beyond what you have copied or stolen?" (732). In 1924, D. H. Lawrence voiced similar concerns: "All that is visible to the naked European eye, in America, is a sort of recreant European. We want to see the missing link of the next era." What the world now knows as American art is not the imported European esthetics that dominated the nineteenth century but the work of pioneers who transformed their media as they redefined Americanness by infusing European forms with an indigenous energy and vision. The action and field painting of Jackson Pollock, the choreography of Martha Graham, the murals of Diego Rivera, and the music of Violeta Parra are examples of what has come to be appreciated abroad as American art. It is no coincidence that at some point in their careers each of these artists communed with what Lawrence called the "daemon of the continent,"[2] the American Indian. The art critic Alberto Busigani traces Pollock's rebellion against European painting to the "practices of the American Indians, especially the sandpaintings of the Navajos,"[3] and Graham counts the Kachina dances of the Southwest as "one of the greatest inspirations of my entire life."[4] Rivera sought to recreate in his murals the vision and esthetics of indigenist America, believing in an artistic return to the classical pre-Columbian cultures, and Parra incorporated American Indian instruments, vocal tones, and languages into her political folk music. It is not surprising that the radical reinterpretations of European forms into the terms of American experience that we find in such influential movements as Abstract Expressionism, Modern Dance, Mexican Muralism, and the South American *nueva canción* should direct our attention to the cultures of the continents' original inhabitants.

Whitman himself recognized the importance of American Indian culture, asking in a letter of 1883 if the United States was to proceed "cheerfully accepting and using all the contributions of foreign lands from the whole outside globe—and then rejecting the only ones distinctly its own—the autochthonic ones?" (CP:554). Whitman's own "free verse" is certainly a contribution of the magnitude of those of Pollock, Graham, Rivera, or Parra in claiming for poetry a distinctly American form, a parallel rebellion against what he branded, in the same letter to Emerson, as "authorities, poems, models, laws, names imported into America" (734). It is Whitman's voice that constitutes Lawrence's "missing link" to the influential poetry of the twentieth century, yet a link, as such, anticipates antecedents as well as successors. Was Whitman's revolution as freely invented as the rootless American protagonist who makes himself up? If so, would not "its neck bend right and left wherever it goes" (734), as Whitman criticized his contemporary writers, changing directions as quickly as Huck Finn and Israel Potter change clothes? On the contrary, in Whitman's poetry we recognize a more rooted quality than mere self-invention, the primal voice of a maternal tradition that genuinely seems to belong to the American land and people. It has been recognized as such far from the nineteenth-century context of Whitman's Manhattan, as we have seen, even in the remote territory of Araucania, Chile, where Neruda first encountered it. Yet many of the critics who have pursued the sources of Whitman's originality have turned, on the basis of contradictory biographical documentation of the poet's desultory readings, clippings, and interests, in the least native directions, filling bibliographies with studies on Whitman and the Upanishads, Whitman and the Italian opera, Whitman and Hebrew poetry, and Whitman and the French Symbolists. A truly universal poetry, as Whitman's also is, could and perhaps should contain parallels with such diverse international traditions, yet these directions hardly promise to demonstrate that to which Whitman really links the particularly American genius of a poet like Neruda. In speaking of imported literary models, whose "costume and jewelry prove how little they know nature," Whitman asks a more basic question: "Where is a savage and luxuriant man?" (734).

In his introduction to a collection of essays on ethnopoetics, Jerome Rothenberg makes the crucial observation that

When the industrial West began to discover—and plunder— 'new' and 'old' worlds beyond its boundaries, an extraordinary countermovement came into being in the West itself. Alongside of the official ideologies that showed European man to be the apex of the human pyramid, there were some thinkers and artists who found ways of doing and knowing among other peoples as complex as any in Europe and often virtually erased from European consciousness. Cultures described as 'primitive' and 'savage' . . . were simultaneously the models for . . . forms of art and poetry so different from European norms as to seem revolutionary from a later Western perspective. It was almost, looking back, as if every radical innovation in the West were revealing a counterpart . . . in the traditional worlds the West was savaging.[5]

What Rothenberg is discussing is not merely the intellectual sympathy for the primitive that informs Rousseauian or German Romanticism, based on the "savage" as an Adamic emblem of the innocence lost to "civilized" man. The maternal tradition does not necessarily employ the American Indian as a symbol or artifact at all, as Longfellow or Robert Penn Warren, Santos Chocano, or Octavio Paz have, but rather, it incorporates a poetics and persona that correspond to the complex and sophisticated model present in American Indian poetry. When Roy Harvey Pearce, for instance, in his critical study of North American "savagism," notes that "towards the end of the eighteenth century, budding American poets lined up, in a not very orderly fashion, either on the primitivistic or anti-primitivistic side,"[6] he means "primitivistic" in terms of a sympathetic treatment of the American Indian as a literary subject, not the mode in which these poets wrote, which was universally British-derived. "What is at stake," Brotherston makes clear in his commentary on the maternal tradition in Latin American poetry, "is not writing which depicts or is simply *about* Indians, creoles or Negroes, etc. . . . Our concern is the more radical impingement of what these people had and have to say poetically, of their different poetic languages, on that of Latin America."[7] Vast amounts of American literature have been produced about the American Indian, yet little of this romantic genre has assumed either an American Indian vision or poetics in place of an exclusively European perspective on its exotic subject matter.

The maternal tradition in American poetry, on the other hand, has developed from an extended interpenetration of two cultural sources, that which Brotherston calls the "imported paternal heritage" and the "violated local or 'mother' cultures."[8] Not only in the Americas but in many modern nations, cultures are, more often than not, characterized by this subtle merger of the aboriginal and the imported. Even European cultures are still deeply marked, and are often distinguishable from each other, by the persistent influences of their original tribal inhabitants, whose traditions survived Romanization and even these tribes' eventual decimation or assimilation. In the same sense, "the foundations of modern North America rest firmly on a solid bed of ancient civilization," insists the anthropologist Jack Weatherford in writing about the extensive Indian pyramid site of Cahokia along the Mississippi, adding that "our culture and society today descend from ancient Cahokia as much as from medieval London, Renaissance Rome, and ancient Athens."[9] Mary Austin, an early twentieth-century pioneer in the translation of American Indian poetry, was the first to introduce this point of view in approaching North American literature. In her seminal essay, "The American Rhythm" (1923), she argues that "it ought not be necessary to justify the relationship between Amerind and American verse, seeing how completely we have accepted the involvement of Hellenic and Pelasgian influences in the best of Greek literature. Nobody denies the intermingled strains of British, Celtic and mixed Nordic elements in the best of English, or refuses to see . . . the aboriginal Teuton informing the literature of Germany."[10]

The blending of the European and the indigenous in the Americas has proved markedly different in the northern and southern hemispheres, which has deeply affected the manner in which the American Indian voice has surfaced in various national poetries. Since few Iberian wives or families accompanied their colonist husbands on their single-minded quest for the instant wealth of New World gold, most of these conquistadors began what were often second families with American Indian women, engendering the myth of the European father/Indian mother that permeates *Canto general*. Neruda describes Arauco, the American Indian province of which he was a native, as "a cold uterus / made of wounds, mauled, / raped, conceived" (IV:4:78), the conquistador Balboa as a "mortal bridegroom" (III:10:51), and Alvarado as a Spaniard who "ravished the nuptial rose of the tribe" (III:6:48).

Neruda repeatedly employs his father's surname, Reyes, as a conquistador name, while he consistently associates the mother who died shortly after his birth with the Indian, although there is no evidence that she was in fact so. In *El viajero inmóvil,* Emir Rodríguez Monegal writes that Neruda's "perhaps irrational feeling that his blond father belonged to the invading and conquering race and that his mother was made of dark indigenous clay was to dominate his personal mythology from this moment and impregnate *Canto general.*"[11] This private metaphor, however, points to the public truth that many Latin American cultures are as predominantly mixed or mestizo as the racial backgrounds of their populations, and various movements within Latin American art have adopted a nationalistic Indianism in order to address not only a past but a present reality.

The Northern European colonists of the United States, on the other hand, were for various reasons settlers in search of the permanence of land and new homes, and were thus accompanied by wives and families or followed by eligible European mates. The centuries-long war of this racially unmixed stock to strip the North American Indian tribes of their ancestral lands resulted not only in a widespread genocide of native populations, but in the subsequently powerful, subconscious presence of the vanishing Indian in North American culture, as analyzed by Richard Slotkin in *Regeneration through Violence.* Slotkin's main argument is essentially Gary Snyder's assertion that "the American Indian is the vengeful ghost lurking in the back of the troubled [North] American mind."[12] Although not many nineteenth-century North Americans could claim American Indian mothers, the pervasive Pocahontas myth in the poetry and fiction of this era strongly suggests the profound association between the maternal and the Indian, perhaps accounting for the paucity of white women protagonists in the fiction of most nineteenth-century male writers: White women were extraneous to their American metaphor of the romance between white male civilizers and dark mother nature.[13]

Whitman only hints at such a filial relationship with Pocahontas, and such a deep identification with the Indian mother, in "The Sleepers," in which his own mother tenderly shares a long communion with a vanished "red squaw":

Her hair, straight, shiny, coarse, black, profuse,
    half-envelop'd her face,
Her step was free and elastic, and her voice sounded
    exquisitely as she spoke.
. . . .
O my mother was loth to have her go away,
All week she thought of her, she watch'd for her
    for many a month,
She remember'd her many a winter and many a summer,
But the red squaw never came nor was heard of there again.

(6:430)

Many of Whitman's twentieth-century North American inheritors have avowed, much more deliberately than Whitman, an American Indian "mother" as the source of their Americanness and of the native tradition that their poetry represents. Carl Sandburg, William Carlos Williams, and Hart Crane all devoted poems to this American Indian mother, often in the person of Pocahontas, as did Vachel Lindsay in these lines from "Our Mother Pocahontas":

> The forest, arching low and wide
> Gloried in its Indian bride.
>
> . . . .
>
> John Rolfe is not our ancestor.
> We rise from out the soul of her.
>
> . . . .
>
> We here renounce our Teuton pride:
> Our Norse and Slavic boasts have died:
> Italian dreams are swept away,
> And Celtic feuds are lost today.[14]

In a similar fashion, in "The Dance" section of his Whitmanian epic *The Bridge,* Crane supplies, according to Leslie Fiedler, all of the Pocahontas mythology that Whitman suggests but left out.[15] In *In the American Grain,* Williams identifies the American land with the voice of an Indian mother, the "She" who lures De Soto into the depths of the conti-

41

nent, and as a modern poet seeking to connect with that lost voice, he acknowledges the almost ghoulish quality of attempting to reclaim its spiritual authenticity: "The land! don't you feel it? Doesn't it make you want to go out and lift dead Indians tenderly from their graves, to steal from them—as if it must be clinging even to their corpses— some authenticity."[16] According to Michael Castro, in his treatment of these three Whitman inheritors who "extend and develop these seed-like perceptions found in Whitman" regarding the American Indian:

> Lindsay, Crane and Williams all lacked firsthand contact with living Indians and all based their writing on an imaginative and symbolic revival of peoples who were alive for them primarily in spirit. But more important, these poets shared the intuition that intimacy with the land and its spirit was central to a new, ex-panded American consciousness and identity and that the Indian was somehow the key to this needed contact and consciousness.[17]

As with Whitman's long absent squaw, these visions of the Indian mother are, for twentieth-century North American poets, haunting cultural memories rather than the nurturing, earth-body presence iden-tified as the native mother in Neruda's work. Octavio Paz has rightly observed that "North Americans are concerned with the problem of their origins because what previously existed in America, the native world, was completely destroyed. The United States is built on the void left by destroyed Indian cultures."[18]

While a more conscious attention to American Indian culture has characterized the maternal tradition in Latin American poetry, well into this century the tradition has emerged in North American poetry primarily through what Slotkin assumes to be the "result of sponta-neous developments in American writing, rather than the deliberate use of Indian sources," since the North American "heritage had through long years in the wilderness become a mixture of the Indian and the European."[19] Even though Neruda, more deliberately than Whitman, identifies his voice with that of the American Indian in order to define the authentic American, a consideration of Whitman's poetry in terms of the American Indian model aligns into meaningful perspective many of the contradictions as well as the unconscious assumptions inherent in his work. Although neither Whitman nor Neruda were Indianists, as were their contemporaries Thoreau and Paz, both began to compose their major work within the contexts of unprecedented Indianism among the artists and writers of their eras, cultural moments that might help to elucidate the origins of the styles and personae they adopted. The quite conscious savagism of North American Transcendentalism and Latin American Marxism were the specific backgrounds out of which the relatively unconscious shamanist poetics of both Whitman and Neruda developed, and a review of their relationships to these cultural movements is essential to understanding their kinship with the American Indian. In paralleling these two distinct movements, one recurrent constant emerges: Whether in the Northern or Southern continents and in spite of the often exaggerated and naive perceptions about indigenous peoples upon which they are based, Indianist eras are always times of revolutionary transformations of the American identity, as if wrestling with Lawrence's "daemon of the continent" proved the catalyst for assuming a renewed sense of purpose and place.

II

"Indians," it is claimed, was Thoreau's dying word, and if so, it was as much an answer to Whitman's question about "a savage and luxuriant man" as to the larger Transcendentalist quest for the natural, de-Europeanized American. Beginning in 1850, Thoreau filled eleven notebooks with his observations on a disappearing race that, as his interactions with the Indian guide Joe Polis in *The Maine Woods* indicate, he was never quite able to understand. This was due not only to his own romantic over simplification, but also to what he considered the "corruption" of the remaining Indians with whom he came into contact. While Thoreau was moving in what he assumed to be their direction, the Indians he knew were moving in what they assumed to be his direction, a classic miscommunication between colonizers and colonized. "So while missionaries and official philanthropists were trying to convert Indians," observes Robert Sayre in *Thoreau and the American Indians,* "other Americans—authors, artists, soldiers and many more—were in various ways converted, too, 'Indianized.' There was no other way, apparently, of having the land free of the enemy, and becoming a part of the land which still held in it the enemy's ghosts." In attempting to rethink their way from the outmoded systems of the old culture toward the wisdom-in-nature of the new, the Transcendentalists, each in his own way, encountered the "savage," and their visions were deeply influenced by the individual angles of these encounters. "The reborn white savage or Transcendental Indian," concludes Sayre concerning Thoreau's own confrontation, "could incorporate [the Indian's] virtues, metaphysically eating him as the Indian warrior ate the heart of his enemy,"[20] an image bound to disturb Thoreau as much as it might intrigue Melville, so different were their "savage" visions.

Unlike Thoreau, Whitman evidenced no pronounced interest in the prevalent savagism of his era, nor was he "inclined to lead a sort of Indian life among civilized men," of which Hawthorne accused Thoreau. If Thoreau is the "first imaginary Indian,"[21] as Harold Beaver calls him, Whitman is the first Indian of the imagination. Whitman's encounter with the Indian seems to have taken the form of his fellow North Americans, Pollock's and Graham's, in the opening of the artistic imagination, exploding closed European models with an "original energy" that resembles an American Indian esthetic and vision. "Whitman, less cerebral than Thoreau," writes Slotkin, "perhaps lived up to some of the implications of *Walden* better than its author. . . . Whitman's 'barbaric yawp' sounded like Indian war cries of bloodlust and sexual threat over the rooftops of the assaulted town, and was perhaps more dramatically effectual as a statement of identification with the Indian character and spirit of the wilderness and the erotic impulses of the subconscious mind."[22]

"There is only so much of the American Indian left," wrote Thoreau in 1842, "as there is of the American Indian in the character of this generation."[23] The American Indian stands as a focal point of much of pre-Civil War North American literature due to the Florida war of the 1830s and 1840s, during which the Cherokees and Seminoles were largely exterminated, and the even more programmatic genocide of other tribes forced from their lands during the westward relocation of the same era. During the period of 1820–1850, many Indian biographies and histories appeared, in addition to Schoolcraft's translations of Indian literature, and a sentimental "protest" poetry burgeoned in the literary periodicals in defense of the brutalized but noble Indian. Works such as Seba Smith's *Powhatan,* Mrs. Sigourney's *Pocahontas,* or Epres Sargent's "The Last of His Tribe" were all mournful dirges for the plight of the Indian written in a decidedly minor romantic key, akin to the abolitionist verse of the epoch.[24] Events such as the capture of Chief Osceola, or the use of bloodhounds to hunt down Seminoles in Florida swamps, provided topics for literary works increasingly popular among a public seeking mythic roots in a land that they were coming to occupy almost exclusively. As the actual threat of their presence diminished, the image of the Indian was incorporated both more frequently and positively into the literature of the day: "Where there ain't no Indians," observed Jim Bridges, a mountain man of the 1830s, "that's where you find them thickest."[25] Slotkin traces the gradual rouging of the white man and bleaching of the red man in the varied attempts to create a national epic and a North American hero: from the American-as-captive of Thompson's *New England Crisis* of 1676 to the American-as-avenger of Wolcott's "Brief Account . . . of John Winthrop" of 1725; then, in turn, from the American-as-farmer who moves comfortably between both white and red worlds, as seen in Dwight's *Greenfield Hill* of 1794, to the American-as-hunter, one who adopts an Indian role and view of nature as he becomes a "refiner" of the savage, as presented in Bryan's *The Mountain Muse* of 1813. Within this context, the pantheist Thoreau's strained meeting with the Protestant Joe Polis in the 1850s bears a certain logic in terms of the progressive role reversal already functioning in the literary imagination. And Whitman's poetics appear as an almost inevitable product of this process.

This evolution of the transformed identities of white-man-as-nature-initiate and red-man-as-tamed-Christian culminates in 1855, a year in which Longfellow published his "Song of Hiawatha" and Whitman the first edition of *Leaves of Grass.* The two works bear a strangely inverted relationship to each other that shows a certain significance in the coincidence of their publications, the first important crossroads in North American poetry. Longfellow selected an obscure European verse form, the trochaic dimeter of the Finnish *Kalevala,* to create a romantic narrative in which a sentimentally Europeanized and desexualized Indian becomes a Christian hero: the Indian as Tennysonian angel. Whitman, on the other hand, uses the devices of an oral, tribal poetry to create himself as the "savage," sexually charged hero of a long lyric of nature initiation, one in which he reveals himself as "hankering, gross, mystical, nude" ("Song of Myself":20:47): the poet as barbarian. Just as the bleached red man becomes a cultural insider as an appropriately poetic subject, the barbarian poet establishes his identity as a cultural outsider, a white Indian who has, in the ways thought most offensive, gone native. "Hiawatha" represents the apogee of the dead-ended Europeanizing of the North American experience, and Longfellow is the last of the serious nineteenth-century poets in that tradition. Whitman, on the other hand, emerges as a "renegade," a type defined in North American Indian fiction, according to Roy Harvey Pearce, as "a man who has willfully given himself over to savagism and deliberately turned against civilization."[26] Lawrence calls Whitman the "first white aboriginal" with "the true rhythm of the American continent speaking out in him,"[27] and even a newspaper of his day described the poet as "a pretty fair specimen of . . . a polished Aborigine."[28] As such, he is the first of the various "holy barbarians" who have gone on the righteous warpath against white North American sensibilities, assuring a certain breed of North American poet an archetypal role as a menacing heathen. In his memorable essay "Paleface and Redskin" (1939), Philip Rahv chooses this perennial cultural metaphor to describe the split personality of North American literature. He uses this comparison not only to determine the primary differences between the maternal and paternal literary sensibilities but to identify Whitman as the original "redskin," celebrating native rhythms and instincts to the eternal consternation of Europeanized "palefaces" such as Longfellow and James.[29]

In addition to Lawrence's "aboriginal" and Rahv's "redskin," others among Whitman's noted readers have referred variously to the poet, with either a positive or negative connotation, as "primitive" (Yvor Winters), "barbaric" (George Santayana), "savage" (Gerard Manley Hopkins), or "crude" (Ezra Pound).[30] What these writers mean by "primitive" and its synonyms is, more accurately, non-European, with little interest in the precise relationship Whitman might bear to the often complex forms of an oral, tribal poetry that were part of an American Indian heritage under active investigation by several of Whitman's admired contemporaries during the period in which he began composing *Leaves of Grass*. For this generation of writers, the American

Indian was in the air, so to speak, to an extent not equaled again until the 1960s, when a broader interest in Whitman and the entire maternal tradition in poetry was enthusiastically awakened. Yet as attractive as the proposition might be, the striking similarity between Whitman's and American Indian poetics does not confirm influences or indicate sources. During the early readings that informed his writing, however, we do know that Whitman was to some extent aware of the "primitive" direction in which he was moving. "The primitive poets," he noted, "their subjects, their style, all assimilate. Very ancient poetry of the Hebrew prophets, of Ossian, of the Hindu singer and ecstatics, of the Greeks, of the American aborigines, the old Persians and Chinese, and the Scandinavian Sagas, all resemble each other."[31] Whitman's recognition of the essential similarity between these models, what he calls in the same notebook entry "the florid, rich, first phases of poetry," suggests that he was aware of the poetics of the oral tradition, which he was to incorporate into his own writing. Most important, his inclusion of the American Indian poets in the august company of the classical ancients indicates that he had possibly read Schoolcraft's translations of their poetry and was at least familiar with their tradition as a means of connecting his own word to the American land: "And for the past, "he writes in "Starting from Paumanok," "I pronounce what the air holds of the red aborigines" (16:22). Other notebook passages indicate a similar familiarity and respect, such as the fragment of Shoshone Indian poetry from his commonplace book included in *Specimen Days* (CP:270). The overt sympathies expressed in a poem such as "Unnamed Lands," included in the 1860 edition of *Leaves of Grass,* suggest why the poet may have been assigned, out of the numerous agencies in the Department of the Interior, to his brief stint at the Bureau of Indian Affairs five years later:

> O I know that these men and women were not for
> nothing, any more than we are for nothing,
> I know that they belong to the scheme of the world
> every bit as much as we now belong to it.

> Afar they stand, yet near to me they stand,
> Some with oval countenances learn'd and calm,

Some naked and savage, some like huge collections
   of insects,
Some in tents, herdsmen, patriarchs, tribes, horsemen,
Some prowling through woods, some living peaceably
   on farms, laboring, reaping, filling barns. . . .

(372)

"Yet near to me they stand": Despite this avowed empathy for the "primitive," there is little evidence to suggest that Whitman consciously adopted an American Indian poetics in the same manner that, for instance, another important modern primitivist, Pablo Picasso, intentionally distorted European forms to fit an African esthetic.

What such a comparison intends is to define a model, in this case a relevant one involving a certain cultural logic. No model, however, can contain the *whole* of Whitman, as F. O. Matthiessen recognizes in *American Renaissance* with the three tentative analogies he suggests of oratory, opera, and the ocean. The common perception that Whitman's style and prophetic persona are necessarily derived from the Bible perhaps more accurately indicates that, of all those primitive poetic forms that Whitman includes in the above passage, the Hebraic is the only poetry with oral, tribal origins with which his readers are familiar. The Hebraic prophet did enact the shamanic role within his originally tribal nation, yet this original function as well as its poetics have been transformed in their absorption into European culture, as we see in the King James Bible, a prose translation of Hebrew verse. To assume a biblically prophetic model for such an essentially pagan poet, one whom Matthiessen claims went "still farther than Emerson in throwing overboard church and dogma, even the tenets of Quakerism,"[32] is to confine him to that inappropriate category reserved in European literature for all unrhymed mysticism of dubious origins: the biblical. The language of literary criticism, out of its limited experience with any such literature except the biblical, tends to foster partial approaches to Whitman, resulting only in isolating what appear as stylistic irregularities that terms such as *trope, irony, ambiguity,* and *tension* cannot explain. On the other hand, Whitman's use of repetition, apostrophe, litany, parallel structure, compound elements, essential detail, tribal grouping and the lyric present, supported by the shamanistic persona that emerges in the poems, can be understood not as the eccentric elements of an invented style, nor as a stew of assimilated oratorical, operatic, or biblical rhetorics, but as a natural unity of effects present in all oral, tribal poetry, particularly the American Indian.

III

In *Homage to the American Indians* (1970), the Nicaraguan poet Ernesto Cardenal writes that "the dictator-sacrificer-who-tears-human-hearts," together with the United Fruit Company, "came to pierce with arrows / the orphan, the widow, the wretched one. / They have eaten Quetzal, they have eaten it fried." As an important religious symbol of the Maya-Quiché, the quetzal bird here takes on the significance of all American Indian culture, which in this context has been degraded and exploited, and is identified with the suffering of the downtrodden. While for the Transcendentalists the American Indian served primarily as a philosophical symbol of natural man, for twentieth-century Latin American Indianist writers the Indian has been transformed into a largely political symbol of the oppressed, often associated with revolution or a committed degree of social activism. Whereas the North American metaphor for European-indigenous relations has been one of erasure, a lingering invisibility accompanied by a prevailing guilt, haunting sadness, and reverent loss, the Latin American metaphor has been rape, one that engendered not only a mixed progeny but present poverty and corruption, arousing anger, vengeance, and, ultimately, a revolutionary hope based on a promised return. In the same poem, which is a meditation on the meaning of the Mayan calendar, Cardenal ends with the calendar-unit *Cuceb,* which "means revolution / literally 'Squirrel' (that which spins) / It will then be the end of their cupidity and greed."[33] For both nineteenth-century North American and twentieth-century Latin American savagists, the American Indian defines the New World paradise, either lost or regained, and points the way to a pre- or post-Christian Eden as the ultimate meaning of America.

The place that the American Indian has occupied within Latin American literature, however, differs markedly from the role that the

Indian has played in North American literature. Despite many broad similarities, the indigenous cultures of the two hemispheres are themselves different. Unlike the preliterate hunting and herding tribes that occupied much of the United States, several southern native cultures were characterized by an urban classical civilization that rivaled medieval Europe in technology and other major civilizations in the arts and sciences, particularly architecture, astronomy, and medicine. Their influences were consequently less easily erased than in North America and, some might argue, came to predominate over the Spanish in certain areas. The first book published in the New World, for example, was a bilingual Christian text in Spanish and Nahuatl (1539); the first nativist writer, and the greatest prose writer of the colonial era, was an Incan-Spanish mestizo, Garcilaso de la Vega el Inca (1534–1615); and the first example of American free verse was a poem published in 1778 by Granados y Gálvez as a tribute to ancient Mexican culture, in the form of a presumed text by the fifteenth-century poet-king Nezahualcoyotl. The purely imaginative merger with the American Indian that takes place during the course of North American poetry is from its inception in Latin America more of an actual blending, forming the basis for as much of a sociopolitical identity as a mythic one. "Over the centuries the principal Indian languages . . . have undoubtedly declined," observes Brotherston, "but they have far from disappeared from oral and written literature, and have continued to 'win over' poets in Latin America."[34] One of the first poets so influenced was the best poet of the colonial era, the Mexican nun Sor Juana Inéz de la Cruz (1648–1695), who composed verses in both Spanish and Nahuatl. In addition, an important predecessor of Neruda was the conquistador Alonso de Ercilla y Zúñiga, who celebrated the same tribes native to Neruda's province in his extended epic *La Araucana* (1569–1589), for which Neruda rewards him in *Canto general* by referring to him as the only "blond eagle" who "will not drink the chalice / of blood" (III:22:64). Yet de Ercilla's Chief Caupolicán is, much like Longfellow's Hiawatha, portrayed in neoclassical cadences as a sentimentalized "noble savage" converted to Christianity before his death, underlining the sad inevitability of his defeat yet his brave resistance to the triumphant Spanish. De Ercilla's epic served as the foundation for a romantic school of savagism both in New World and European literature, in which this hallmark "inevitability" of the passing of the native world is elegized in terms of a Wordsworthian loss of childhood.

Andrés Bello's epic *América* (1823) represents a turning point in the Latin American view of this "inevitability," and as the first Latin American poem to name, in the Whitmanian sense, the American landscape, with its flora, fauna, and local heroes, employing the native vocabulary, it represents a direct antecedent to *Canto general*. Although Bello predictably laments the loss of Edenic innocence, another element surfaces in the poem with references to the violated Indian world: "the first progeny of her fertile breast / Before the curved plow raped her soil / Or the foreign ship visited her parted shores." [35] Bello's message, Brotherston finds, is that "the upstart Spanish will not for long 'usurp' the kingdom of the sun. Of course, it was out of just such sympathies as these that the Indianist cult sprang, in early nineteenth-century politics and literature." [36] During the era of the struggles for colonial Independence, the American Indian became emblematic of the noble "native" world as opposed to the corrupted "foreign" world of Spanish domination, and the liberators were seen as native sons avenging a maternal honor lost at the hands of an alien rapist. Even after the newly created American oligarchies, freed of colonial rule, turned their attention to Europe during the *modernista* era, the American Indian remained a symbol not of a lost innocence but of a nationalist pride, particularly in the face of any foreign threat. In his essay "Nuestra América" (1891), José Martí identifies the maternal soul of the continent with the mestizo or "natural man," as opposed to any encroachment of colonial European culture: "The imported book, therefore, has been defeated in America by the natural man. . . . The autochthonous mestizo has defeated the exotic creole. There is no struggle between civilization and barbarity, only between false erudition and nature." [37] Even such a cosmopolitan poet as Rubén Darío, who proudly claimed mestizo ancestry, asserts Latin defiance of North American aggression, in "A Roosevelt" (1904), on the part of an "ingenuous America that has Indian blood," mentioning Moctezuma in the same breath as Columbus. [38] The American Indian as a symbol of the proudly independent Latin American soul also served as a basis for the turn-of-the-century movement *mundonovisimo*, best represented by Santos Chocano's *Alma América,* which attempts to assimilate into a modern national identity the disparate elements of indigenous and creole cultures. Santos Chocano claims that as a Latin American, he is "twice epic," representing the best of both the native and the European worlds, and like Darío defies Anglo-Saxon America with his dark, Incan blood.

By the 1920s, however, the romantic use of the Indian as an "original" theme, sung in patriotic counterpoint to European points of reference, had evolved in the context of a new political consciousness that found in the Indian a symbol not of lost innocence or nationalist pride but of the oppression of the Latin American masses. Several related movements developed, notably in the predominantly Indian countries of Peru and Mexico, and although their perspective was populist, their ideology Marxist, and their purpose didactic, their artists consciously adopted an American Indian esthetic and cosmology, transcending the purely thematic or decorative use of the Indian as a protest symbol toward an art at once public yet visionary. Among these artists were the Andean novelists Alcides Arguedas, Jorge Icaza, and Ciro Alegría; the Mexican muralists Diego Rivera, Davíd Alfaro Siquieros, and José Clemente Orozco; as well as the poets Vallejo and Neruda. Neruda was living abroad during the fermentative era of the 1920s, during which Victor Raúl Haya founded the revolutionary ARPA party in Peru, one based on reunification through indigenous Inca culture, as well as on land reform, antioligarchic and anticlerical ideals. During the same period, José Carlos Mariátegui launched the Indianist-Marxist literary journal titled *Amauta,* the Quechua word for "sage."[39] Neruda did not make contact with these movements until after his political conversion to Marxism during the Spanish Civil War, and his subsequent return to the Americas after the end of that war and his father's death. During the three-year period beginning in 1940 in which he served as Chilean Consul General to Mexico, he became associated with the muralists as well as other politicized artists and intellectuals involved in the cultural program of the Mexican Revolution, with its call for a redemption of the pre-Conquest heritage: "We had to begin from before the beginning," as Octavio Paz defined the revolutionary thrust of this epoch.[40] During this time, Neruda attempted to publish a Chilean literary review titled *Araucania,* possibly modeled after the influential *Amauta,* whose only issue featured the portrait of an Araucanian Indian woman on its cover. The project was promptly cancelled by his government, which declined to be represented abroad as "a nation of Indians."[41] Yet it was to their common American Indian heritage that Neruda, as a Chilean, attributed his profound connection to Mexico, particularly to its fervently Indianist culture of that epoch: "I felt myself intertwined [in Mexico] because every Chilean's roots extend under the earth and come out in other regions. . . . Lautauro was related to Cuauhtémoc,"[42] he explained, referring to the legendary Araucanian and Aztec warriors who resisted the Spanish.

This was also part of the twelve-year period during which Neruda was composing *Canto general,* first published in Mexico in 1950. The cultural context in which Neruda's book appeared might best be characterized by Octavio Paz's *El laberinto de la soledad,* published in the same year, in which a central figure in Paz's analysis of Mexican history is the Latin American version of Pocahontas, the violated Indian mother, *La Chingada:* "It is appropriate to associate her with the Conquest, which was also a violation, not only in the historical sense but also in the very flesh of Indian women. The symbol of this violation is doña Malinche, the mistress of Cortés."[43] It was appropriate that Neruda's book was first issued as a subscription edition illustrated by Rivera and Siquieros, both of whom were Indianists to a much greater extent than Neruda, choosing to illustrate, Brotherston points out, "the only lines from the whole of *Canto general* which suggest that America had reached a high point of culture and intellectual development *before* the European conquest."[44] Unlike Neruda, however, Rivera and his wife, Frida Kahlo, were both "imaginary Indians" as well as genuine "Indians of the imagination." Their idealistic, colorful Indianism recalls on a grander scale the nineteenth-century primitivist enthusiasms of Thoreau who, pondering a New England arrowhead, wrote: "Such are our antiquities. These were our predecessors. Why, then, make so great ado about the Romans and the Greeks, and neglect the Indian? . . . Celebrate not the Garden of Eden, but your own."[45] Rivera and Kahlo had the same perspective but, far beyond arrowheads and shards, a more classical garden to celebrate. Kahlo, although half German, adopted traditional tribal dress and art forms while Rivera, in the late 1940s, began construction of the first Mayan-Aztec pyramid to be built in the Americas in a thousand years, his own elaborate tomb, which he filled with over forty-two thousand pieces of pre-Columbian art. The effect of this cultural moment can certainly be perceived in *Canto general,* in which Rodríguez Monegal observes that "the poet writes as if he were descended only from the oppressed indigenous race and his language and traditions were Araucanian, Guaraní or Nahuatl."[46] In 1945, Neruda began writing the section of *Canto general* that anchors the book in an Indian cosmology and poetics, "Alturas de Macchu Picchu," one month after he officially became a member of the Communist party, events that Hernán Loyola considers "twin expressions of the same internal reality."[47]

This marriage between Latin American Indianism and communist political ideology, incongruous as it may seem, has its origin in the collectivist ideals that Marx and Engels found in Lewis H. Morgan's study of the Iroquois nation, mentioned in the subtitle of Engels's *The Origin of the Family, Private Property and the State* (1884). This influential book is Engels's revision of Marx's notes on primitive communism informed by his study of American Indian society in the final years of his life. According to Jack Weatherford in *Indian Givers,* a reevaluation of the indigenous contributions to hemispheric culture, the kinship states of the Iroquois "became in Marxist theory the ideal to which industrial communism would return once the workers smashed private property, classes and the state. The final communist society would be an industrialized version of the Iroquois social system."[48] If Marxism has supplied the modern ideology, American Indian culture has provided a twin spirituality that has continued to inspire revolutionary movements in Latin America to this day, as recently as the Tupac Amaru guerrillas or the brutally Maoist *Sendero Luminoso* movement in Peru. Less violent guerrilla groups of the 1960s adopted tribal names, such as the Uruguayan Tupamaros, and members of the Chilean resistance to Pinochet used legendary Mapuche warrior *noms de guerre,* much in the spirit of Neruda's compensatory myth in *Canto general* of an Indian father who would rectify the wrongs of the European one and claim the violated continent for the future: "I searched for you, my father, / young warrior of darkness and copper" (I:1:14). Roy Harvey Pearce comments that the Transcendentalists "constructed analyses in which they tried to move from the idea of a past savage perfection to one of a future civilized perfection. The latter was to be analogous to but not identical to the former."[49] This observation certainly seems true of the Indianists of both hemispheres. While for the North American writers of the Transcendentalist era, a unity with nature, or an instinctive innocence, was the lost Indian paradise to be recovered, for the Latin American Indianists, which form Neruda's background, the return is not to innocence but to a collectivist power for the dispossessed Indian masses. This cultural difference curiously corresponds to the gradual historical shift that Weatherford traces in popular culture between the early nineteenth-century image of the American Indian as a healer, as exploited by the traveling medicine shows selling tonics of Indian roots and barks, and the early twentieth-century image of the Indian as a warrior, as reflected in the wild West show and cowboy movie.[50]

Although Whitman and Neruda share an American Indian poetics, their basic directions are anchored in both culturally and historically different views of the meaning of the aboriginal. As the masculine projection of a robust, rootless country, Whitman seeks to unite with the primal geography of the eclipsed Indian mother. Neruda, on the other hand, seeks to avenge the dishonored Indian mother still present in the fertile American soil. Whitman's impetus is toward an ahistorical animal innocence, or sexuality; Neruda's is toward redressing historical injustices, or politics. Yet here the sexual and the political become converse dimensions of each other. Whitman's sexuality is framed politically in terms of a revolutionary democracy of working-class lovers, and Neruda's radical politics are given a sexual shape, in which the disenfranchised indigenous male reclaims the birthright of his masculinity.

Both of these perspectives, the innocent and the vengeful, are anchored in an identification with the primitive roots of America (Whitman's populist grass / Neruda's "tree of the people"), and therefore their tribal personae were perceived in a familiar manner as a "savage" threat to the "civilized" order. Whitman's renegade poetics made of him, at times literally, a censurable sexual outsider, as Neruda's, on several occasions, turned him into an exiled political outlaw. Yet both were poets representative of the broad directions of their eras. Whitman's persona is as much a product of the nineteenth-century North American quest for an Emersonian, prehistorical *in illo tempore* as Neruda's persona is the result of a twentieth-century Latin American faith in a posthistorical Marxist utopia that will restore the sun of the Incas.

Although Neruda's vision contains a blend of American Indian cos-

mology and political ideology that attests to his 1930s and 1940s
Indianist background, there is, as with Whitman, once again little evidence to suggest that Neruda ever studied American Indian poetics or
consciously attempted to graft its techniques onto his own language.
A quotation in Quechua from Tupac Amaru I does stand untranslated
as the epigraph to "Los Conquistadores" in *Canto general,* yet such an
Indianist affectation is rare in his work. What emerges in his poetry
is not a display of borrowings from American Indian poetry and mythology decoratively set against a recognizably Spanish romantic voice
and persona, as we find in Paz's poetry, but rather a unity of incantational and organizational effects, together with the development of the
complex shamanistic persona, which harmonize into a voice that reso-
nates from an oral tradition outside the European. Perhaps even more
significant than Neruda's and Whitman's Indianist cultural contexts is
the fact that both were raised during eras when the native presence was
a dominant feature of the American landscape. Neruda's parents were
among the first white settlers on the indigenous lands of the fiercely
independent Araucanian Mapuche tribe, a region finally ceded to the
government in 1881, only twenty-five years before the poet's birth.
Neruda describes his family history in this territory in "Viaje por las
costas del mundo":

> *La agonía de los guerreros, el final de una raza que parecía inmortal,*
> *pudo hacer posible el que mis padres, después de uno pacto en que el Go-*
> *bierno de Chile reconoció los araucanos como ciudadanos libres de la*
> *República de Chile, con todos sus derechos y perrogativas, pudieran lle-*
> *gar con los primeros 'pioneers' en un viejo coche de alquiler, atrevesando*
> *varias leguas de territorio desconocido hasta entonces, hasta la nueva*
> *capital de la frontera poblada por los chilenos. Ésta se llamó Temuco*
> *y ella es la historia de mi familia y de mi poesía. Mis padres vieron la*
> *primera locomotora, los primeros ganados, las primera legumbres en*
> *aquella región virginal de frío y tempestad.*

(OC:II:562)

The warriors' death rattle, the end of a race that seemed immortal, after a treaty in which the Chilean government recognized the
Araucanians as free citizens of the Republic, with all rights and
privileges, made it possible for my parents to come with the first

'pioneers' in a rented jalopy, crossing stretches of land unknown until then, to the new frontier capitol settled by Chileans. It was called Temuco and this is the story of my family and my poetry. My parents witnessed the first locomotive, the first livestock, the first vegetables in that virginal province of cold and storm.

Margarita Aguirre, one of Neruda's biographers, noticed that when she returned to this hometown of Temuco, "listening to the Indians reminded me of the Nerudian accent."[51] Neruda was raised in a frontier house typical to a territory that Manuel Durán describes as "Indian land, very much like Oregon or Montana at the end of the 19th century."[52] There the young Neruda was enchanted by the sound of Mapuche words, many of which he later accumulated in chants of Araucanian place-names, flora, and fauna. The Chilean Sergio Bocoz-Moraga finds that in his poetry Neruda "summons the magical, musical sounds contained in the humble Mapuche language . . . the rumors, the smells, the beloved sights and sounds of his mysteriously beautiful landscapes and seascapes."[53]

Whitman was born more than a decade before the forced westward Indian relocation of the 1830s, on an island he proudly called by its Indian name, Paumanok. Like Neruda, he was also attuned to the "wailing word" of American Indian chants that, during his lifetime, he saw disappearing from the landscapes that formed them. In a poem of 1887, "Yonnondio," a title that Whitman glosses as an Iroquois lament, the poet himself laments the passing of their word:

> A song, a poem of itself—the word itself a dirge,
> Amid the wilds, the rocks, the storm and wintry night,
> To me such misty, strange tableaux the syllables calling up;
> Yonnondio—I see, far in the west or north,
>   a limitless ravine, with plains and mountains dark,
> I see swarms of stalwart chieftains, medicine-men, and warriors,
> As flitting by like clouds of ghosts, they pass and are
>   gone in the twilight,
> (Race of the woods, the landscapes free, and the falls!
> No picture, poem, statement, passing them to the future:)
> Yonnondio! Yonnondio!—unlimn'd they disappear;

Today gives place, and fades—the cities, farms,
    factories fade;
A muffled sonorous sound, a wailing word is borne through
    the air for a moment,
Then blank and gone and still, utterly lost.

(524)

In dismissing the possible derivative sources in the analogies that he presents to Whitman's poetry, F. O. Matthiessen finally does suggest an atavistic return to such a "wailing word" as the ultimate origin of Whitman's poetics: "Whitman's desire to give up borrowed cadences altogether came from his crude reliving of the primitive evolution of poetry."[54] In following this evolution, perhaps both Whitman and Neruda intuitively followed a similar evolution worked out during thousands of years of close contact with these same landscapes to which they were responding.

It is precisely such an atavistic process that Mary Austin finds as the basis of the "landscape line," a loose poetic measure that is related to natural topography and the physicality of the poet, one which she posits as the crucial link between American Indian and modern American poetry. Austin lived for sixteen years among the native peoples of the Southwest, where she "became convinced as early as the first years of the present century that American poetry must inevitably take, at some period in its history, the mold of Amerind verse, which is the mold of the American experience shaped by the American environment,"[55] as she writes in "The American Rhythm," introducing her anthology of American Indian "re-expressions." Austin was among the first American writers to consciously propose an anthropologically oriented poetics based on body, breath, movement, natural environment, and archaic ritual, and therefore to associate the parallel forms of modern American and American Indian poetics:

> In so far as verse forms are shaped by topography and the rhythm of food supply, the aboriginal American was singing in precisely the forms that were later to become native to the region of Spoon River, the Land of Little Rain, and the country of the Corn-huskers. It was when I discovered that I could listen to aboriginal

verses on the phonograph in unidentified Amerindian languages, and securely refer them by their dominant rhythms to the plains, the deserts and woodlands that had produced them, that I awoke to the relationships that must necessarily exist between aboriginal and later American forms. This was before 1900, before there was any movement more than was indicated by Whitman and the verse of Stephen Crane, which at that time I had not seen. Whitman I knew slightly, though here I confess that my interest in him swelled perceptibly in the discovery of how like the Indian's his method is.[56]

Although Austin's work, influential during the 1920s and 1930s, has been largely eclipsed and her methods of translation superseded by contemporary ethnopoeticists such as Jerome Rothenberg, her ideas remain a significant bridge not only between anthropology and poetry, but between primitive and modern poetics and between Whitman and his "poets to come." "Almost anybody might have predicted the rise of a new verse form in America,"[57] she claims, in response to the uniqueness of the American landscape and experience. In this sense, the evolutionary similarities between North and Latin American poetries of which Paz writes are rooted in the parallel contours of this response.

The true character of this response, however, is not, as many American artists have mistakenly attempted, to become an "imaginary Indian," but to follow what William Carlos Williams elucidates as the lesson of Daniel Boone, "to be *himself* in a new world, Indian-like. If the land were to be possessed it must be as the Indian possessed it. . . . as a natural expression of place."[58] If poetry follows as a "natural expression of the place," as does the work of such Indians of the imagination as both Whitman and Neruda, it would then direct its readers back to what Austin calls "the rhythms in which the land had already expressed itself"[59] as an ideal cultural model. In his preface to an anthology of contemporary Native American poets, Duane Niatum writes of "this sense of coming from the land and not to it" as the continuing basis of a poetics "that gives the Native American voice its clarity and range."[60] Whitman was the first non-Indian American to practice such a poetics, for as he writes in his "Preface 1855," the genuine American poet "responds to his country's spirit. . . . he incarnates its geography and natural life and rivers and lakes" (711). Whitman perceived the close identification between the American Indian and the native topography that the poet incarnates, and insisted that "of all those men and women that fill'd the unnamed lands, / every one exists this hour here or elsewhere, invisible to us" ("Unnamed Lands," 373). Gary Snyder, one of Whitman's North American inheritors, explains his own relationship to the racial memory incarnate in the American landscape in a way that may have been as true for Whitman and Neruda: "For modern Americans, the invisible presence of the Indian, and the heart-breaking beauty of America, work without fasting or herbs. We make these contacts simply by walking the Sierra or Mohave, by singing and watching."[61]

3
Ritual Speech:
I, the Song

I
the song
I walk here
—*Modoc song*

I n "An Indian Bureau Reminiscence," a brief description in *November Boughs* of his six-month tenure at the Department of the Interior during 1865, Whitman writes in eulogistic tones of the innate grandeur of the vanishing race, mentioning that he was often in close proximity to "Omahas, Poncas, Winnebagoes, Cheyennes, Navahos, Apaches, and many others. . . . Many wear head tires of gaudy-color'd braid, wound around thickly—some with circlets of eagles' feathers. Necklaces of bears' claws are plenty around their necks. Most of the chiefs are wrapped in large blankets of the brightest scarlet." Although he admired "some of the young fellows," he finds that the most authentic beauty "was borne by the old or elderly chiefs, and the wise men," and he confesses what should not surprise any reader of his poetry: "There were moments, as I look'd at them or studied them, when our own exemplification of personality, dignity, heroic presentation anyhow . . . seem'd sickly, puny, inferior" (CP:577–79). Whitman often paid visits to these Indian dignitaries at their lodgings, and upon at least one occasion, as his biographer Justin Kaplan relates, had himself introduced by an interpreter as "the poet-chief. . . . The poet-chief says that we are really all the same man and brethren together, at last, however different our places, and dress and language."[1] Whitman, like Neruda, also directed such displays of universal solidarity toward workers, soldiers, prostitutes, slaves, and all of the ungathered members of the great American tribe for which the poet felt he spoke as its "poet-chief." Although we may assume that this was a term invented solely to communicate sympathy with visiting American Indians, the idea seems strongly appropriate to the poetics that Whitman developed. Given the centrally complex role of the word-sender or shaman within American Indian cultures, Whitman's admired "wise men," the corresponding function of a poet-chief provides a close parallel to the personae that both Whitman and Neruda elaborated in their work. More than simply a prophet, the shaman is a namer, singer, word-conjuror, storyteller, spirit-guardian, tribal-unifier, healer, and psychic voyager: the individual apart who represents the whole.

In considering the multifaceted roles of the shaman in relation to the poetic personae of Whitman and Neruda, the most fundamental is that of the word-sender. Language is the medium in which Whitman and Neruda approximated the various functions of the shaman, and it is their particular sense of language that most clearly identifies their work with the American Indian. One aspect of this language which readers of Whitman and Neruda may notice is that they are reading writing that simulates a "speech event." The event of their poetry is the voice of the poet: "I pronounce" or "I sing." The titles themselves point to a spoken or sung presentation. *Canto general* is one of the five of Neruda's volume titles that contain the words *canto* or *canción,* in addition to the title of his autobiography, *Confieso que he vivido,* which suggests a speech act. The book titles within *Canto general* include: "América, no invoco tu nombre en vano," "Canto general de Chile" "Los ríos del canto," and "Coral de año nuevo para la patria en tinieblas." The 1892 edition of *Leaves of Grass* contains fifteen poems entitled "songs," together with numerous others that indicate speech or song, such as "I Sing the Body Electric," "Chanting the Square Deific," or the poem placed first in this edition, "One's-Self I Sing." The reader, in the role of listener, might also notice that the writers, in the role of speakers, introduce a poetry that at times seems to be almost arbitrarily divided into the self-contained units of "poems" or sections of poems. "I utter and utter," Whitman intones in "A Song of the Rolling Earth" (1:220), asserting the equally rolling, conjunctive nature of his speech, which overwhelms most European concepts of the written poem. In oral poetry, according to Ruth Finnegan's study of the subject, "units like 'lines,' 'verses,' 'stanzas'—even 'poems' and 'cycles' are relative,"[2] redefined by each performance in the same sense that each successive edition of *Leaves of Grass* reshaped the poetic material. Neither do oral poems have titles, Finnegan adds, recalling the titleless format of Whitman's 1855 edition as well as the numbered sequencing of untitled sections, both poems in themselves yet also poem-parts, in *Canto general* and *Leaves of Grass*. What emerges from Whitman and Neruda is not so much the constructed poem, but rather a voice that could continue indefinitely pronouncing its own presence into being with the frequent anaphoras with which it presents itself, as in this passage from *Canto general* about Neruda's country:

> *Salí a encontrarte hijos por la tierra,*
> *salí a cuidar caídos con tu nombre de nieve,*
> *salí a hacer una casa con tu madera pura,*
> *salí a llevar tu estrella a los héroes heridos.*
> (VII:1:529)

> I went to find children for your land,
> I went to embrace the hopeless with your snowy name,
> I went to build a home with your pure wood,
> I went to take your star to the wounded heroes.
> (214)

Or in these lines from Whitman about Neruda's continent:

> I see the Brazilian vaquero,
> I see the Bolivian ascending mount Sorata,
> I see the Wacho crossing the plains, I see the incomparable
>   rider of horses with his lasso on his arm,
> I see over the pampas the pursuit of wild cattle for their hides.
> ("Salut au Monde!":7:143–44)

The traditional structure of the English or Spanish poem propels it with a clockwork mechanism through introduction, conflict, and resolution toward closure. These are largely absent from the poetry of both Whitman and Neruda, seemingly open at both ends, beginning and ending according to the dictates of a poetics that, by the use of compound elements, emphasizes the continuity of speech.

In their poetry, unlike the traditional European lyric, voice is not merely one of several elements subordinated into the functioning of the poem, but alone determines the length and shape of the poem as well as of its lines. To a great extent, the "saying" *is* the poetry, and the poem, as a structure, is a thematically or rhythmically measured interval of voice. Although this voice may be written, Whitman emphasizes that "pronunciation is the stamina of language,—it is language" (AP:12). In "A Song of the Rolling Earth," Whitman cautions the reader that the writing must not be confused with the words, nor the typography with the voice that is speaking in his poetry:

> Were you thinking that those were the words, those
>   upright lines? those curves, angles, dots?
> No, those are not the words, the substantial words are in
>   the ground and sea,
> They are in the air, they are in you.
>
>   (1:219)

A writer as speaker necessitates a reader as virtual listener: For ritual speech to exist, it must be received. Neruda tells his listener that his voice, identified as "I," "is not such a distant bell," but as with Whitman's "words" in the above passage, "when you welcome me, you welcome / yourself" (X:12:285–86). C. Carroll Hollis, in *Style and Language in Leaves of Grass,* describes this use of language as illocutionary, which means speech acts that "carry out what they are saying as they are being said."[3] This requires both that a speaker speak, as well as a hearer hear, in order to be completed. The actions implied in such Whitmanian and Nerudian illocutions as "I name," "I speak," "I sing," "I give," "I celebrate," "I pronounce," and "I bequeath" assume a power of language and an authority of the speaker that are rare outside of religious or legal ceremonies, and are certainly foreign to modern literature. Yet their use is consistent with the empowering sense of language present in oral cultures such as those of the American Indian. When the Iroquois shaman sings that "I plant the Tree of the Great Peace,"[4] he uses language with an illocutionary authority similar to Whitman's when he announces into being the essential qualities of the American character:

> I announce a life that shall be copious, vehement, spiritual,
>   bold,
> I announce an end that shall lightfully and joyfully meet its
>   translation.
>
> I announce myriads of youths, beautiful, gigantic,
>   sweet-blooded,
> I announce a race of splendid and savage old men.
>
> ("So Long": 504)

In her essay "Orfeo en utopía," Jean Franco finds an identical oral quality in *Canto general* generated by the "use of rhetorical resources that create a sacred 'aura' around the words." As in Whitman's poetry, one of these oral devices "gives the impression that an act is being completed by very pronunciation of the words."[5] In "Los enemigos," for example, Neruda simultaneously judges and punishes the early oppressors of the American people:

> *Para el verdugo que mandó esta muerte,*
> *pido castigo.*
>
> *Para el traidor que ascendió sobre el crimen,*
> *pido castigo.*
>
> *Para el que dio la orden de agonía,*
> *pido castigo.*
>
> (V:3:504)

> For the executioner who ordered this death,
> I demand punishment.
>
> For the traitor who rose above the crime,
> I demand punishment.

Ritual Speech: I, the Song

For him who gave the order of agony,
I demand punishment.

(190)

Such illocutionary forms of language, which both Hollis and Franco mark as fundamental to the oral qualities of Whitman and Neruda, indicate the power invested by both poets not only in the speaker-listener relationship but in voice itself.

According to Whitman, this voice emanates from a body: "Human bodies are words, myriads of words, / (in the best poems re-appears the body. . . .)" ("Rolling Earth":1:219). The body as the basis of voice, and voice as the medium of poetry, is a major theme permeating most of his work: "A true composition in words," Whitman insists, "returns the body, male or female" (AP:27). It was the physicality of the sound of the word that first drew Whitman to oratory, a fascination with the primal power of speech, and his early notes indicate that he intended to speak rather than write his "lectures." Lacking any social or theological program, not to mention any talent for the lectern, Whitman turned to poetry, yet his poems are not such in any previous sense of the word. In considering the speech acts employed in his poetry, Hollis has concluded that Whitman "was so convinced that he had to get beyond the printed line to communicate the force of his beliefs with the direct immediate effect he found listening to Elias Hicks and Father Taylor that he wrote as if he were doing so in order to make it come about."[6] As a journalist and printer, Whitman's early dissatisfaction with the limitations of print is evident in these lines from the 1855 version of "A Song of Occupations": "I was chilled with the cold types and cylinder and wet paper between us. / I pass so poorly with paper and types. . . . I must pass with the contact of bodies and souls" (TV: I:84n). What his poems became is an incantational poetry written down, songs made of talk marks. Whitman was aware of the oral tradition in poetry, and in "The Perfect Human Voice," indicates not only the value he places on voice but suggests this as the direction of his own "language experiment":

Beyond all other power and beauty, there is something in the
quality and power of the right voice (*timbre* the schools call it)

that touches the soul, the abysms. It is not for nothing that the Greeks depended, at their highest, on poetry and wisdom's vocal utterance by *tete-a-tete* lectures—(indeed all the ancients did). . . . I sometimes wonder whether the best philosophy and poetry perhaps waits to be roused out yet, or suggested, by the perfect physiological human voice. (CP:674)

It is arguable whether Whitman himself possessed that perfect voice, or if what various early biographers describe as "a high-pitched voice" limited his oratory to the page. A taped version, however, has recently been discovered of a wax cylinder reputedly recorded by Whitman in 1890, reading the poem "America." One listener finds the voice to be "strong, deliberate," not unsurprisingly marked by a distinct New York accent in which "earth" is pronounced "uth." This recorded version confirms the biographer Horace Traubel's description of the poet's voice as "strong and resonant."[7]

Neruda also intended his poetry, particularly that of the middle and later periods, as oral presentation. "No book has been able / to wrap me in paper, / to fill me with typography / . . . to bind my eyes," he writes in "Oda al libro (I)."[8] One of Neruda's translators, Alastair Reid, recognized the oral nature of the poet's work trying to render his voice into English: "He wrote in a speaking voice, he was a sayer, he addressed subjects—and objects—directly."[9] Franco also emphasizes that as the basis of Neruda's poetry, "the poetic word is, above all, a spoken word."[10] In "La palabra," from *Plenos poderes* (1962), Neruda announces, as did Whitman, that this word is not an abstract visual cipher but originates in a body as a voice, identical with the primary act of creation:

> *Nació*
> *la palabra en la sangre,*
> *creció en el cuerpo oscuro, palpitando,*
> *y voló con los labios y la boca.*
>
> .   .   .   .
>
> *Salió*
> *de las tinieblas*
> *y hasta ahora no hay trueno*

Ritual Speech: I, the Song

que truene aún con su ferretería
como aquella palabra,
la primera
palabra pronunciada:
tal vez sólo un susurro fue, una gota
y cae y cae aún su catarata.

(OC:II:974)

The word
was born in the blood,
grew in the dark body, beating,
and took flight through the lips and mouth.

. . . .

It emerged
from the darkness
and until now there is no thunder
which ever rumbles with the iron voice
like that word,
the first
word uttered—
perhaps it was only a ripple, a single drop,
and yet its great cataract falls and falls.[11]

Much like Whitman, in his role as public poet Neruda fashioned his poetry for a national, if not globally humanitarian purpose, one demanding an oral presentation: "We write for people so simple that very often, very often they cannot read. Poetry, nevertheless, existed on earth before writing and printing. Because of this, we know that poetry is like bread and must be shared with everyone, the lettered and the country people, with our whole vast, incredible, extraordinary family of peoples."[12] Neruda became known in his own country as a popular troubadour, tirelessly visiting cafés and *peñas,* factories, schools, and mining camps to recite a poetry that García Lorca characterized as "closer to blood than to ink."[13] José Santos Chocano describes the unusually liturgical quality of that famous voice in the following account:

Pablo Neruda, hidden behind his mask of impassivity, begins
a reading of his poems. His voice has a veiled nasality; his pro-

nunciation is lazily dragged out; altogether his recitation gives an impression of languor and monotony. It seems to me that he prays his poems. In the same way that the faithful repeat their litanies, in a chorus that seems to rock and sway in sleep-inducing rhythms. . . . The poet manages in his recital to infuse something of a liturgical emotion.[14]

This was a voice known by all of the Chilean people, although the majority of his books were read only by the literary few. Neruda marks as "the most important event of my literary career"[15] the reading he gave in 1938 to a group of uneducated porters in the bustling Central Market in Santiago, and its emotional reception, during a period when he was moving from the hermetic literary language of *Residencia en la tierra* toward the more oratorical qualities of *Canto general*. This was the moment at which he began to incarnate the American bardlike qualities that Whitman prophesied but never assumed in the public life of his nation.

The oral character of Whitman and Neruda's poetry, written during an age of eye-oriented, printed literature, points to differing, if not archaic, assumptions about the nature of language itself. Taking into account the multiplicity of his or her social functions, the American Indian shaman is not, as we presently understand the word, an artist. At the basis of the apparent simplicity yet deep complexity of American Indian poetics is the inherent confusion between what we self-consciously know as art and life. In all of the languages of the five hundred original North American Indian cultures, and in most of those from the southern hemisphere, there is no word for "art" apart from the spiritual or tribal functions that any esthetic creation might serve. This creation is non-mimetic, that is, it is not a copy or shadow of the real but incorporates reality, in its essence, and becomes the thing itself. For the word-sender, the singing of poems is sacred and practical rather than secular and artistic. The purpose is to name, mythify, initiate, heal, unify, or psychically transport, rather than, as we understand the artistic function, for individual self-expression, entertainment, or purely esthetic pleasure. Beauty is not a secondary reflection of goodness but, as with the Pueblos, "good" and "beautiful" are the same word.[16]

In "The Poet" (1843), Emerson proposes a similar sacred and practical poetics, seeking "in vain for the poet . . . with sufficient plainness

or sufficient profoundness . . . [to] chaunt our own times and social cir-
cumstance. . . . the northern trade, the southern planting, the western
clearing, Oregon and Texas are yet unsung. Yet America is a poem in
our eyes." Emerson calls for both an ecstatic seer and a national bard as
"Namer and Language-maker," realizing that "this expression or naming is not art, but a second nature, grown out of the first, as a leaf out of
a tree." [17] Whitman was the fulfillment of Emerson's call, and in much
the same sense, Whitman did not develop as a poet until he forgot about
"art" and "beauty," as demonstrated by his pre-1848 verses, which are
mediocre at best. As Emerson exhorts, Whitman intended his words
for a spiritual and national purpose, and so closely identified were his
words with that purpose that he could advise the reader that "this is
no book, / Who touches this touches a man" ("So Long," 505). In "A
Backward Glance o'er Travel'd Roads," he warned those who ignored
his purpose only to judge his esthetics: "No one will get at my verses
who insists upon viewing them as a literary performance . . . or as aim-
ing mainly toward aestheticism" (CP:731). Shunning what elsewhere
he referred to as the "*beauty disease*" (CP:482), Whitman boasted of his
persona in an anonymous self-review of *Leaves of Grass* that "the effects
he produces in his poems are no effects of artists or the arts, but effects
of the original eye or arm, or the actual atmosphere, or tree, or bird." [18]

Neruda, on the other hand, was an accomplished romantic and avant-
garde poet, the author of eight celebrated volumes, when his political
conversion during the Spanish Civil War precipitated his startling metamorphosis into a Whitmanesque poet identified with a collective social
purpose as well as the naming and unifying of America. Even before
the publication of his politically oriented *Tercera residencia* in 1947, he
had embraced the anti-esthetic principles of what he called an "impure"
poetics,[19] considering himself, as his biographer Volodia Teitelboim
testifies, "a man responsible to his country and humanity. He wanted
to be useful." [20] Readers who "have considered his work exclusively as
poetry have found themselves faced with a poet who neither wants to
nor can be analyzed in only esthetic terms," explains Rodríguez Monegal, echoing Whitman's protest.[21] To illustrate Neruda's disavowal of
the purely "literary performance," when a copy of his acclaimed but
anguished *Residencia en la tierra* (1935) was discovered in 1949 next
to the body of a young suicide, with the page opened to the under-

lined verse "It happens that I'm tired of being a man," he made a public renunciation of his former poetry and forbade that it be reprinted, claiming that these poems "don't help anyone to live but to die. If we examine anguish—not the pedantic anguish of snobs but that other authentic human one—we see it is the way that capitalism rids itself of those mentalities that could prove hostile to it in the class struggle."[22] Neruda claimed that in subsequent books he intended "to exaggerate the superabundant tone of happiness. Happiness never kills anyone."[23] Neruda's optimism, like Whitman's, is fundamental to his purpose, one that took precedence over esthetics, dissolving the distance between the poet and his message. As in Whitman's conclusion to "Song of Myself"—"I stop somewhere waiting for you" (52:89)—Neruda closes *Canto general* with his voice unifying speaker and listener: "my hand holds your hand" (XV:28:399). For both these poets as well as the shaman, the nature of language itself precludes the distance that art, as we know it, assumes between speaker and audience, signified and signifier, man and nature.

In "Nature," Emerson formulates a theory of language that corresponds to—and was undoubtedly influenced by—Friedrich von Schiller's delineation of "naive" poetry, in which nature is victorious over the self-consciousness of art and the "sign disappears completely in the thing signified."[24] "As we go back in history," Emerson writes, "language becomes more picturesque, until its infancy, when it is all poetry; or all spiritual facts are represented by natural symbols." What Emerson and Schiller are both referring to is the function of language in primitive, oral culture, in which the name of a thing contains, or participates in, its spirit so that to name is to evoke. Both lament the passing of a Golden Age of such primal poetry, with Schiller harking back to the Homeric epics and Emerson to the Edenic world of children and those he calls "savages." Both agree with the romantic precept, as Emerson explains it, that "the corruption of man is followed by the corruption of language," and that the language of modern poets is "fossil Poetry," not the living word.[25] "To such a degree could Emerson perceive the primitive in all great art," observes Matthiessen, "that for him the true poet is the primitive one who is capable of making "the word one with the thing."[26] The modern function of language is to refer, to breach the gap between man and nature, art and reality, signs and signified. The primitive function is to evoke by naming, as Adam does in the prelapsarian garden, a sense of language in which, as Neruda writes in "La palabra," "words give glass quality to glass, blood to blood / and life to life itself." [27] For Schiller, poets "will either *be* nature, or they will *seek* lost nature." [28] Emerson hoped for "naive" poets, those who would be nature, to rise like new Adams from the American experience to "pierce this rotten diction and fasten words again to visible things." [29] Just as Whitman lived out the wildness of the more theoretical Thoreau, as a poet he incarnated the relationship between nature and language that Emerson greeted with recognition "at the beginning of a great career" (730). Yet in his understanding of the innate similarity between aboriginal American poetry and the classic Greek and Hebrew bards, Whitman was one step beyond Emerson, who believed the racist caricatures of the phrenologists enough to dismiss the American Indian in a letter to none other than the author of "Hiawatha": "The dangers of Indians are, that they really are savage, have poor, small, sterile heads— no thoughts." [30] Had Emerson investigated their thoughts, he would have discovered the primitive conjuror or naive poet whom both he and Schiller idealized.

Since the North American Indian cultures had no written languages, and all but the Maya and Aztec civilizations of the southern hemisphere were likewise preliterate, all poems were sung or chanted: an "event." In his introduction to an anthology on American Indian poetics, Brian Swann comments that "a truly sacramental sense of language means that object and word are so fused that their creation, the 'event,' is itself creative. . . . For the Indian there was great power in words. The story, the 'event,' was often regarded as having a life of its own." [31] To ritually pronounce the word "tree," for example, is a powerful event because the sound contains the spirit of treeness; the word is an independent entity and the word-sender or song-poet, as this function of shamanism is variously called, is a powerful figure because he or she is the guardian and activator of such spiritual treasure. For the American Indian, language is "the source of a world in itself," Kenneth Lincoln writes in an essay in the Swann volume. "The primacy of language interfuses people with their surroundings and natural environment—an experience or object or animal or person lives inseparable from its name." [32] In this sense, to extend Emerson's metaphor from the economic panic that he employs in "Nature," language for the American Indian is not merely a symbolic paper currency unbacked by gold bullion, but is wealth itself. "I have always been a poor man," confessed a Navajo, "I do not know a single song."[33]

"I and mine do not convince by arguments, similes, rhymes," Whitman explains, "We convince by our presence" ("Open Road": 10:155). In his chants, as in American Indian poetry, Whitman eschews the purely referential function of language for the evocative, and therefore the incantational. He is concerned that words be infused with presence, that names conjure physical and spiritual entities, and that the reader, as listener, is not merely referred to an experience by language but rather immersed in the experience of his language:

> Stop this day and night with me and you shall possess the
>   origin of all poems,
> You shall possess the good of the earth and sun, (there are
>   millions of suns left,)
> You shall no longer take things at second or third hand, nor
>   look through the eyes of the dead, nor feed on the
>   spectres in books. . . .
>
> ("Song of Myself":2:30)

Whitman's so-called lists or catalogs of people, places, movements, activities, or things are not used rhetorically but are intended to ritually name into presence an experience in which his audience participates. In *An American Primer,* Whitman stipulates that this incantational use of language should, as in American Indian poetics, constitute a "world in itself": "A perfect writer would make words sing, dance, kiss, do the male and female act, bear children, weep, bleed, rage, stab, steal, fire cannon, steer ships, sack cities, charge with calvary or infantry, or do anything that man or woman or the natural powers can do" (AP:6). Arranging and rearranging the words, as Whitman often did in his notebooks and revisions, alters the reality that the "event" of naming creates. "The way in which many of his notes show him making use of language in the fashion of the primitive conjuror," Matthiessen has noticed, demonstrates "his belief that he could summon up a state or quality simply by articulating its name."[34] "All words are spiritual," Whitman asserts, and "*names* are magic" (AP:1 and 18). A poetics based on this sense of language, in which the word participates in the spirit of the thing named, makes of words palpable essences that do not reflect a reality but rather, like the American Indian, create one. Whitman tells us, for instance, that the farmers' words are almost edible: they "partake of ripeness, home, the ground—have nutriment, like wheat and milk" (AP:24). As R. W. B. Lewis remarks in his essay about Whitman as the "New Adam," "There is scarcely any poem of Whitman's before, say, 1867, which does not have the air of being the first poem ever written. . . . And the process of naming is for Whitman nothing less than the process of creation. . . . The things that are named seem to spring into being at the sound of the word." [35]

Neruda also assumed quite seriously the role of New World Adam, considering the vast landscapes of preconquest America that he surveys in the first book of *Canto general* as "My land without name, without America" (I:1:14). In these "lands without name / or numbers," Neruda, as self-proclaimed "Incan of the loam," first names the trees and vegetation, then in subsequent sections, respectively, the animals, birds, rivers, minerals, and finally the native inhabitants of the principal civilizations. As with Whitman, the names partake texturally of the entities named, with the native ones exhibiting a sonorous lushness that conjures the uniquely American topographies: jacaranda, ceibo, caucho, guanaco, puma, quetzal, toucan, Tequendama, Bío-Bío, chibcha, Chichén, and Macchu Picchu, among many. Jack Schmitt, the translator of *Canto general*, observes that Neruda's poetry provides "obsessive catalogs of Mapuche placenames, the flora and fauna, the entire vast, humming nature of the southern rainforest." [36] Like Whitman's naming of his own continent and Andrés Bello's even earlier naming of the elements of South American geography, Neruda was among the first poets of the modern era to stabilize in print many of the vernacular names assigned to Latin American natural phenomena and therefore to formally and securely fasten the Spanish-American language to its reality. Like the American Indian shaman, Neruda guards the spirit of place in his language, for it is a language received directly from the land and transmitted to his tribe through naming. In this passage from book I, "La lámpara en la tierra," he speaks with the Bío Bío river of his childhood Araucania:

> *Pero háblame, Bío Bío,*
> *son tus palabras en mi boca*

Ritual Speech: I, the Song

las que resbalan, tú me diste
el lenguaje, el canto nocturno
mezclado con la lluvia y follaje.
Tú, sin que nadie mirara a un niño,
me contaste el amanecer
de la tierra, la poderosa
paz de tu reino, el hacha enterrada
con un ramo de flechas muertas,
lo que las hojas de canelo
en mil años te relataron,
y luego te vi entregarte al mar
divido en bocas y senos,
ancho y florido, murmurando
una histora color de sangre.

(4:323)

So talk to me, Bío Bío,
yours are the words that
roll off my tongue, you gave me
language, the nocturnal song
fused with rain and foliage.
You, when no one would heed a child,
told me about the dawning
of the earth, the powerful peace
of your kingdom, the hatchet buried
with a quiver of lifeless arrows,
all that the leaves of the cinnamon laurel
have told you for a thousand years—
and then I saw you embrace the sea,
dividing into mouths and breasts,
wide and flowering, murmuring
a tale the color of blood.

(20–21)

Neruda recognized in Whitman's poetry a language similar to that which he received from the Bío-Bío, one that also told of "the dawning / of the earth" and echoed its American Indian legacy, one so identified with the land and its spirit that to name involved the Adamlike power to create. "There are in our countries rivers which have no names, trees nobody knows, and birds which nobody has discovered," Neruda remarked. "Our duty, then, as we understand it, is to express what is unheard of. Everything has been painted in Europe. But not in America. In that sense, Whitman was a great teacher. . . . He had tremendous eyes to see everything—he taught us to see things. He was our poet." [37] Both Whitman and Neruda recognized in the Adamic function of their own language the ancient race of poets, "the red aborigines," that preceded them in naming the American landscape, one that vanished in North America, as Whitman laments,

> Leaving natural breaths, sound of rain and winds, calls
>   as of birds and animals in the woods, syllabled to us
>   for names.
> Okonee, Koosa, Ottawa, Monongahela, Sauk, Natchez,
>   Chattahooche, Kaqueta, Oronoco,
> Wabash, Miami, Saginaw, Chippewa, Oshkosh, Walla-Walla,
> Leaving such to the States they melt, they depart, charging
>   the water and land with names.
>
> ("Paumanok":16:26)

II

The poetic techniques derived from the magical sense of language inherent in an oral tradition differ markedly from those in the European literary tradition. Concepts such as metrics, syllabics, rhyme scheme, irony, paradox, tension, ambiguity, conceit, or resolution do not help to elucidate either American Indian poetry or that of Whitman or Neruda: A different vocabulary of literary terms is required to discuss poetry of this dimension. Manuel Durán comes close to providing a set of useful concepts when he catalogs those techniques Neruda employs in *Canto general* that are similar to those used by Whitman in *Leaves of Grass:* "the use of constructive parallels, a system of thought balance in which a verse cannot stand alone, but is dependent on the following verse to complete its thought; rapid enumeration characteristic of inspired speech; reiteration in varying forms, and extensive alliteration, both designed to produce rhythm within the free verse and an almost chanting, hypnotic quality to the lines."[38] Significantly, this list parallels one that Jerome Rothenberg presents in *Technicians of the Sacred* concerning the intersections between primitive and modern poetry,[39] and to the various qualities of vernacular speech that Richard Bridgman locates in North American fiction in *The Colloquial Style in America*, in which he emphasizes that "the oratorical mode shares the characteristics of the colloquial."[40] That the similarities between the poetic techniques of Whitman and Neruda should conform both to the essential qualities of primitive poetry and to the patterns of colloquial American speech suggests not only an oral tradition as the foundation of both poets' work, but that their assumptions about the relationship between incantational language and "the people" are not merely romantic postures but, to a great extent, are valid premises. This connection between ritual and everyday speech is explored by Dennis Tedlock in an essay on Zuñi ceremonial language, one that points toward the basis of an oral poetics:

> I speak of a *text*, even though the Zuñis do not have a *manuscript* of the beginning. But there is a way of fixing *words* without making visible *marks*. As with alphabetical writing, this fixing is done by a *radical simplification* of ordinary talk. Ordinary talk not only has words in it, in the sense of strings of consonants and vowels, but it has patterns of stress, of emphasis, of pitch, of tone, of pauses and stops that can move somewhat independently of the sheer words. . . . To *fix a text* without making *visible* marks is to bring *stress* and *pitch* and *pause* into a fixed relationship with the *words*. The Zuñis call this *ana k'eyato'u*, 'raising it right up,' and we would call it chant.[41]

Chant is a means of streamlining, then "fixing," the connective and emphatic patterns of colloquial speech, employing repetition, parallel structure, enumeration, compound elements, and the alliterative and onomatopoeic techniques common to the qualities that Durán, Rothenberg, and Bridgman list in their individual contexts. An oral poetics would include these terms, in general, as well as those more specific to a particular culture, such as the use in American Indian poetry of apostrophe, oral emphatics, essential detail, tribal grouping, and the lyric present, also common in the poetry of Whitman and Neruda.

Using such a vocabulary to approach their poetry reveals not only their proximity to an American Indian model, but the demanding complexity inherent in the apparent simplicity of their "free verse."

One of the units most basic to the chant is repetition. In *Oral Poetry,* Finnegan concludes that many scholars accept it "as a touchstone between 'oral' and 'written' styles. . . . 'Repetition' is sometimes seen as part of the primaeval nature of 'primitive man'—the supposed typical bearer of the oral tradition."[42] In this sense, section 14 of "Starting from Paumanok," to take one example, is not intended as a geography lesson, in which case a catalog might be appropriate, but as the creation in language of a "world in itself," as in American Indian poetry, using words not as signs but as presences. Whitman's insistence on using "aboriginal names" rather than English ones, as in the title of this poem, indicates the powerful fusion between word and place that both he and Neruda recognized in these names:

> Exulting words, words to Democracy's lands.
>
> Interlink'd, food-yielding lands!
> Land of coal and iron! land of gold! land of cotton,
>   sugar, rice!
> Land of wheat, beef, pork! land of wool and hemp!
>   land of the apple and the grape!
> Land of pastoral plains, the grass-fields of the world!
>   land of those sweet-air'd interminable plateaus!
> Land of the herd, the garden, the healthy house of adobie!
>
> (24)

The repetition of "land" is intended neither to emphasize a point nor to persuade the reader into adopting a certain perspective, as it would be used as a rhetorical device in oratory. It is employed, first, to cohere the disparate nouns—from coal to grapes to herd, incrementally and nonhierarchically, with preference to none—into the growing vision of a sweeping landscape and, secondly, to evoke this reality into being by the repeated intoning of its name. If "land" does contain the spirit of the entity to which it refers, its repetition twenty-four times in this section of the poem should be sufficient to plant it firmly beneath our feet, a specific land, that of "Eire, Huron, Michigan," filled with the specific riches of gold and sugar. The more the word is repeated, the larger or stronger its presence becomes, as in the Navajo "Night Chant," in which the rain god is evoked with this litany:

> With your moccasins of dark cloud, come to us
> With your mind enveloped in dark cloud, come to us
> With the dark thunder above you, come to us soaring
> With the shapen cloud at your feet, come to us soaring
> With the far darkness made of the dark cloud over your head,
>   come to us soaring[43]

With each incremental repetition, the rain god emerges, from head to foot, as a dark cloud.

Neruda uses such repetition to chilling effect in book IV, "Los libertadores," summoning up the heart of the dead conquistador Pedro de Valdivia as "we," a group of Araucanian Indians, perform "the rites of the earth" and devour it, mouthful by mouthful:

> '*Dame tu frío, extranjero malvado.*
> *Dame tu valor de gran tigre.*
>
> . . . .
>
> *Dame tu caballo y tus ojos.*
> *Dame la tiniebla torcida.*
> *Dame la madre del maíz.*
> *Dame la lengua del caballo.*
> *Dame la patria sin espinas.*
> *Dame la paz vencedora.*
> *Dame el aire done respira*
> *el canelo, señor florido.*'
>
> (2:390)

> 'Give me your coldness, evil foreigner.
> Give me your great jaguar's bravery.
>
> . . . .
>
> Give me your horse and your eyes.
> Give me your twisted darkness.

Ritual Speech: I, the Song

Give me the mother of maize.
Give me the horse's language.
Give me the homeland without thorns.
Give me victorious peace.
Give me the air where the cinnamon laurel,
the blossoming eminence, breathes.'

(86)

What is incrementally invoked, bite by bite, with each repetition of "give me" is, more than the "twisted darkness" of the heart, the tearing hunger for vengeance of the singer, from the cold, foreign first morsel to the fragrant breath of satisfaction at the end.

In American Indian poetry, as in Whitman and Neruda's, the spirit of a thing is summoned in a direct apostrophe by the chanting of its name, whether it be landness, soaringness, or a human heart. The apostrophe to supposedly inanimate objects is an inherent characteristic of American Indian poetry used consistently by both Whitman and Neruda, in which the chants are as much to, as about, the objects they name. These are not catalogs in an organizational or rhetorical sense, but are apostrophes that animate, sensualize, and spiritualize the presence of those things named, as in the address to rain in the "Night Chant." In "Song of Myself," Whitman chants into being the elaborated landscape of his own body, addressing it in the same fashion as he does the larger anatomy of the country with which he identifies it in "Landscapes projected masculine, full-sized and golden" (29:58):

Translucent mould of me it shall be you!
Shaded ledges and rests it shall be you!
Firm masculine colter it shall be you!
Whatever goes to the tilth of me it shall be you!
You my rich blood! your milky stream pale strippings
    of my life!
Breast that presses against other breasts it shall be you!
My brain it shall be your occult convolutions!
Root of wash'd sweet-flag! timorous pond-snipe! nest
    of guarded duplicate eggs! it shall be you!
Mix'd tusseld hay of head, beard, brawn, it shall be you!

Trickling sap of maple, fibre of manly wheat, it shall
   be you!
Sun so generous it shall be you!

(24:53)

In a parallel fashion, in *Canto general* Neruda uses the apostrophe to
name into being both his continent and himself as metaphors for each
other, progressively identifying throughout the work the primordially
American elements of the first book with the autobiographical details
of an expanding "Yo soy," as the final book is titled. With a fusing
erotic energy similar to Whitman's, in these lines from book XIV, "El
gran océano," Neruda claims the marine night as his wife, addressing
the landscape-as-female-body common to his poetry, as opposed to
the fairly typical landscape-as-male-body apostrophe of the Whitman
passage:

> *Ámame sin amor, sangrienta esposa.*
>
> *Ámame con espacio, con el río*
> *de tu respiración, con el aumento*
> *de todos tus diamantes desbordados:*
> *ámame sin la tregua de tu rostro,*
> *dame la rectitud de tu quebranto.*

(24:690)

> Love me without love, bloody wife.
>
> Love me with space, with the river
> of your respiration, with the increase
> of all your brimming diamonds;
> love me without the truce of your face,
> grant me the rectitude of your exhaustion.

(370)

In his later *Odas elementales* (1954), Neruda transformed the apostrophe into a radically simplified, elongated, incantational form of direct
address to everything from artichokes and winter to salt and socks. In

these odes, Neruda, like the American Indian shaman, demonstrates his interrelation to all things in "a cosmos that is personalized," as Joan Halifax writes in her study of shamanism, *The Wounded Healer*. For Neruda as well as the shaman, "rocks, plants, trees, bodies of water, two-legged and four-legged creatures, as well as those creatures who swim or crawl—all are animate, all have personal identities."[44] This passage from "Oda a la papa" illustrates how Neruda, with an address to the personalized spirit of a quite ordinary form of food, finds an ancestral kinship with the elements around him:

> *Papa,*
> *te llamas,*
> *papa*
> *y no patata,*
> *no naciste con barba,*
> *no eres castellana:*
> *eres oscura*
> *como nuestra piel,*
> *somos americanos,*
> *papa,*
> *somos indios.*
>   (OC:II:305)

> Tater,
> you're called
> a tater
> not a potato,
> you weren't born bearded,
> you're not a Castillian,
> you're dark
> as
> our skin,
> we're Americans,
> tater,
> we're Indians.

Ritual Speech: I, the Song

In an Eskimo poem, "Magic Words for Hunting Caribou," another form of food is addressed with a similarly musical simplicity and a strong sense of familiarity:

> You, you, caribou
> yes you
> > long legs
> yes you
> > long ears
> you with the long neck hair—
> From far off you're little as a louse:
> Be my great swan, fly to me,
> big bull
> > cari-bou-bou-bou.[45]

The contemporary Sioux shaman Lame Deer, in explaining the relationship between the commonplace and the spiritual in American Indian culture, suggests the significance of the apostrophe for those who believe each element of the physical world contains a spirit that must be named, acknowledged, addressed, and finally integrated into the mythic whole, as Neruda attempted in his three volumes of *Odas elementales:*

But I'm an Indian. I think about ordinary, common things like this pot. The bubbling water comes from the rain cloud. It represents the sky. The fire comes from the sun which warms us all. . . . The meat stands for the four-legged creatures, our animal brothers, who give of themselves so that we should live. The steam is living breath. It was water; now it goes up to the sky, becomes a cloud again. These things are sacred. We Sioux spend a lot of time thinking about everyday things which in our mind are mixed up with the spiritual. . . . We Indians live in a world of symbols and images where the spiritual and the commonplace are one.[46]

Throughout *Leaves of Grass,* Whitman, like the American Indian, "mixes up" the spiritual with the everyday, addressing the divine "inside and out," shocking nineteenth-century North American sensibilities in "Song of Myself" by finding "The scent of these arm-pits aroma finer than prayer" (24:53). "Whatever is commonest, cheapest, nearest, easiest, is Me," Whitman writes in the same poem (14:41), with the capitalized Self indicating, in Transcendentalist script, the fusion of the quotidian with the Emersonian Oversoul. Such an attitude accompanied Neruda's move away from esthetics toward collective purpose and forms the basis of his 1935 manifesto calling for an impure poetry of "useful objects in repose: wheels that have rolled across long, dusty distances with their enormous loads of crops or ore, charcoal sacks, barrels, baskets, the hafts and handles of carpenters' tools,"[47] in short, many of the spiritually illuminated, commonplace objects that he would later sing to directly in his odes.

In addition to the use of the second person to apostrophize the spirits of ordinary phenomena, "you" is also employed by Whitman and Neruda to emphasize the oral nature of their written medium by directly addressing the listener or listeners, assuring that their word is received. Both poets considered their word as the seed of the universal grass or tree of life, which would germinate not only in the earth but upon entering the ears of their audience, a primal concept of language recalled in the mythic insemination of the Virgin Mary by the Holy Spirit in the guise of a dove whispering its powerful word in her ear. In book X, "El fugitivo," Neruda addresses first the collective listeners, *vosotros,* those who helped him during his clandestine flight from political persecution in Chile during the 1940s:

> *A todos, a vosotros,*
> *los silenciosos seres de la noche*
> *que tomaron mi mano en las tinieblas, a vosotros,*
> *lámparas*
> *de la luz inmortal, líneas de estrella,*
> *pan de las vidas, hermanos secretos,*
> *a todos, a vosotros. . . .*
>
> (12:604)

> To all, to you
> silent beings of the night

who took my hand in the darkness, to you,
lamps
of immortal light, star lines,
staff of life, secret brethren,
to all, to you. . . .

(285)

In the last lines of the poem this collective you becomes intimate, individual, the ideal listener, *tú:* "to you, the one who unknowingly has
awaited me, / I belong and acknowledge and sing" (286). According to
Hollis's calculations, the 1856 edition of *Leaves of Grass* contains 162 direct questions to the audience, whereas in British and North American
poetry until the twentieth century, he counts none.[48] While the romantic poet's audience is primarily the poet himself or a distant beloved,
in much of Whitman and Neruda's work their audience is either the
lover, the ideal listener, or the tribal gathering. Although in Neruda's
work the numerous individual and collective addresses are distinguishable, as we have seen, by the *tú* and *vosotros* forms, in Whitman's poetry
they are at times ambiguously and significantly entwined by the use
of the uniform English second person, as if the lover, the listener and
the tribe were the same "you." As an oratorical device to establish the
speaker-listener relationship, the use of the direct "you," in either statement or question form, is largely absent from American Indian poetry
because, by the nature of the presentation, this relationship is never in
question. What is frequently employed, however, as by Whitman and
Neruda, is both the collective imperative and an actual or implied form
of call-and-response.

The imperative is normally used in American Indian poetry within
the context of a spell, that is, a set of directions, as opposed to a prayer
(a request) or a song (a description), as John Bierhost defines these
genres in the introduction to his anthology of American Indian poetry,
The Sacred Path.[49] The anaphoric repetition of the imperative in this
Pawnee song is undoubtedly directed toward a collective purpose:

Remember, remember the circle of sky
the stars and the brown eagle
the supernatural winds . . .

Ritual Speech: I, the Song

Remember, remember the great life of the sun
breathing on the earth . . .

Remember, remember the sacredness of things
running streams and dwellings
the young within the nest . . .[50]

Neruda's spell-like conclusion to "Alturas de Macchu Picchu" works in
a similar way, structured throughout by a dominantly anaphoric use of
the *vosotros* form of the imperative not only to address collectively the
spirits of the dead Incan builders of the city but to unite the greater tribe
of the living audience for whom his voice speaks, as established by the
imperatives of the previous "American love" sequence in section VIII:

> *Dame el silencio, el agua, la esperanza.*
>
> *Dame la lucha, el hierro, los volcanes.*
>
> *Apedgadme los cuerpos como imanes.*
>
> *Acudid a mis venas y a mi boca.*
>
> *Hablad por mis palabras y mi sangre.*
> (12:344)

> Give me silence, water, hope.
>
> Give me struggle, iron, volcanoes.
>
> Cling to my body like magnets.
>
> Hasten to my veins and to my mouth.
>
> Speak through my words and my blood.
> (42)

Whitman uses the imperative form of direct address consistently
throughout *Leaves of Grass,* not only to collectivize his audience but

also to punctuate the longer lyrical passages with the immediacy of his voice, insisting that we "come," "behold," "allons," "see" or "hear." Much as Neruda ends his most famous poem above, Whitman concludes his "Song of Myself" with a spell-like series of imperatives: "look for me under your boot-soles" and "Failing to fetch me at first keep encouraged, / Missing me one place search another, / I stop somewhere waiting for you" (52:89).

Whitman and Neruda's rhetorical questions addressed to their audience, although not a form specifically related to American Indian poetry, involve one that largely is: the question-answer antiphony. The call-and-response motif is common to much oral, tribal poetry, although the repetitive response is seldom included as part of the translation. This element of the African oral tradition has survived intact in black church services in the United States. In this segment of a Panamanian Kuna chant, for example, there are two voices, one the narrating chief and the other the responding chief (RC):

> (8) They came to enter their golden seats in
>   God's listening house.
> RC: Indeed.
> (9) All the female relatives all the nieces
>   (women) you came to enter with me.
> RC: Indeed.
> (10) All the bird grabbers (midwives) really
>   arrived and the hammock makers.
> RC: Indeed.
> (11) Those who make molas arrived those who
>   string beads arrived.
> RC: Indeed.[51]

Hollis finds that a similar but implied call-and-response structure is inherent in many of the rhetorical second-person questions in Whitman's poetry. For instance, the conclusion to "Song of the Open Road," in Hollis's reading, would be:

> Will you give me yourself?
> [I will]
> will you come travel with me?

[I will]
Shall we stick by each other as long as we live?
[We shall]

(15:159)

As a common rhetorical device in Whitman, Hollis claims that ending
this poem with a series of questions

> is successful here chiefly because of the *shall-will* usage. Remember that the form used in a question (whether *shall* or *will*) anticipates the same form in the answer. Here, when the answer is not vocalized at all, it nevertheless flashes through the reader's mind. The poet expects (and presumably will get) from the each "Will you?" . . . the "I will" reply, implying consent, promise or resolve. For the last line of the poem—and note that he shifts to the first-person plural—the answer is consequent upon one's having just vowed to take to the open road with the poet. . . . The point here is that the persona speaks directly to the reader, in the present tense and time, with sufficient seriousness and sincerity that we give him that necessary 'willing suspension of disbelief' and respond, however fleetingly, to his query.[52]

In book XIV, "El gran océano," Neruda reverses these roles of questioner and responder to engage the readers collectively (*vosotros*) and more explicitly in an extended dialogue:

> *Me habéis preguntado qué hila el crustáceo*
>   *entre sus patas de oro*
> *y os respondo: El mar lo sabe.*
> *Me decís qué espera la ascidia en su campana*
>   *transparente? Qué espera?*
> *Yo os digo, espera como vosotros el tiempo.*
>
> (17:680)

You've asked me what the crustacean spins
    between its gold claws
and I reply: the sea knows.

Ritual Speech: I, the Song

> You wonder what the sea squirt waits for in its
> transparent bell? What does it wait for?
> I tell you: it's waiting for time like you.
>
> (360)

As Hollis suggests, the reading of oral poetry does require a certain "willing suspension of disbelief" on the part of the reader to convert it into the record of a speech event, which is what our translations of American Indian poetry represent. As translations, these are even one level further removed from the sound of the word. Whether the intended or original magic is lost is difficult to say. Yet when we turn to these texts, such as they are, it is evident that form is an integral result of function, even if that function, in its original scope, is lost or transformed. In the same sense, the ritualistic function of a Kachina-inspired Martha Graham choreography may not survive in the Modern Dance concert, yet it still defines the movement on stage, just as the power of certain speech acts defines the written and silently read stylistics of Whitman and Neruda's poetry.

The transposition in their work of oral into written poetry, or the resulting tension between the visual and auditory, is central and marks their poetry as different from American Indian song. Reading Whitman, his stylistics make us aware, through the eye, not only of his voice but of the "many uttering tongues" of speech itself:

> My voice goes after what my eyes cannot reach,
> With the twirl of my tongue I encompass worlds
>   and volumes of worlds.
>
> Speech is the twin of my vision, it is unequal to
>   measure itself.
> It provokes me forever, it says sarcastically,
> *Walt you contain enough, why don't you let it out then?*
>
> ("Song of Myself":25:55)

Yet even the ways in which Whitman and Neruda translate the elements of speech into those of vision occur in patterns typical to oral poetry. Like blues songs, the individual "lines" of American Indian songs are often punctuated by the words "say" or "listen." Like the repetition of the call-and-response, however, this has seldom become part of the translation. In her chant, the contemporary Mazatec shaman María Sabina sings

> I am a sap woman, a dew woman, says
> I am a fresh woman, a woman of clarity, says
> I am a woman of light, a woman of the day, says
> I am a woman who looks into the insides of things, says [53]

In a Cherokee song, we find the oral emphatic "listen":

> listen   I'll grind your saliva into the earth
> listen   I'll cover your bones with black flint
>
> . . . .
>
> listen   I'm bringing a box for your bones
>   A black box
>   A grave with black pebbles
> listen   your soul's spilling out
> listen   it's blue [54]

In a Kuna chant, we find the oral emphatic "don't you hear it is said don't you hear it is said" at the end of each line, as well as other combinations involving "say" and "hear." [55] In section 18 of "Starting from Paumanok," Whitman uses much the same pattern, transforming "listen," "hear," or "say" into "see":

> See, streamers streaming through my poems,
> See, in my poems immigrants continually coming
>   and landing,
> See, in arriere, the wigwam, the trail, the hunter's
>   hut, the flat-boat, the maize-leaf, the claim,
>   the rude fence, and the backwoods village,
>
> . . . .
>
> See, ploughmen ploughing farms—see, miners digging
>   mines—see, the numberless factories,
> See, mechanics working at their benches with tools—

see from among them superior judges, philosophs,
    Presidents, emerge, drest in working dresses,
See, lounging through the shops and fields of the States,
    me well-belov'd, close-held by day and night,
[Hear] the loud echoes of my songs there—read the hints
    come at last.[56]

(27)

Each of the images introduced by "see" is intensely visual, and the imperative affirms the power of vision repeatedly infused throughout the poem. Yet after the twelfth such repetition of "see," the visual command is transposed under a cumulative weight into: "*Hear* the loud echoes of my songs there—*read* the hints come at last." Through an incantatory synesthesia, Whitman converts vision into a song that is heard, seemingly liberating his words from the limitations of paper and ink. He then refocuses this "seeing" and "hearing" into the immediate act of "reading," acknowledging his audience and the words on the page through which he is communicating at the very moment he transforms vision into song, image into speech. In the imperative-structured spell that concludes the final section to part I of *Canto general*, Neruda chants the oral emphatics of "look" and "listen" to perform a similar act of synesthesia between seeing and hearing:

Mira las lanzas descansando.
Escucha el susurro del aire
atravesado por las flechas.
Mira los pechos y las piernas
y las cabelleras sombrías
brillando a la luz de la luna.

Mira el vacío de los guerreros.
No hay nadie. Trina la diuca
como el agua en la noche pura.

Cruza el cóndor su vuelo negro.
No hay nadie. Escuchas? Es el paso
del puma en el aire y las hojas.

Ritual Speech: I, the Song

No hay nadie. Escucha. Escucha el árbol,
escucha el árbol araucano.

No hay nadie. Mira las piedras.

Mira las piedras de Arauco.
                              (I:6:329–30)

Behold the spears at rest.
Listen to the whispering air
pierced by arrows.
Behold the breasts and legs,
the dark hair
shining in the moonlight.

Behold the warriors' absence.

There's no one. The diuca finch trills
like water in the pure night.

The condor cruises its black flight.

There's no one. Do you hear? It's the puma
stepping in the air and the leaves.

There's no one. Listen. Listen to the tree,
listen to the Araucanian tree.

There's no one. Behold the stones.

Behold the stones of Arauco.
                              (26–27)

In considering the original versions of American Indian poems, Michael Castro warns that "their dimensions of music, movement, and relation are more complex, more physical [than the translations], for they are literally embodied in their singers. The translation, because it shifts the ground of the poem from the media of the singer's body and voice to the medium of the page, can only provide, at best, the roughest equivalent of the original."[57] Yet if Whitman and Neruda have lost the purely oral/aural magic present in American Indian poetry, by using such emphatics to induce a visual/oral synesthesia they generate a different but equally powerful magic inherent in the writing down of oral poetry. Readers are made aware not only of the voice of the poet but that this voice emanates from a physical body, one progressively identified as a microcosm of the land the poet sings. The effect, as in American Indian shamanism, is that the land itself sings through the manifest voice and body of the poet: "My land without name . . . / your aroma climbed up my roots to the glass / raised to my lips, up to the slenderest / word as yet unborn in my mouth" (*Canto general*:I:1:14). The rhythmic trajectory of the word—from land to body to mouth to poem to ear—is based in Whitman and Neruda's poetry on essentially oral devices common to what Rothenberg calls "the animal-body-rootedness of 'primitive' poetry," in which there is "recognition of a 'physical' basis for the poem within a man's body—or as an act of body & mind together, breath &/or spirit."[58] The effect of this in Whitman and Neruda's poetry is to convince readers that they are listeners and the poetic "I" is not only a song but, as Whitman proclaims in "The Sleepers," "I am a dance" (1:426).

III

In American Indian poetry, the power of the word gives reality to language as a "world in itself," since words are used not to duplicate the world but to pronounce it into existence. In *An American Primer,* Whitman names into being a cosmos in itself of words as sensual objects, caressing their palpable textures at length:

> Words of the Laws of the Earth,
> Words of the Stars, and about them,
> Words of the Sun and Moon,
> Words of Geology, History, Geography
> . . . .

Ritual Speech: I, the Song

> Words of the Body, Senses, Limbs, Surface, Interior,
> Words of dishes to eat, or of naturally produced
>   things to eat,
> Words of clothes,
> Words of implements,
> Words of furniture, . . .
>
> (AP:26–27)

In "Como era España," a poem in *Tercera residencia,* Neruda creates what is certainly a "country in itself" by utilizing fourteen four-line stanzas to conjure Spain by incanting only the richly resounding names of its towns:

> *Argora, Torremocha, Argecilla,*
> *Ojos Negros, Salvacañete, Utiel,*
> *Laguna Seca, Cañamares, Salorino,*
> *Aldea Quemada, Pesquera de Duero.*
> (OC:I:276–77)

Even though these uses of language create a nonreferential world in the sense that the signifier is fused with the signified, this does not imply that words are cheapened or fade into meaninglessness, as in the nonreferential language of such American avant-garde works as Huidobro's *Altazor* or Stein's *Bee Time Vine,* in which the connection between signifier and signified is largely broken. Quite the contrary, as Old Torlino, a Navajo shaman, proclaims in this chant:

> I am ashamed before the earth;
> I am ashamed before the heavens;
> I am ashamed before the dawn;
>
> . . . .
>
> Some of these things are always looking at me.
> I am never out of sight.
> Therefore I must tell the truth.
> *I hold my word tight to my breast.* [59]

Language is "held tight," never used wastefully, because of the spiritual reality in which it participates, akin to the biblical injunction against using in vain the names of God.

American Indians, legendary for their silence, construct songs with exacting, ecological detail, employed to suggest large, unstated complexities:

> The water bug is drawing
> the shadows of the evening
> toward him on the water.[60]

As in the visual arts of the American Indians, what is captured is essence, not appearance. Writing on the primitive creation of animal images, art historian Herbert Read explains that the American Indian artist selects "just those features which best denote [the animal's] vitality, and by exaggerating these and distorting them until they cohere in some significant rhythms and shape, he produces a representation which conveys the very *essence* of the animal."[61] Likewise, in American Indian poetry this essential detail is precise, for, as Lincoln writes, the "language remains spare, neither more nor less than the evoked 'thing' itself."[62] Carl Sandburg was sufficiently struck by the similarity between this quality of American Indian poetry and Imagism to remark wryly, in a 1917 edition of *Poetry* magazine dedicated to American Indian translations, that "suspicion arises definitely that the Red Man and his children committed direct plagiarism on our modern imagists and vorticists."[63] Ironically, what so fascinated the cosmopolitan Pound about Chinese and Japanese poetry was being discovered by several of his stateside contemporaries in the then recently published translations of American Indian poetry, that is, the "direct treatment of the 'thing'" together with "absolutely no word that did not contribute to the presentation," according to the *Imagiste* manifesto published in *Poetry* only four years prior to its aboriginal issue.[64] In view of the anthropological and linguistic theories concerning the origins of the American Indian peoples as extensions of the same neolithic Siberian tribes that also migrated throughout Asia, it is not surprising that we should find the concise, concrete juxtapositions of a form such as the haiku, for instance, as an important element in American Indian poetry, and that this quality would have awakened such an enthusiastic recognition among modern American poets.

As inheritors of Whitman, each in his own way, perhaps both Sandburg and Pound were already sensitized to the distinctly non-European poetics of succinctly juxtaposing concrete phenomena into "images" to convey poetic meaning, an approach they later rediscovered in the exotica of Asian and American Indian poetry.[65] Certainly one of the more ground-breaking qualities in Whitman's poetry is that amid the apparent wordiness of its incantational structures, haikulike "essential details" suggest whole unspoken stories or spheres. These details are usually exaggerated or distorted in a way that depicts essence rather than appearance, and are presented, usually in a single line or two, with an exacting precision. Here are three of the more memorable from "Song of Myself":

> Leaving me baskets covered with white towels swelling
> the house with their plenty.
>
> > (3:31)

> The malform'd limbs are tied to the surgeon's table,
> What is removed drops horribly in a pail.
>
> > (15:42)

> Fog in the air, beetles rolling balls of dung.
> > (24:52)

In this manner, Whitman creates whole worlds with few words, each of the details odd in itself yet suggesting an essential characteristic. Whitman's details are often urban and journalistic, while those in American Indian poetry are always harmoniously related to nature, yet they are used in the same way to express the interrelations within a larger picture, and are therefore as exceedingly well defined as Pound's exemplary "Petals on a wet, black bough."

Although Neruda is a master of the use of "essential detail," his presentation is, on the whole, notably less imagistic than Whitman's, depending line by line on the metaphoric use of language rather than the unadorned presentation of the concrete. Although there are many passages such as the above conclusion to book I of *Canto general* ("Behold the spears at rest"), which do create metaphor by the imagistic juxtaposition of simple details, Neruda's tendency is toward the more European simile and what might be called the wrought or completed metaphor, in which the poet makes the connection in his language that the American Indian or Whitmanian image merely suggests. For example, each of these brief passages from a Mescalero Apache poem, "Song of Myself," and *Canto general*, respectively, establishes a metaphor about birds:

> The black turkey in the east spreads his tail
> The tips of his beautiful tail are the white dawn[66]

> The litter of the grunting sow as they dug at her teats,
> The brood of the turkey hen and she with her
>   half-spread wings,
> I see in them and myself the same law.
>
>   (14:41)

> *Los ilustres loros llenaban*
> *la profundidad del follaje*
> *como lingotes de oro verde*
> *recién salidos de la pasta*
> *de los pantanos sumergidos,*
> *y de sus ojos circulares*
> *miraban una argolla amarilla,*
> *vieja como los minerales.*
>
>   (I:3:319)

> Illustrious parrots filled
> the depths of the foliage,
> like ingots of green gold
> newly minted from the paste
> of sunken swamps

and from their circular eyes
yellow hoops looked out,
old as minerals.

(17)

All three poets describe the animals by the use of "essential details" that oddly emphasize a part of the animal in order to capture the essence of the whole: the tips of the turkey's tail feathers, the sow's teats and the half-spread wings of the turkey hen, and the round yellow eyes of the bright green parrot. Yet the American Indian and Whitman excerpts both suggest an implicit relationship between, in the former, the black turkey and night, and in the latter, the poet and a natural maternity. Neruda, however, makes the relationship between the parrot and its environment explicit by means of a simile (like gold) and a metaphor (minting): The parrot is a brilliant distillation of the greenery that surrounds it, and is to its background what a gold ingot is to the earth, a conceit continued by the comparison of their eyes to coins. Neruda often employs startling metaphoric fusions that display his surrealist background, such as addressing the earth as a "green uterus," calling the condor a "solitary monk of the sky," or juxtaposing "iron" and "vapor" to describe the Amazon river (I:1, 2 and 4). Far from the simple declarative rigors of Imagism and even beyond the limits of the European romantic tradition, Neruda frequently seems determined to metaphorically fuse together every known element in the universe by means of the adjectival *de* construction. John Felstiner has suggested that such language indicates "a primitive sympathy with the inanimate world [which] also accounts for him wanting to converse with Macchu Picchu, the Bío-Bío River, the ocean, and for the *sílabas, palabras, idioma* and *silencio* he hears in them."[67] Although Whitman and Neruda differ in these several points concerning the exact nature of their expression, what they more generally share is the incantatory impulse, as an Arekuna Indian song goes, to "leave nothing unnamed."[68]

As in American Indian poetry, Whitman and Neruda's "essential details" are often chanted in lengthy accumulations, in which they are panoramically linked. Parallel construction, one of the principal devices of American Indian poetry, is employed by both Whitman and Neruda in order to "rhyme" parallel worlds. "Instead of rhyming words (the poem as unifying technique)," Lincoln points out that "the [Indian] songs rhyme perceptions, moods, natural objects, the world as word (the poem as unifying association)."[69] In the Navajo "Song of the Black Bear," these three lines are so associated:

> With zigzag lightning darting from the ends
>   of my feet I step,
> With zigzag lightning streaming out
>   of my knees I step,
> With zigzag lightning streaming from the tip
>   of my tongue I speak.[70]

Although the repetitively conjunctive linking of elements in a chant is democratic in that all manner of unrelated phenomena may be included with unsubordinated grammatical equality, therefore perhaps defining a quintessentially American poetic form, parallel structure is a means of repetition used to establish the complex hierarchies between these elements existing within a given group. In the Navajo song, the electric energies of walking, running, and speaking are not equal, but are rhymed, as are those parts of the body that accomplish them. The repetition with an increment of "zigzag lightning" enlarges its presence with each recurrence until speech culminates as the most energetic of these functions, electricity running up the body from toe to tongue. The rhyming of dissimilar particulars by parallel construction, together with the enlarging of presence by means of repetition, gives American Indian poetry what Margot Astrov calls its "magically coercive quality."[71] The nature of this rhyming is exacting and often antithetical, as in this Papago song:

> An eagle is walking,
> Toward me it is walking.
> Its long feathers blow in the breeze.
>
> A hawk is running,
> Toward me it is running.
> Its down feathers ruffle in the wind.[72]

The first stanza is mirrored in the second with a notable intensification of effect, from "eagle," "walking," "blow," and "breeze" to "hawk," "running," "ruffle," and "wind." In considering the possibly Asian origins of American Indian forms, it is significant that classical Chinese poetry employs a complex system of similar antitheses, strictly codified in manuals of poetically balanced oppositionals to which poets refer, yet used in the same manner as in American Indian poetry to rhyme natural elements through parallel structure.[73]

Parallel structure is one of the principal poetic devices in Whitman and Neruda's poetry, and both poets use this technique in order to establish interrelations between the elements enumerated in their chants. Here, for example, is a grouping of animals in "Song of Myself":

> Where the panther walks to and fro on a limb overhead,
>   where the buck turns furiously at the hunter,
> Where the rattlesnake suns his flabby length on a rock,
>   where the otter is feeding on fish,
> Where the alligator in his tough pimples sleeps
>   by the bayou,
> Where the black bear is searching for roots or honey,
>   where the beaver pats the mud with his paddle-shaped
>   tail; . . .
>
> (33:61)

The central rhyme within these lines is between the various animals, their activities and habitats, as structured in parallel phrasing. The acts of walking, turning, sunning, feeding and sleeping in the first three lines seem to proceed from the greatest to the least levels of energy, following an atavistic movement from air to earth to water to swamp to roots, from complex mammal to amphibious reptile. The fifth line, with its searching and patting, reverses this direction toward the proverbial busyness of the beaver, perhaps in preparation for the energetic flight of the "over" section to follow in the poem. "Where" expands in increments with each repetition the presence of the complex interdependency of the natural world until it includes, at length in this section, a harmonious unity of almost all natural life. The "tough pimples" used to characterize the alligator is a distorted yet economical detail that strangely captures its essence, as do the "flabby length" of the rattlesnake and the "paddle-shaped tail" of the beaver.

Such details rhyme in both character and construction in the Whitman excerpt into a "tribe" of animal associations in a manner remarkably similar to Neruda's presentation of "Algunas bestias" that inhabit pre-Columbian America in book I:

> *Era el crepúsculo de la iguana.*
>
> *Desde la arcoirisada crestería*
> *su lengua como un dardo*
> *se hundía en la verdura,*
> *el hormiguero monacal pisaba*
> *con melodioso pie la selva,*
> *el guanaco fino como el oxígeno*
> *en las anchas alturas pardas*
> *iba calzando botas de oro,*
> *mientras la llama abría cándidos*
> *ojos en la delicadeza*
> *del mundo lleno de rocío.*
> *Los monos trenzaban un hilo*
> *interminablemente erótico*
> *en las riberas de la aurora,*
> *derribando muros de polen*
> *y espantando el vuelo violeta*
> *de las mariposas de Muzo.*
>
> (2:318)

> It was the twilight of the iguana.
>
> From its glistening battlement
> a tongue
> darted into the verdure,
> the monastic anteater trod
> the jungle with melodious feet,
> the guanaco fine as oxygen
> in the wide brown heights

was wearing boots of gold,
while the llama opened candid
eyes in the delicacy
of the world covered with dew.
The monkeys wove
an interminably erotic thread
on the shores of dawn,
leveling walls of pollen
and startling the violet flight
of the butterflies from Muzo.

(16)

As the sun of this "twilight" section is setting, the eye is rising by grouping the animals not according to geographical location but rather from the lowest to the highest of their habitats, spanning the continent from the lizards of the jungle floor, up through the guanacos and llamas of the Andean *altiplano,* toward the monkeys in the rain-forest treetops and finally to the air-borne butterflies native to a province of Colombia. As in the Whitman passage, several of the biospheres of the country are integrated in a parallel manner into a single interdependency. All of these animals are diurnal and nonpredatory and are defined as glistening, melodious, fine, candid, erotic, and pollinating; that is, procreative and innocent, idyllically involved in darting, treading, wearing golden boots, opening their eyes, and weaving. In the second part of this section, a dark mirror image of this tribal moiety is introduced:

[Era la noche de los caimanes,]
la noche pura y pululante
de hocicos saliendo de légamo,
y de las ciénagas soñolientas
un ruido opaco de armaduras
volvía al origen terrestre.

El jaguar tocaba las hojas
con su ausencia fosforescente,
el puma corre en el ramaje
como el fuego devorador
mientras arden en él los ojos

Ritual Speech: I, the Song

alcohólicos de la selva.
Los tejones rascan los pies
del río, husmean el nido
cuya delicia palpitante
atacarán con dientes rojos. [74]

(318–19)

It was the night of the cayman,
the night pure and pullulating
with snouts emerging from the ooze,
and from the somnolent swamps
an opaque thud of armor
returned to the earthy origin.

The jaguar touches the leaves
with its phosphorescent absence,
the puma bolts through the foliage
like a raging fire,
while in him burn
the jungle's alcoholic eyes.
Badgers scratch the river's feet,
sniff out the nest
whose throbbing delight
they'll attack with red teeth.

(16–17)

This group is nocturnal and predatory, one identified with a primordial night of "snouts emerging from the ooze," evolving from the reptilian battleground of dinosaurs (whose armor foreshadows the arrival of the conquistadors) to the carnivorous mammals that ignite the jungle. In a carefully reflected antithesis to those of the "twilight," here the heavenly ascent becomes a demonic descent through the night to animals that glow, bolt, burn, scratch, sniff, and attack, with the "red teeth" of the amphibious badgers approaching the river where, beneath the jungle floor, "in the depths of the almighty water," as this section ends, "lies the giant anaconda / like the circle of earth, / covered with ritual clays, / devouring and religious." As in the Whitman passage, the parallel construction interrelates in terms of an atavistically determined hierarchy the seemingly "chaotically enumerated" members of well-defined natural clans. As in American Indian poetry and in Whitman, the animals are economically evoked through the precise rendering of oddly essential details: from the darting tongue of the iguana, gold boots of the guanaco, and erotic thread of the monkeys to the emerging snouts of the caymans, alcoholic eyes of the puma and red teeth of the badgers. Finally, it is the oppositional nature of the parallel structure of this section that so unerringly recalls the eagle/hawk antithesis of the Papago song quoted above: the exacting reflection between opposed but closely related animals such as the iguana/cayman, anteater/armored swamp creature (dinosaur), guanaco/jaguar, llama/puma, badger/monkey, and, consummately, butterfly/anaconda, with the latter being a massive projection of the larval stage of the former. Through the use of parallel construction and essential detail, what is evident in this section of *Canto general* is an imagination strongly related to the antithetical organizational techniques of the American Indian, based on a means of classification far different from the European.

The classic European view of the enumerative organization in Whitman and Neruda's poetry is perhaps best represented in Leo Spitzer's essay, *La enumeración caótica en la poesía moderna* (1945), in which, among others, the two poets are compared on the basis of their "chaotic" or heterogeneous enumerations. Spitzer claims that it is "to Whitman whom we owe these catalogs of the modern world, broken to pieces in a dust cloud of heterogeneous things that are, nevertheless, integrated in his grand and majestic vision of the All-in-One." Without the unifying quality of Whitman's pantheistic faith, however, Spitzer maintains that modern poets such as Neruda use this disordered "bazaar style" to exhibit a disgust before the disjunctive absurdity of daily life. Spitzer is correct on two important points. First, for Whitman "the stylistically heterogeneous series assumes a metaphysically conjunctive function."[75] And secondly, although he considers only the first two volumes of *Residencia en la tierra*, Neruda's chaotic catalogs in these works do reflect a crisis of sensory disconnection that the poet suffered during his prolonged isolation at remote consular posts in Asia, as in these lines from "La calle destruida":

> *Sobre las poblaciones*
> *una lengua de polvo podrido se adelanta*

Ritual Speech: I, the Song

rompiendo anillos, royendo pintura,
haciendo aullar sin voz las sillas negras,
cubriendo los florones del cemento, los balurates
de metal destrozado,
el jardín y la lana, las ampliaciones de fotografías
    ardientes
heridas por la lluvia, la sed de las alcobas,
    y los grandes
carteles de los cines en donde luchan
la pantera y el trueno,
las lanzas del geranio, los almacenes llenos
    de miel perdida,
la tos, los trajes de tejido brillante,
todo se cubre de un sabor mortal
a retroceso y humedad y herida.

                   (OC:I:218–19)

Over the towns
a tongue of rotted dust advances,
breaking rings, gnawing painting,
making the black chairs howl voiceless,
covering the cement rosettes, the bulwarks
    of shattered metal,
the garden and the wool, the enlargements of
    ardent photographs,
wounded by the rain, the thirst of bedrooms,
    and the huge
movie posters on which struggle
the panther and the thunder,
the geranium's lances, the stores filled
    with spoiled honey,
the cough, the suits of shiny weave,
everything is covered with a mortal taste
of retreat and dampness and injury.[76]

While using the same conjunctive patterns common to his later work, the effect of such deliberately jarring juxtapositions is to defeat any degree of belonging, either of the poet to his body, that body to the world, or the elements of the world to each other, underlining the pathos of a radically disconnected materiality common to surrealist writing. Yet when we compare the elaborated unities and balanced antitheses of the above passages from Whitman and Neruda to these lines from *Residencia en la tierra,* we cannot find what Spitzer calls a disordered "Babelism" in either Whitman or in the Neruda of *Canto general* and his works thereafter.

On the contrary, what we observe in these poets is a means of classification that may deny the traditional European logic of genus/species, cause/effect, and time/space, yet one that at the same time presents us with a unified vision of a world naturally organized along the lines of "tribal" or "family" resemblances, as in this grouping (set off by semicolons) from "Song of Myself":

> The quadroon girl is sold at the auction-stand,
>   the drunkard nods by the bar-room stove,
> The machinist rolls up his sleeves, the policeman
>   travels his beat, the gate-keeper marks who passes,
> The young fellow drives the express-wagon, (I love him,
>   though I do not know him;)
> The half-breed straps on his light boots to compete
>   in the race,
> The western turkey-shooting draws old and young, some
>   lean on their rifles, some sit on logs,
> Out from the crowd steps the marksman, takes
>   his position, levels his piece; . . .

(15:42)

The unifying principle within this tribal group is men as defined by their activities, both in terms of anatomy (arms, feet, hands, separately, and in the fourth line, arm-hand-foot coordination) and of a forward movement (nod, roll, travel, pass, drive, compete, race, draw, step) to the western frontier. The combination of anatomy and movement suggests an underlying phallic organization, alluded to in the love aside of the third line and culminating in the last with the dramatically colloquial description of the marksman. This phallic focus is underlined by the initial image, seemingly incongruous, of the quadroon girl at auction: Young quadroon women, prized for their beauty, were largely bought and sold as concubines. Unifying this phallic family are named and implicit essential details that serve as totem identifications: the quadroon's sexual function, the drunk's stovepipe, the machinist's arm, the policeman's club, the gate-keeper's pen, reins, straps, rifles, logs, all directed not only westward but to the violence of the leveled "piece" and to the ritual assertion of masculinity common to that culture, the frontier turkey-shoot. Most of Whitman's basic assumptions about the Westward Expansion, slavery, democracy, masculinity, work and the sexuality of "adhesion" and "calamus" are evident in the way these lines interrelate. The sexual violence with which Whitman frames this group indicates the disturbing relationship between slavery and the Westward Expansion, as well as the ambivalence he feels as both an abolitionist and an expansionist, as though the frontier gun of the final image were aimed at the slave girl of the first. Far from the intentional chaos of the early Neruda lines, these enumerated details, like those in the bestiary from *Canto general,* reflect a harmony of complexly nuanced particulars natural to other, more primitive means of classification.

Anthropologists such as Claude Lévi-Strauss and Emile Durkheim, who have studied the totemic classifications of tribal peoples, have discovered methods of organizing both nature and society that bear a strong resemblance to Whitman and Neruda's. The tribal families of animals enumerated in the Whitman and Neruda passages are, like the groupings that Durkheim investigates in *Primitive Classification,* "systems of hierarchized notions. Things are not simply arranged . . . in the form of isolated groups, but these groups stand in fixed relationships to each other and together form a single whole." Durkheim finds that primitive social classifications precisely reflect the divisions observed within the natural world, so that different groups within the tribe are identified with the tribal groupings in nature, which may be dependent on color, direction, habitat, number, or a subtle combination of several such means of classification. The principal division within a tribe (of animals, for instance) is into halves or moieties, as in the diurnal/nocturnal separation in Neruda's bestiary passage, which are further divided into clans (by altitude, let us say, as Neruda does) and then into subclans (by shape or size, for example, as Neruda suggests). "Among certain Sioux," Durkheim explains, "there is a section of the tribe which is called red, and which comprises the clans of the mountain lion, buffalo and elk, all animals characterized by their violent instincts; the members of these clans are from birth warriors, whereas the farmers, people who are naturally peaceful, belong to clans of which the totems are essentially pacific animals."[77] Among the Zuñi, clans are identified by natural phenomena divided into seven primary directions; the sun and eagle tribes belong to the zenith direction, the frog and water tribes to the nadir direction, the tobacco, maize, and badger tribes to the southern direction, and so forth. "Indeed, what we find among the Zuñi," Durkheim concludes,

> is a veritable arrangement of the universe. All beings and facts in nature, 'the sun, moon, and stars, the sky, earth and sea, in all their phenomena and elements; and all inanimate objects, as well as plants, animals and men,' are classed, labelled, and assigned to fixed places in a unique and integrated 'system' in which all the parts are co-ordinated and subordinated one to another by 'degrees of resemblance.'[78]

In American Indian poetry, these "degrees of resemblance" are then abstracted from the natural phenomena the songs address into groupings of essential details. As Claude Lévi-Strauss writes in *The Savage Mind* about a song of the Osage (southern Sioux), "Each animal is thus decomposed into parts, according to a law of correspondence (muzzle=beak, etc.) and the equivalent parts are regrouped among themselves and then altogether in terms of the same relevant characteristics."[79] As we have seen in the passages from Whitman and Neruda, essential detail is the aspect of tribal grouping whereby the partial resemblances between diverse phenomena are isolated, exaggerated, and used as a means to identify these phenomena into what perhaps seem "chaotic," yet are in reality complexly harmonized families. This Osage song, for example, abstracts the blackness from each of its various totemic clan animals (the puma, golden eagle, young deer, and others) in order to group them into a ritual "black thing" song that goes, in part:

> Behold the soles of my feet, that are black in color,
> Behold the tip of my nose, that is black in color,

Ritual Speech: I, the Song

> Behold the tips of my ears, that are black in color,
> Behold the tip of my tail, that is black in color.[80]

In a similar manner, the male-activity section from "Song of Myself" abstracts both the moving and phallic qualities of each man's action in order to group them as a "clan of the firing gun." Here Whitman, like the American Indian song-poet whom Lincoln describes, "groups words in parallel phrases and rhymes thoughts, as though words also gather tribally, corresponding in kinship."[81]

In *Shaking the Pumpkin,* Jerome Rothenberg presents this kinship principle at work in these three clans of Navajo correspondences chanted as songs:

cotton	smoke
motion	cloud
clouds	rain
	acceptance
Frog	breathing in
hail	
potatoes	
dumplings[82]	

On the broadest level, such a sense of tribal kinship is the organizing principle for much of the enumeration in Whitman and Neruda's poetry. Tribal grouping is at work in all of the longer sections of *Leaves of Grass,* in which seemingly unrelated, haikulike images are chanted in clans, often set apart from each other by semicolons. It is also present in the multiple elements that certain individual lines combine, as in these from "Song of the Broad-Axe," which clearly echo the Navajo correspondences:

> Citadel, ceiling, saloon, academy, organ, exhibition-
>   house, library,
> Cornice, trellis, pilaster, balcony, window, turret,
>   porch,
> Hoe, rake, pitchfork, pencil, wagon, staff, saw,
>   jack-plane, mallet, wedge, rounce,

Chair, tub, hoop, table, wicket, vane, ash, floor,
Work-box, chest, string'd instrument, boat, frame,
    and what not,
Capitols of States, and capitol of the nation of
    States. . . .

                        (9:192)

Each line is an organic grouping in terms of shape, use, means of construction, or phase of the building process, and the section moves, line by line, from top to sides to bottom to enclosed spaces to emblematic edifices, culminating in the symbolic center of the nation—its first house, so to speak—the national capitol building. As in the Zuñi classifications, this suggests a "veritable arrangement of the universe" at work. The various clans in the tribe of housebuilding are invoked in each line: first line, high and imposing; second, supportive and angular; third, long and thin; fourth, flat and round; and fifth, wooden and hollow, a hierarchy natural to the construction process.

The reader's perplexity over oddly placed inclusions in such tribal groups parallels the anthropologist's when confronted with seeming irregularities in certain primitive classifications, such as the Osage association of the eagle as a land animal. Lévi-Strauss explains that "in Osage thought eagles are associated with lightning, lightning with fire, fire with coal and coal with the earth. The eagle is thus one of the 'masters of coal,' that is, a land animal." Thus, Lévi-Strauss contends that "the principle underlying a classification can never be postulated in advance. It can only be discovered *a posteriori* by ethnographic investigation, that is, by experience."[83] One likewise wonders why Whitman the teetotaler would include "saloon" among the clan of the high and imposing, as well as why Whitman the carpenter would place "wagon" at the center of a clan of long, thin tools. As with the Osage classification of the eagle, either historically remote or particularly private chains of associations are no doubt responsible for several of Whitman's more curious classifications, and nineteenth-century cultural history or Whitman's biography may prove for his readers what "ethnographic investigation" is for the anthropologist. Could "wagon" be associated with one of its parts, such as the axle, handle, or "tongue," with its function

110

in transporting carpentry tools, or perhaps with its driver? Whitman's "adhesion" to wagon and stage drivers was an important aspect of his life prior to the first publication of this poem in 1856. Harold Aspiz claims that during the 1850s Whitman "systematically visited hospitalized stage drivers: 'Yes, I knew all the drivers [on the Broadway stages] then,' recalled the poet," who visited about fifty at the New York Hospital during that period.[84] One can only speculate, but perhaps "wagon," through a homoerotic association with its drivers, assumed membership in the long, thin clan, as certainly suggested in the line from the previously quoted phallic grouping in "Song of Myself": "The young fellow drives the express-wagon, (I love him, though I do not know him)." As in the classifications of the Sioux or Zuñi, Whitman's tribal groupings interrelate into a whole, and often we must read between groupings to discover the "degrees of resemblance" that establish the clan memberships of certain seemingly misplaced inclusions.

To an even greater extent than Whitman, Neruda bases much of his poetics on the weaving together of words whose meanings have been established in previous contexts. Yet almost as if he were exhausted of private associations by the generally opaque hermeticism of his first two *Residencias,* Neruda's tribal groupings in *Canto general* are either anchored in a common historical culture or in nature, although occasionally certain associations also require either the biographer or the cultural historian. In a direct address to Recabarren, founder of the Chilean Communist party, Neruda enumerates a tribe of properties that demonstrates his poetics at work even in transparent lines of the most politically committed poetry:

> *Tú eres la patria, pampa y pueblo,*
> *arena, arcilla, escuela, casa,*
> *resurrección, puño, ofensiva,*
> *orden, desfile, ataque, trigo,*
> *lucha, grandeza, resistencia.*
> (IV:39:450)

You're homeland, pampa and people,
sand, clay, school, home,

resurrection, fist, offensive,
order, march, attack, wheat,
struggle, greatness, resistance.
(140)

Here the intermingling of the earth clan (pampa, sand, clay, wheat) with the battle clan (resurrection, fist, offensive, order, march, attack, struggle, resistance) and the family clan (homeland, people, school, home, greatness) invokes the tribe of patriotic Indian warriors with whom Latin American revolutionary movements have often identified. The order of elements in the battle clan reflects, as does the arrangement of the lines in Whitman's housebuilding tribe, the steps prescribed for revolution, from the "resurrection" of political consciousness to the "resistance" against oppression. The earth clan includes the four principal topographies of the Chilean landscape and their workers—nitrate miners (pampas), coastal fishermen (sand), rain-forest Indians (clay), and farmers (wheat)—the exact nature of each having been established by their inclusion in other clans throughout *Canto general*. "Clay," for instance, is repeatedly identified as a member of the Indian, mother, river, and Araucania clans introduced within the first three books of the work, that is, with the tribe of those elements representing the spiritual, familial, and geographical roots of the poet: "whence I come . . . from a silent mother of clay" (I:4:20), a mother of a "mineral race . . . like a cup of clay" (I:6:24). "Clay," in Neruda's poetry, signifies more than damp earth. It is a word webbed with associations of the dark Indian mother whom he lost at birth and whom he recovered in the rainy landscapes of Araucania. Throughout his later poetry, it becomes further identified with his third wife, Matilde, an Araucanian with the American Indian blood that his natural mother possessed only in the poet's imagination.

The cross-referencing in Neruda's poetry of frequently repeated key words—stone, genital, syllable, blood, clay, fire, cup, pure, root, wave, wing, and arrow, among many—is a means of creating another "veritable arrangement of the universe." Each element carries with it a network of multiple memberships in various tribes, moieties, clans, and subclans of meaning established not only throughout this particular work but throughout his body of poetry. What may initially appear as a simplistic, even annoying, repetitiveness in his poetry is, as in American Indian classification, in reality a means of interlocking these complex clans of meaning into a whole.[85] For the Zuñi song-poet, for example, the use of the word "tobacco" indicates south, and exists in relationship to other southern clan elements such as "maize" and "badger," just as "bear" indicates west. "Bear eating tobacco" would indicate the southwest, together with other combinations of color, number, and place established by the natural qualities assigned to the two clans. Neruda is as much involved as American Indian song-poets in creating the "world in itself" of language and, in his later works in particular, presents the reader with simple-sounding combinations of common words such as "stone," "bird," and "crystalline" that have accumulated through tribal grouping complex associative meanings throughout his work.[86] Felstiner raises this concern, observing that "if the common words for things, 'bird' and 'moon' and 'dew,' sometimes make [Neruda] sound facile or repetitive, maybe his aim is just that, to speak in common. He doesn't worry whether the language will fail him, any more than a swimmer worries whether water will be there for the next stroke."[87] Neruda is confident of the language in which he swims because by slow accretions of meaning he has created it.

In *Canto general*, Neruda's enumerations concern either a past or present historical reality, or they represent groupings within nature, and as a distinguished ornithologist and conchologist, his passion for the naming and classification of natural American forms is evident throughout this and subsequent books:

> *Estoy, estoy rodeado*
> *por madreselva y páramo, por chacal y centella,*
> *por el encadenado perfume de las lilas:*
> *estoy, estoy rodeado*
> *por días, meses, aguas que sólo yo conozco,*
> *por uñas, peces, meses que sólo yo establezco,*
> *estoy, estoy rodeado*
> *por la delgada espuma combatiente*
> *del litoral poblado de campanas.*
>
> (VI:17:525)

Ritual Speech: I, the Song

I am, I am surrounded
by honeysuckle and wasteland, by jackal and lightning,
by the enchained perfume of lilacs:
I am, I am surrounded
by days, months, waters that I alone know,
by fingernails, fish, months that I alone establish,
I am, I am surrounded
by the slender combatant foam
of the seaboard full of bells.

(210–11)

Yet if this is classification, even of the primal order that Durkheim and Lévi-Strauss elucidate, what are its dimensions? Where does it begin and end? In groupings such as this one, or that of Whitman's house-building tribe, readers may wonder about the criteria for the inclusion or exclusion of elements. Whitman does not exhaust either the implements or aspects of construction any more than Neruda here begins to name everything in nature that surrounds him. These nouns, adjectives, proper names, motions, qualities, feelings, and landscapes clustered in their work are, as in American Indian poetry, "compound-elements, each clearly articulated and with plenty of room for fill-in (gaps in sequence, etc.)," as Rothenberg describes the same process in all oral poetry. "The 'spectator' [is a] (ritual) participant who pulls it all together."[88] The compound-element structure of such tribal groupings means that the organization is essentially open ended and the elements, to some degree, interchangeable. The effects of this in Whitman and Neruda's poetry are threefold. First, this structure is magnified from the line to the stanza to the individual poem and ultimately to the works themselves, lending a mosaic organization to the clustered, untitled sections grouped as poems, each of which in turn occupies the place of a nonhierarchical compound-element in the open ended arrangement of the book. Just as the meaning of lines or stanzas exists independently of the inclusion or exclusion of particular compound-elements, *Leaves of Grass* and *Canto general* are both mosaic compositions of sections within sections, each of which is a self-contained, nonlinear contribution to the democratic growth of the whole. Secondly, the conjunctive structuring of continuous elements mirrors the fragmentation of vernacular speech. As Bridgman observes about the compound structure of colloquial prose, "The vernacular speaker offers those actions in an unsubordinated series, just as he does physical objects. . . . This focuses attention upon the single unit of action as it is caught and isolated between commas and conjunctions."[89] As in speech, our attention is focused more on the passing units of a potentially endless series—"by honeysuckle and wasteland, by jackal and lightning"—than on any conscious syntax of subordination, a quality inherent to written language. In this passage, the stuttering repetition of "I am, I am" enhances this effect, because what compound-elements produce is a form of stuttering in which words move forward one at a time but not in their relationship to each other. Yet the third effect is that this speech is ritualized or "raised right up," as the Zuñis call it, by the rhythmic unifiers of repetition and parallel construction ("surrounded"; the "by" and "I alone" constructions), which bind the diverse, seemingly endless elements ("fingernails, fish, months") into a ceremonial, hypnotic flow, inviting the readers/listeners, as Rothenberg claims, "to pull it all together," and in doing so, transporting them to another, more suspended sphere.

IV

Ceremony is what Whitman and Neruda are performing in their poetry, and another of the factors that ritualistically align the groupings of compound-elements is a decisive unity of time. Hollis finds an almost exclusive use of the lyric present tense in Whitman's poetry, with 94 percent of the poems in the 1860 edition written in the present tense.[90] In "The Lyric Present," George Wright maintains that in the exclusive use of the simple present tense in poetry, "the actions described seem suspended, removed from the successiveness of our ordinary time levels, neither past, present, or future, neither single nor repeated, but of another dimension entirely."[91] For example, in the line "I sing the body electric," when does Whitman sing? Does he sing in the moment he is writing (then why not the present progressive "am singing") or in the moment the reader reads the words? Since no habituality is indicated by a frequency adverb, does he sing once, and if so, when? A book constructed 94 percent in this tense takes on a dreamlike, ceremonial quality, for according to Wright, the lyric present communicates

> a sense of elevation and, often, of solemnity which seems appropriate to visionary experience. . . . When poets use the tense, therefore, to describe their own actions or those of others, these actions acquire a faintly or strongly ceremonial character. This is especially true in first-person examples, where the poet, in announcing his ceremonial actions, seems to be playing a priest-like role.[92]

The first-person use of the lyric present is priestlike because the illocutionary nature of the speech points to a spiritual power that the speaker assumes, one that translates words into action, such as Whitman's "I speak the pass-word primeval, I give the sign of democracy" ("Song of Myself":24:52). When this tense is used to describe others, it makes their actions or qualities seem like eternally mythic conditions of the cosmos: "The pure contralto sings in the organ loft" (15:41); that is, she does not sing in any historic time in memory, but as if in a continual vision or religious ritual, in original time.

American Indians refer to this lyric present as "dreamtime." According to Joseph Epes Brown, "Events or processes transmitted through oral tradition tend to be recounted neither in terms of time past or time future in a lineal sense. Indeed most native languages have no such tenses to express this. They speak rather of a perennial reality of the now."[93] All of American Indian poetry takes place in the lyric present, which, as in Whitman's poetry, bears witness to its strongly ceremonial form and purpose. More than a mere stylistic device in either of these poetries, it serves as a means of making sacred the ritual occasion of utterance. As Mircea Eliade explains in *The Sacred and the Profane,* the lyric present or dreamtime is the "eternal mythical present that is periodically reintegrated by means of rites." The distinguishing factor of religious man, according to Eliade, is that "he refuses to live solely in what, in modern times, is called the historical present; he attempts to regain a sacred time that . . . can be homologized to eternity."[94] Whitman, as an example of this religious consciousness, does not speak of beginnings or endings, but of a mythic present outside of reference to the historical past or future, in which

> There was never any more inception than there is now,
> Nor any more youth or age than there is now,
> And will never be any more perfection than there is now,
> Nor any more heaven or hell than there is now.
>
> ("Song of Myself":3:30)

This mythical time of religious ceremony is a recurring original time that cannot be located in history and is, therefore, decidedly pre- or non-Christian. Eliade believes that Christianity "radically changed the experience and concept of liturgical time, and this is because Christianity affirms the historicity of the person of Christ." The Christian interpretation of Whitman to the contrary, both Whitman and American Indian song-poets share a concept of time that is not only religious but archaic or "pagan" in nature and ceremonial in form, marking a ritualized return to a mythic present, to what Eliade considers the "presence of the gods, to recover the strong, fresh, pure world that existed *in illo tempore.*"[95]

This recurring *in illo tempore* of American Indian dreamtime and of Whitman's lyric present is the paradise lost that Christianity locates at the beginning and Marxism at the end of the historical time in which both are grounded, inspiring faith in a redemptive individual return after death or a utopian collective future after revolution. Unlike the pagan Whitman, Neruda, as a Marxist, is a participant in this historical process, integrating dates, names, deeds, governments, and political policies into *Canto general,* basing whole books on historical figures and the dramatic recreation of significant events from the landing of the conquistadors to the beginnings of the Cold War. For example, books III, IV, and V are devoted, respectively, to the conquerors, the liberators, and the dictators of most of the countries of Latin America, in almost exhaustive detail. Yet rather than a chronological narration, Neruda alternates continually between several verb tenses—the narrative past tense, the present narrative, the present progressive, and the lyric present—frequently within the same section or even within the same stanza. Neruda often positions his voice in the present narration of an historical event, only to distance himself with the past narrative and to comment finally in the lyric present. The effect of this is a blurring of the present into the past and the past into the suspension of a mythic time. Although factually accurate, for the most part, events are grouped by theme or region in a mosaic rather than a linear fashion, and the unities of time and place are often more mythic and auto-biographical than historical. Neruda acknowledged to Julio Cortázar that *Canto general* is "an achronological monstrosity," which Cortázar considers "proof that Latin America is not only outside of European historical time but has a perfect right and, what is more, the piercing obligation to be so. . . . *Canto general* decided to make a *tabula rasa* and begin anew."[96]

Like that other comprehensive twentieth-century saga of the Latin American experience, García Márquez's *Cien años de soledad,* Neruda's is a narrative spun in a spiral of overlapping recurrences approaching the archetypal at the same time as it engages a sense of historical background.[97] There are two seemingly opposed impulses at work within *Canto general,* which Saúl Yurkievich terms the poetics of the "mythic-metaphoric" and of the "militant-testimonial," and which he views as an antagonistic duality coexisting within Neruda's poetry:

> One, the mythic, postulates a backward motion, a return to the uterus, going back to an origin granted by the past; it is a nostalgic version, fed by the desire to recover the bounty of beginnings; it situates us in natural time, cyclical, without advance, in the eternal return. . . . The other, a historicist poetic, assumes a future time of continual progress, vectorial, directed toward a future where the bounty is located; the golden age is not at the beginning, but at the end, once the social revolution is won.[98]

Yurkievich is correct in identifying a strain of politically committed, occasionally propagandistic poetry woven throughout the denser, more archetypal texture of *Canto general.* This testifies to the Cold War background during which the book was edited (1947–49), just as Whitman's propagandistic outbursts about the Westward Expansion of his era inadvertently frame a more ahistorical vision. "Neruda, poet of a

continent whose peoples have been condemned to plunder, to poverty
and stagnation," explains Yurkievich, "cannot rest content with a natural, primitive, paradisiacal vision,"[99] or with the robust innocence and
social optimism of Whitman's mid-nineteenth-century United States,
which he so much admired. Yet Neruda—never a realist, socialist or
otherwise—is less concerned with using poetry to record history or to
document its failures than in lifting his version of the past onto the
level of a genesis myth so that it might enter into history and thereby
help to change it. Lines such as these use the lyric present to transpose
historical reality into the suspension of dreamtime:

> *De noche y día veo los martirios,*
> *de día y noche veo al encadenado,*
> *al rubio, al negro, al indio*
> *escribiendo con manos golpeadas y fosfóricas*
> *en las interminables paredes de la noche.*
>
> (VI:10:522)

> Night and day I see martyrdom,
> day and night I see the enchained—
> Whites, Blacks, Indians—
> writing on the night's interminable
> walls with bruised phosphoric hands.
>
> (207)

Like Whitman, Neruda is celebrating the cosmogony of the birth and
survival of his tribe in a world that may be unjust and misdirected but
that, nevertheless, is constantly being reborn. The Spanish poet Gabriel
Celaya has perceptively identified the exact stratum of genesis that
Neruda's dreamtime occupies by calling him "the poet of the Third Day
of Creation, *par excellence:* a great sacred dinosaur, serpentine, viscous,
cold and sweet, primordial, magnetic more than energetic, hypnotic,
materially or minerally as fascinating as a precious stone or a dragon
from the Tertiary Age."[100] *Canto general* begins with the creation of
the earth ("La lámpara en la tierra") and concludes with the creation
of the waters ("El gran océano"), and "in between are abundant poems
that recall the 'day of origin,'" as Yurkievich points out: "The original,

in this perspective, is literally a return to the source, to reiterate what from the beginning of time is renewed as the sacred model."[101] Even the blackened hands of the oppressed miners of Tarapacá are "hands that break planets, / and raise the salts to heaven," repeating "the celestial history: 'This / is the first day upon the earth'" (IV:38:6:134).

What *Canto general* represents is the type of narrative that American Indians know as an "origin story: a tale of an 'earlier world' that often explains present conditions," as Kenneth M. Roemer defines this genre in his essay on "Native American Oral Narratives." *Canto general* combines three types of origin stories: the creation narrative, such as the Maya-Quiché *Popul Vuh,* to which Neruda links his origin story of the American creation by beginning "Before the wig and the dress coat" (I:1:13); the emergence narrative, such as those that trace the trials of the Navajo ancestors in becoming a people, and such as those books Neruda dedicates to the conquerors, liberators and dictators of the Americas, as well as the "Canto general de Chile"; and the migration tale, which might be compared to book X, "El fugitivo." "In all of the origin stories," Roemer explains, "whether they be creation, emergence, or migration tales, the characters are divinities or prototypes of people and animals—the Navajo call them 'mist people.'"[102] "Mist people" seems an excellent way to characterize the Indian warriors, slaughtered tribes, cruel conquerors, liberators, and early dictators whom Neruda introduces in the first part of the work as the recurring prototypes of the Communist party leaders, martyred masses, invading imperialists, nationalists, and modern dictators whom he presents cyclically as the current reality. The origin stories do not occur exclusively in the chronological past, Brown makes clear, but "rather they tell of processes which are of eternal happening; the same processes are recurring now and are to recur in other cycles."[103]

Neruda's "mist people," no strangers to the broadest social bases of Latin America, continue to appear in the "pantheons" of voices channeled by shamans in contemporary mestizo and Afro-Caribbean possession cults. The cult of María Lionza in Venezuela, for example, includes a pantheon of Indian caciques and heroic liberators, a local version of the fourth book of *Canto general,* "Los libertadores." At the height of this Venezuelan pantheon is the spirit of the Liberator, Simón Bolívar, who regularly addresses the faithful through the mouths and bodies of possessed shamans. The tribal origin story that these mediums perform is a religious ceremony blending the nationalistic and historical with the mythic and cosmological, much like Neruda. According to Francisco Ferrandiz, who has investigated the nationalist elements in this cult, these rituals provide their marginal devotees with "the voice of the true protagonists of historical events. In the mouths of the mediums, oral tradition and popular knowledge are at the same time reproduced, amplified and transformed in nature."[104] The historical actions in *Canto general* are likewise amplified and transformed, or, as Yurkievich puts it, "scrambled, entangled, invaded by the turbulent imagination that transmits human happenings into mythological instances, into cosmogonic forces."[105]

Neruda's pantheon of historical voices, like those of the cult of María Lionza, sing what North American Indians call an "inside song,"[106] the point of which is to reaffirm unity and to heal, not to tell a chronological story whose full context is expressed in words alone. A reader unfamiliar with Latin American history or culture would be as lost in the mythic labyrinth of *Canto general* as the uninitiated at a possession cult ceremony. Neruda is speaking to his tribe of the initiated, not to outsiders seeking a chronicle, epic history, or objective perspective. For Neruda, the origin story of the Latin American peoples is an "inside song" rooted in a history transformed into myth, out of which springs the lyric elements of a ritualized speech that so closely identifies his work with the word-conjuring of Whitman. Both poet-chiefs adopted techniques that correspond to those of the American Indian song-poets, as singers, namers, and storytellers. In doing so, they developed personae that approximate the mask the shaman puts on as he gathers the tribe around him to participate in the hypnotic chant of what the Zuñis call *chimiky' ana'kova,* or "that which was the beginning."[107]

4
This Ecstatic Nation: Tribe, Mask, and Voice

> This ecstatic Nation
> seek—it is yourself—
> —*Emily Dickinson*

*T*he speakers in *Leaves of Grass* and *Canto general* do not step forward as characters already familiar from the pages of European romantic poetry, although several surface romantic traits can mislead us into thinking so. Whitman and Neruda's voices do resemble those of Wordsworth and García Lorca, their most notable European romantic contemporaries, who both adopted the language of what Wordsworth called "a man speaking to men," were associated with such democratic movements as the French Revolution and Spanish Republicanism, and opposed the disruptive industrialism of their times with a return to simpler communities, those of the "solitary reaper" in the English countryside and of the Andalusian country people with their gypsy folklore. Yet neither of the European poets offered his own persona, on an epic scale, as an emblem of communal reintegration. The cultural unity of the English or of the Andalusians as a homogeneous people, of course, is never in question in their work. The lyric "I" of these poets remains private and singular rather than public and collective, a voice distanced from the social center, childlike, often nostalgic, rather than one vocalizing the identity of a people in transition. Even the biblical persona of a truly prophetic poet such as Blake stands apart from the vision that it presents, an outsider circling like Joshua the walls of a society it seeks to change.

Like many romantics, Whitman and Neruda appear to set themselves at the center of their work, yet these "selves" lack a verisimilitude of recognizably human dimensions. In Rimbaud's phrase, their "I is Another," one that not only speaks but acts in mythic proportions, with a mysteriously anointed authority, as if generated not merely from the personality of an individual writer but from the soul of a nation. What Neruda learned from Whitman, as Frank Menchaca phrases it, "is that 'I' is not only Another but 'I' is Others."[1] In "The Sleepers," Whitman waves his hands like magic wands over the "wretched features" of a host of the physically and psychically ailing, as if to draw them into his own healing magneticism and reincorporate them into the lost collective wholeness he represents: "I dream in my dreams all the dreams of the other dreamers, / and I become the other dreamers" (1:331–32). In "Alturas de Macchu Picchu," Neruda mounts the ancient Incan citadel, surveying across the ages the misery of those who constructed it, a labor identified with the ongoing oppression of the American masses, whom he attracts to his "body like magnets" so that they might "speak through my words and my blood" (II:13·42). Whitman and Neruda's ideas of a spiritual democracy, their creation of a masklike "I" as a microcosm of a collective "we" that their word unifies and animates, the multiplicity of voices that speak through this mask, and their identification of their own magnetic anatomy and biography with the geography and history of their nations point to a New World model rather than the romantic one: the poetic persona suggested by Whitman's term *poet-chief,* which parallels the role of the tribal shaman in American Indian cultures.

The ceremonial cosmogony in Whitman and Neruda's poetry is identified with the formation and growth of their own continents, just as the American Indian song-poet celebrates the legendary establishment of his tribe as simultaneous with the origins of the universe. In their poems of "A Nation announcing itself," as Whitman writes in "By Blue Ontario's Shore" (2:340), they fulfill another of the complex shamanic roles in addition to those of singer, namer, spirit-guardian, and word-conjuror: They act as tribal unifiers. "Like the warrior, the song-poet lives individually for the sake of the tribe," Kenneth Lincoln points out. "He does not celebrate himself separately, his vision apart from the natural world, but sings his kinship in the tribal circle." Since the song-poet is the guardian of the tribal language, his role is to preserve unity among all those who use it. This is because, according to Lincoln, "a common tribal language is essential. Oral traditions gather the people tribally, as they poeticize the common speech. . . . The word is tribal bond."[2] Just as the song-poet names into tribes, moieties, and clans of relationship the diverse elements of nature, he pronounces into unity the differing but related members of the tribe. "The world of the human and the world of nature and spirit are essentially reflections of each other in the shaman's view of the cosmos," as Joan Halifax explains in *Shaman: The Wounded Healer*.[3] The shaman lends to human diversity the unities he finds in nature, so that their classification, as defined by Durkheim and Lévi-Strauss, is as much of society as of nature, and the language and mask of the shaman form an essential bridge between the cosmic body and the body politic. "Fall behind me States! / A man before all—myself, typical, before all," Whitman writes in "Blue Ontario" (14:351), anticipating Neruda, who announces, "I'm people, innumerable people" (X:13:287).

For Whitman as for Neruda, not only the idea of The People but their presence as an audience is central to their identities as poets. In twenty-seven of the North American native languages, the name of the tribe simply means "the people," as the name of the Araucanian Mapuche tribe signifies "the people from the earth." Whitman christens his own tribe with a Greek derivation meaning essentially the same: Democracy. Like the shaman, Whitman and Neruda do not celebrate their own particularities except that they are or should be indicative of the natural harmony of the whole, or as Whitman writes in "Starting from Paumanok":

> I will not make poems with references to parts,
> But I will make poems, songs, thoughts, with reference
>   to ensemble,
> And I will not sing with reference to a day, but
>   with reference to all days,
> And I will not make a poem or the least of a poem
>   but has reference to the soul. . . .
>
> (12:23)

The word of the shaman, as a tribal bond, originates from the tribe, not from the individuality of the shaman. This is what Whitman calls "*the poem . . . that comes from the Soul of America*" ("Blue Ontario":1:340). As in Neruda's metaphor in these lines from "El fugitivo," this word is germinated by the shaman and returned to the tribe as a necessary spiritual food:

> *El maíz te lleva mi canto*
> *salido desde las raíces*
> *de mi pueblo, para nacer,*
> *para construir, para cantar,*
> *y para ser otra vez semilla*
> *más numerosa en la tormenta.*
> (X:13:606)

> The corn brings you my song,
> risen from my people's
> roots, to be born,
> to build, to sing,
> and to be seed again
> more numerous in the storm.
> (287)

Yet this model of tribal harmony, attractive as it may be, hardly seems to correspond to the social complexities that Whitman and Neruda faced as nineteenth- and twentieth-century poets. The United States and Chile are not hunting-and-gathering tribes or hivelike ancient citadels led by poet-chiefs, but historical amalgamations of disjunctive peoples and classes divided along the complicated lines of power and hierarchy, as represented by their economic systems and forms of government. The relationship between spiritually communal ties and the complex structural ones of the modern nation states that Whitman and Neruda celebrate is clarified by Victor Turner in *The Ritual Process,* in which he defines

> two major 'models' for human interrelatedness, juxtaposed and alternating. The first is of society as a structured, differentiated and often hierarchical system of politico-legal-economic positions with many types of evaluation, separating men in terms of 'more' or 'less.' The second, which emerges recognizably in the

liminal period, is of society as an unstructured or rudimentarily
structured and relatively undifferentiated *comitatus,* community,
or even communion of equal individuals who submit together
to the general authority of the ritual elders. . . . The distinction
between structure and communitas is not simply the familiar one
between 'secular' and 'sacred,' or that, for example, between politics and religion. . . . It is rather a matter of giving recognition to
an essential and generic human bond, without which there could
be *no* society.[4]

Examining a range of societies, from the primitive to the most modern, Turner finds in all the often contradictory but fundamental needs
for both structure and communitas, for both differentiation and belonging. The structural ties are usually associated in more primitive
societies with patrilineal organization ("property, office, political alle-
giance, exclusiveness"), and the communal ones with matrilineal organization ("spiritual characteristics, mutual interests and concerns, and
collaterality . . . [that is,] inclusiveness").[5] What the warrior, chieftain,
president, or military leader is to structure, the shaman or poet-chief is
to communitas, of an equal but differing importance. As poet-chiefs,
Whitman and Neruda therefore tried to establish, in the void left by
absent or weakened state religions in the New World, what Henry
Alonzo Myers calls a "spiritual democracy": "Out of the American
democracy of 1855, Walt Whitman constructed an inner complement
to the outer world, a spiritual democracy governed by two principles,
one the unlimited individual, the other the equality of individuals. . . .
there is nothing in the 1855 and 1856 *Leaves* which does not follow
a priori from them."[6] This spiritual democracy was the true meaning of
the social democracy that Whitman encountered in his time and that
Neruda struggled for in his. Both poets constructed their personae as
models of this ideal community of unlimited and equal members, insisting that government and laws do not alone make a nation, but also the
liminal rituals of belonging that, as Turner defines them, partake "of
lowliness and sacredness, of homogeneity and comradeship. . . . a 'moment in and out of time,' and in and out of the social structure, which
reveals some recognition of a generalized social bond that has ceased
to be and has simultaneously yet to be fragmented into a multiplicity

of structural ties."[7] This is the social bond that Whitman emphasizes in the equalizing force of his persona:

> I am of old and young, of the foolish as much
>   as the wise,
> Regardless of others, ever regardful of others,
> Maternal as well as paternal, a child as well
>   as a man,
> Stuff'd with the stuff that is coarse and stuff'd
>   with the stuff that is fine,
> One of the Nation of many nations, the smallest
>   the same and the largest the same,
> A Southerner soon as a Northerner. . . .
>   ("Song of Myself":16:44)

Whitman continues in this section identifying himself with the people of every geographical location in the United States, of every trade and race, claiming "Of every hue and caste am I, of every rank and religion," as if he were, as he considered himself to be from 1855 until the 1870s, the nation's "poetic president."[8]

It is no historical coincidence that both Whitman and Neruda are often associated with the two assassinated presidents, Abraham Lincoln and Salvador Allende, with whom they felt they worked in tandem as their countries' *voces populi,* and upon whom they conferred the blessing of the spiritual democracies that their personae represented. In these personae, they attempted to establish the necessary balance between structure and communitas, between the chief and the poet-chief, between the head of state and the "ritual elder" or equalizing Everyman who must stand at his side. It is also significant that both poets received their shamanic "call" to assume such personae immediately preceding or during the liminal experience of civil wars, when national structures were violently threatened and communitas splintered. As George Hutchinson writes in *The Ecstatic Whitman: Literary Shamanism and the Crisis of the Union,* a revitalizing sense of communitas, associated with shamanic ritual, "comes particularly in times of crisis, whether at a certain ritual moment exemplifying the passage between structural states or in the momentous 'rites of passage' in history . . . shamanism is widely understood as a protective response to extreme environmental hazards or socioeconomic instability and stress."[9] The shaman plays "an essential role in the defense of the psychic integrity of the community," Eliade explains in *Shamanism: Archaic Techniques of Ecstasy,* one that defends "life, health, fertility, the world of 'light,' against death, diseases, sterility, disaster, and the world of 'darkness.'"[10] This is clearly echoed in the summary of his message that Whitman offers toward the end of "Song of Myself": "Do you see O my brothers and sisters? / It is not chaos or death—it is form, union, plan—it is eternal life—it is Happiness" (50:88). Whitman's self-appointed role as healer in the army hospitals of the North American Civil War during the 1860s, together with his wartime rhetoric as champion of national unity in the face of imminent disintegration, was in many ways an acting out of the shamanic persona already present in the first two editions of *Leaves of Grass.* This persona was further developed in *Drum-Taps,* with its insistence to "Thunder on! stride on, Democracy! strike with vengeful stroke!" ("Rise O Days":3:292), on the part of a singer who pronounced communitas into being within a divided nation learning

> . . . from cries of anguish, advancing, grappling
>   with direst fate and recoiling not,
> And now to conceive and show to the world what
>   your children en-masse really are,
> (For who except myself has yet conceiv'd what
>   your children en-masse really are?)
>   ("Long, Too Long America":312)

The widespread fratricide of the North American Civil War was matched in intensity by the Spanish Civil War, during which brother was also pitted against brother in the name of two competing national ideologies, and social community disintegrated even at the elemental level of the family. Neruda, who was serving as Chilean consul in Madrid during the beginning of the war after years of isolation in Asia, reacted not only with a partisan conversion to Marxism, but with the radical change in his poetic consciousness and persona evident in these lines from "Explico algunas cosas" in *Tercera residencia:*

Preguntaréis por qué su poesía
no nos habla del sueño, de las hojas,
de los grandes volcanes de su país natal?

Venid a ver la sangre por las calles,
venid a ver
la sangre por las calles,
venid a ver la sangre
por las calles!

(OC:I:273)

You will ask: why does your poetry
not speak to us of sleep, of the leaves,
of the great volcanoes of your native land?

Come and see the blood in the streets,
come and see
the blood in the streets,
come and see the blood
in the streets![11]

Tercera Residencia is at once a wartime volume parallel to Whitman's *Drum-Taps* and that turning point, unaccounted for in Whitman's development, at which Neruda begins to identify his own voice with the collective one. In "Reunión bajo las nuevas banderas," Neruda realizes, as if for the first time, both his tribal identity and his obligation as a poet to communitas:

Yo de los hombres tengo la misma mano herida,
yo sostengo la misma copa roja
e igual asombro enfurecido:
                              un día
palpitante de sueños
humanos, un salvaje
cereal ha llegado
a mi devoradora noche

para que junte mis pasos de lobo
a los pasos del hombre.
                    Y así, reunido,
duramente central, no busco asilo
en los huecos del llanto. . . .

                              (OC:I:266–67)

I have the same wounded hand that men have,
I hold up the same red cup
and an equally furious amazement:

                              one day
burning with human
dreams, a wild
oat reached
my devouring night
so that I could join my wolf steps
to the steps of man.

                    And thus united,
sternly central, I seek no shelter
in the hollows of weeping. . . .[12]

Following the Civil War, Neruda acted upon his newly committed persona, much as Whitman did during his hospital years, by gathering the "lost tribe" of Spanish Republican refugees and securing their passage to Latin America. For many Latin American Marxists, Spanish Republicanism served as a model and rallying point for their own efforts in opposing the oligarchic structures of their countries, and thus Neruda, upon his own return, carried with him both the ongoing crisis and the shamanic persona that he later infused into *Canto general*.

This role that both Whitman and Neruda assumed in their poetry was traditionally occupied in Europe by religious authority figures who reflected a spiritual hierarchy that validated the temporal one, particularly during any strife threatening that structure. "Priests have always embedded the liminal within highly stable social forms or churches," Hutchinson observes, linking the popular longing for communitas during the pre–Civil War era in the United States to the evangelical Great Awakening.[13] In the nascent democracies of the New World, however, the religious leader has generally been distrusted as representative of a repudiated European hierarchy, as evident in the separation of church and state in the United States' Constitution and in the strong anticlericalism fundamental to democratic movements in Latin America.[14] Yet in these recent republics, integrated into nations on maps only, the need for communal identity among vastly differing groups was met only by the leveling experience of the frontier, where all were equalized and united by the encounter with wilderness. Whitman noticed, however, that as a new civilization replaced wilderness, there was no voice to speak for the spiritual unity of "these States," to establish a national communitas to balance the increasing demands of a national structure. This was the shamanlike role he fashioned for the American bard to replace the priests, for as he writes in the "Preface" to the 1855 edition: "There will soon be no more priests. Their work is done. . . . A superior breed shall take their place. . . . the gangs of kosmos and prophets en masse shall take their place" (727). Whitman's definition of the shamanic American bard was later reworked from this preface into "By Blue Ontario's Shore":

> I heard the voice arising demanding bards,
> By them all native and grand, by them alone can these
>   States be fused into the compact organism of a Nation.
>
> To hold men together by paper and seal or by compulsion
>   is no account
> .   .   .   .   .   .
> Of all races and eras these States with veins full of
>   poetical stuff most need poets, and are to have
>   the greatest, and use them the greatest,
> Their Presidents shall not be their common referee
>   so much as their poets shall.
>
> (9:346–47)

This role as "common referee," as Turner has noted, is the function of the shaman, who "assumes a statusless status, external to the secular social structure, which gives him the right to criticize all structure-bound personae in terms of a moral order binding on all, and also to mediate between all segments or components of the structured system." [15]

Emblematic of its full circumference, the shaman stands both outside and inside of what the contemporary American Indian writer Paula Gunn Allen calls "the sacred hoop" of social and natural interrelatedness, in which "all are seen to be brothers or relatives (and in tribal systems relationship is central), all are offspring of the Great Mystery, children of our mother, and necessary parts of an ordered, balanced, and living whole." [16] Joan Halifax recounts an experience with Matsuwa, a contemporary Huichol shaman in Mexico, which illustrates how shamans maintain the sacred circle of tribal unity with their own magnetic power:

> I remember Matsuwa, at the end of the second night of the
> *Wima'kwari* (drum ceremony), fiercely beckoning individuals
> from disparate social factions to the sacralized ground before him.
> He touched his prayer feathers (*muvieri*) to objects that had be-
> come infused with life energy force (*kupuri*) and transferred the
> precious substance to those who were in need of it. . . . By doing
> this, Matsuwa was equalizing or balancing a social situation that
> was obviously a problem in the community. [17]

During initiation, the shaman masters those liminal forces that strip individuals of their differing identities in the social hierarchy: birth and death, illness and suffering, dream and wilderness. Acquainted with the polarities of male and female, heaven and earth, as well as life and death, the shaman is able to perceive the members of the tribe on this universal level, as Whitman does in his lengthy chanting of those—"The homeward bound and the outward bound"—whom he unites in "The Sleepers":

> The laugher and weeper, the dancer, the midnight
>   widow, the red squaw,
> The consumptive, the erysipalite, the idiot, he
>   that is wrong'd,
> The antipodes, and every one between this and them
>   in the dark,

I swear they are averaged now—one is no better than
    the other,
The night and sleep have liken'd them and restored them.

                                    (7:431)

It is on this important level of tribal unity that several of the seeming dichotomies in Whitman and Neruda's poetry are resolved: the tension between the mystical and the political as well as the corresponding one between individuality and democracy. Whitman and Neruda treat the pronounced individuality of their own personae not, in a romantic fashion, as something setting them apart from other people but as the most common microcosmic model for a nation of individuals: "The American compact is altogether with individuals," as Whitman writes in "By Blue Ontario's Shore" (15:352). This is the role that Emerson prophesied in "The Poet" for his new American bard, one who would be, above all, "representative. He stands among partial men for the complete man, and appraises us not of his wealth, but of the common wealth."[18] In the same poem, Whitman describes how this bard, as the representative individual, lends the cosmic proportion of a "divine average" to the variegated surface of the social structure:

Of these States the poet is the equable man.
Not in him but off him things are grotesque, eccentric,
    fail of their full returns,
Nothing out of its place is good, nothing in its
    place is bad,
He bestows on every object or quality its fit
    proportion, neither more nor less,
He is the arbiter of the diverse, he is the key,
He is the equalizer of his land and age. . . .

                                  (10:347)

Nelson Osorio addresses this question of the collective "I" of "the equable man" in Neruda, observing that "the problem in *Canto general* is that this 'I' is not an 'I' but a 'we.' There is a displacement of the 'I,' as an individual subjectivity figuring in the poem, to an 'I' that implies a 'we.'"[19] Both poets intend that their individuality bind together a collectivity, not through any structural coercion but through the tribal bond of their song, as Neruda hopes in his conclusion to "Qué despierte el leñador":

> *Que nadie piense en mí.*
> *Pensemos en toda la tierra,*
> *golpeando con amor en la mesa.*
> *No quiero que vuelva la sangre*
> *a empapar el pan, los frijoles,*
> *la música: quiero que venga*
> *conmigo el minero, la niña,*
> *el abogado, el marinero,*
> *el fabricante de muñecas,*
> *que entremos al cine y salgamos*
> *a beber el vino más rojo.*
>
> *Yo no vengo para resolver nada.*
>
> *Yo vine aquí para cantar*
> *y para que cantes conmigo.*
> (IX:6:590)

> Let no one think about me.
> Let's think about the whole earth,
> pounding with love on the table.
> I don't want blood to soak
> the bread, beans, music
> again: I want the miner,
> the little girl, the lawyer, the doll
> manufacturer, [the sailor] to accompany me,
> let's go to the movies and set out
> to drink the reddest wine.
>
> I don't want to solve anything.
>
> I came here to sing
> so that you'd sing with me.
> (271–72)

In Neruda's poetry, an accentuated political solidarity is transformed into the much broader sense of what Whitman called "the great word Solidarity"[20] as a basis not only for concerns about economic and social equality but for the metaphysical kinship that unites all natural beings. This sympathetic inclusiveness, as opposed to logical exclusiveness, is fundamental to the thinking of primitive man, whose view of nature, according to Ernst Cassirer in *An Essay on Man,* is

> neither merely theoretical nor merely practical; it is *sympathetic.*
> If we miss this point we cannot find the approach to the mystical world. . . . Primitive man by no means lacks the ability to grasp the empirical differences of things. But in his conception of nature and life all these differences are obliterated by a stronger feeling: the deep conviction of a fundamental and indelible *solidarity of life* that bridges over the multiplicity and variety of single forms.[21]

Like the American Indian song-poet, Whitman and Neruda act as agents of a sympathetic tribalism that identifies the natural unities as it serves the purpose of communitas by unifying the individual with his tribe in an inclusive vision of both nature and society. The essential meaning of their poetry, as well of the shamanic personae they adopted, transcends the purely erotic or political levels of comradeship upon which their poetry is often based. This meaning is best suggested by what is murmured by each participant at the end of the Lakota communal smoking ceremonies: "We are all related."[22]

II

What has often been misunderstood as the megalomania or narcissism in Whitman and Neruda's poetry is, in reality, their attempt to create personae large enough to contain the varying tribal parts they wish to unify: "I am large," Whitman writes in "Song of Myself," "I contain multitudes" (50:74). The most common error made in considering the works of Mr. Walter Whitman, Jr., and of Sr. Neftalí Ricardo Reyes Basualto is to confuse these two writers with their greatest creations, the self-invented personae of Walt Whitman and Pablo Neruda.

It is equally erroneous to approach their complex poetics as though the poetry were written by the untutored personae, such as those who assume the "proletarian" Neruda wrote simple-minded working-class lyrics or those who consider the "rough" and "spontaneous" Whitman's work to be slipshod and raw.[23] Jorge Luis Borges thinks that much of what has been written about Whitman is invalidated by the "summary identification of Whitman, the man of letters, with Whitman, the semi-divine hero of *Leaves of Grass*." Borges counts several of the obvious differences between the two, whom he calls "the friendly and eloquent savage" and the "poor literary man" who invented him:

> This one [the writer] never was in California or in the Platte canyon; that one [the persona] improvised an apostrophe to the second of these places ('Spirit that Formed the Scene') and was a miner in the first ('Starting from Paumanok'). . . . This one was chaste, reserved, and rather taciturn; that one was effusive and orgiastic. To multiply these discrepancies is easy; more important is to understand that this simple, happy vagabond who proposed these verses from *Leaves of Grass* would have been incapable of writing them down.[24]

To confuse the personae with the writers in both Whitman and Neruda's poetry is mistakenly to approach it as a continuation of European Romanticism, in which the poetic persona derives its authority or authenticity, as the root of these words suggests, from the life of its author. *Persona* is the Latin word for mask, and the mask of the romantic poet is, at least in theory, his own maskless face. The "romantic agony" itself became a mask, and the romantic poet often felt obligated to invent a life to fit it. Yet few would doubt that had Wordsworth actually been, let us hypothesize, a millionaire industrialist who penned his poetry of the English countryside in Berlin, and García Lorca a Catalan anthropologist who collected gypsy folklore for the government, the authority of their romantic voices would be seriously weakened, even if their poetry somehow remained the same. Readers who solicit such a romantic "authenticity" from the personae of *Leaves of Grass* and *Canto general* will eventually find Mr. Whitman and Sr. Reyes, if they dig deeply enough, and might be tempted to confuse evidence of a mask with artificiality or insincerity of voice. Such discrepancies encourage the ironic reading given the romantic poet by the adversarial critic, the grand unmasking that has become an obligatory formula of contemporary criticism.

In Whitman and Neruda's case, the distance between man and mask indicates a great deal about the measure and direction of the art, and it is therefore useful to examine carefully both man and mask to understand this distance as a key to the art, not as a means to invalidate it. According to Eliade, the shaman's mask, or, in its absence, the elaborate costume or face smearing, "manifestly announces the incarnation of a mythical personage . . . the costume transubstantiates the shaman, it transforms him, before all eyes, into a superhuman being."[25] Unlike the romantic poet who dramatizes the aspirations and sad limitations of the individual self, through the use of a mask the shamanic performer assumes an otherness that allows him to abandon this self in the ecstasy of his performance, as implied in the Greek root *ekstasis,* a being put "out of place" or self. Yet the audience is not fooled: "Everyone knows that a man made the mask and that a man is wearing it," comments Joseph Campbell on the meaning of primitive ritual; yet the masked performer "is identified with the god during the time of the ritual of which the mask is a part. He does not merely represent the god; he *is* the god."[26] The mask functions not so much as a theatrical device to obscure the face of the performer, but rather as an opening by which the spirit he invokes enters to speak or to move through him, as in the exaggerated performances of mediums in modern Latin American possession cults. Some might argue that neither Whitman's nor Neruda's poetry can be by nature shamanic because of the self-conscious experimentations with the forms of oral poetry and the deliberate self-inventions, assuming that "the performances of 'true' shamans are naive and spontaneous, free of 'artfulness,'" an assumption that Hutchinson points out should be abandoned, "as studies of shamanic role-taking indicate we must."[27] Shamanism is itself not the mask but the role: Whitman and Neruda are not impersonating shamans, but rather, shamanlike, are donning the masks of mythical figures through which the spirits of their lands and the voices of their tribes speak "out of self," ecstatically.

That "savage and luxuriant man"—"Walt Whitman, a kosmos, of Manhattan the son, / Turbulent, fleshy, sensual, eating, drinking and breeding," ("Song of Myself":24:52)—was a mask created by a mid-nineteenth-century New York literary bohemian and health enthusiast who was, in fact, well read, relatively sophisticated, abstemious, and childless. The actual life of the writer, as explored by his more recent biographers Justin Kaplan, Gay Wilson Allen, and Philip Callow, threatens the authority of this voice far less than the romantic confusion of that life with the persona hyperbolically fostered by the poet himself as well as by his disciples, the early biographers John Burroughs, Richard Bucke, and Horace Traubel. The relationship between Whitman and his mask is a complex and mysterious one, and there is little evidence of exactly how or when the part-time housebuilder and undistinguished journalist transformed himself into the magnetic and universal persona presented in the 1855 edition of his book. Although the details of this metamorphosis are missing, what is not in doubt is that, as Henry Miller observed, "no one, scanning his early writings could possibly detect the germ of his future genius. Whitman remade himself from head to foot."[28] Eliade has concluded that the shaman is essentially a sick person who has succeeded in curing himself, and that his ceremonial initiation "transforms the candidate from a possible neurotic into a shaman recognized by his particular society."[29] The distance between Whitman, diagnosed as decidedly neurotic by his Freudian biographical interpreters,[30] and his superhuman persona points not only to his self-invention, but to an initiatory self-curing, largely unaccounted for in his notebooks, by which a sometimes ailing, maternally natured, and isolated literary man assumed the public face of a healthy, masculine, common man of Paul Bunyan dimensions.

There is little evidence of the mythical mask that Whitman was to assume in the 1846 photograph of the author, which Harold Aspiz observantly describes as revealing "a pale young man affecting an effete pose and characterized (to use Whitman's sarcastic term) by a condition of 'delicatesse.'"[31] In *Walt Whitman and the Body Beautiful*, Aspiz demonstrates that perhaps because of this "delicatesse," health, healing, and hygiene are central subtexts in much of *Leaves of Grass*, a work permeated with imagery related to the then-prevalent pseudoscientific theories of hydrotherapy, magneticism, and homeopathy, among others. As a precursor to his book, Whitman originally had intended to advocate these theories in lectures, articles, and a manual to "instill 'Athleticism' in American young men."[32] Yet we also learn that the healer-hero of health, vigor, and the perfection of the American physical form projected in his poetry was the invention of a writer whose family was widely prone to illness and congenital disorders, and that in addition to the later part of his life spent semiparalyzed with a stroke, Whitman was a hypochondriac preoccupied with the symptoms of headaches, constipation, and sluggish energy. Another significant discrepancy between the man and the mask is that a poet who established his persona as a symbol of procreative American masculinity was, according to the extensive documentation in Charley Shively's *Calamus Lovers: Walt Whitman's Working Class Camerados,* a homosexual whose "casual pick-ups or intimate lovers were younger than he and working class."[33] This suggests that the Adonic qualities ascribed to his persona more properly belonged to his partners and underlines the homoerotic subtext most readers have found in his poetry. Of his own nature, the poet once described himself as *"furtive* like an old hen,"[34] one who carefully edited from the idealized biography prepared by his disciple Dr. Richard Bucke passages characterizing him as "a sort of male castrato, a false soprano," and a "motherly soul" with "an almost feminine order of mind."[35] The word *homosexuality,* however, was not introduced in English until the 1880s, and then only as a clinical definition. During Whitman's era, what Lord Alfred Douglas called "the love that dare not speak its name" had no name, and the poet's appropriation of the phrenological term *adhesion,* adapted to celebrate his own version of "manly love," was not the euphemistic evasion it might seem today, but was one of the first attempts to define male same-sex love outside of a pathological, biblical, or purely sexual context.

Of the proletarian carpenter, the man of the people, Aspiz points out that Whitman "could not build houses or handle a saw and hammer well enough to earn a living. The everyday Whitman was something of an aesthete, a friend of artists, and an amateur art collector, whose typical bourgeois pursuits in the 1850s included keeping a store, editing newspapers, and what he called successful 'house building speculations.'"[36] It is also evident that the poet of overflowing spontaneity, of "Nature without check with original energy" ("Song of Myself": 1:29), obsessively revised his poetry throughout several editions, frequently self-censoring the love poems by changing the masculine to feminine. "One of the roughs,"[37] as Whitman advertised his persona in a self-review, was the self-conscious creation of a voracious reader and opera aficionado who disguised himself in print as cleverly as one of Mark's Twain's nineteenth-century con men.

Even more inconsistently, in *Walt Whitman's Concept of the American Common Man* Leadie M. Clark demonstrates that although "the Whitman of *Leaves of Grass* contained all, comprehended all, was willing to accept all" in his spiritual democracy, Whitman, the citizen and journalist, articulated in editorials, recorded conversations, and letters sentiments that were highly unfavorable to American Indians, blacks, and Catholic immigrants. Clark reveals that Whitman was profoundly distrustful of universal suffrage, particularly of the social participation of women except as mothers, and was convinced that only the male "Anglo-Saxon native . . . would form the democratic averages which could ultimately achieve the divine average."[38] Aside from an early involvement in the abolitionist movement, Whitman the man did not lend his voice to other equalitarian issues debated in liberal circles in New York and Boston. The Mohawk writer Maurice Kenny protests the fact that during Whitman's tenure at the Bureau of Indian Affairs, "the worthless treaties were at his fingertips. . . . The horrifying slaughter of innocent Cheyenne and Arapahoe women and children at the infamous Sand Creek Massacre occurred only the preceding November of the year he took his employment . . . how was it that Whitman ignored those death cries?"[39] Was this placid employee, however briefly, of a genocidal government agency the same writer who created himself in poetry as a "luxuriant savage," a white aboriginal shaman? Was this poet who arguably invented modern gay literature a closet case?

The writer whom Aspiz, Spivey, and Clark portray was, in marked contrast to his universal persona, very much a citizen of the mid-nineteenth-century United States, and his foibles, postures, and prejudices must be understood in a context in which certain sexual, racial, and political assumptions remained as yet widely unchallenged. However much contemporary readers may identify with Whitman's persona because of its immediacy and universality, we cannot project onto the writer the standards of our own political or sexual consciousness, much of which we owe to his singularly courageous act of imagination. The persona that the poet invented was his own radical challenge to the limitations of his times, although it dwarfs the rather ordinary nineteenth-century Walter Mitty who created it. In its creation, Whitman found "the man he would like to have been," as Borges observes. "His writing should not be read as the confessions of a man of the nineteenth century, but rather as an epic about an imaginary figure, a utopian figure, who is to some extent a magnification and projection of the writer as well as the reader."[40]

Unlike Whitman, who synthesized the stages of his life projected throughout his successive editions into a cumulative persona combining the elements of Adam (1855), the comrade-lover (1860), the healer (1865), and Columbus (1876), Neruda developed a new persona for almost every major book he published, claiming himself as the "foremost adversary of Nerudism,"[41] an established mode he destroyed with each new publication. Among his more than forty-five volumes, Neruda's major personae include: the lost child (1923); the adolescent lover (1924); the anguished somnambulist (1933); the witness to war (1947); the politicized American singer (1950); the poet of simple objects (1954); the whimsical private man (1958); the autobiographical older poet (1964); and the naturalist and metaphysician of his late work. Each major phase, writes Rodríguez Monegal, produced "not only poetry but a poet. . . . Each dramatization creates and sustains the individual voice and grants it an authority that the private 'I' lacks. Walt Whitman understood this admirably in creating not only a book but a persona." Rodríguez Monegal echoes Borges's complaint about Whitman's readers, however, when he protests that "lamentably, many of those who have analyzed Neruda's work, or have written about it, have not known how to separate the real person (Ricardo Reyes who signed Pablo Neruda) from the successive poetic personae projecting his voice from each of his books."[42] J. M. Alonso is not such a reader, for he does "not think of Neruda as a man, but as what he is: a literary invention made of ink and created through considerable effort of the will and lucidity by one Neftalí Ricardo Reyes, from Temuco, Chile."[43]

The distance between Neruda and his mask is often considerable, especially since the fervent Americanist and Chilean nationalist spent a great portion of his life living abroad in consular positions. Like Whitman, Neruda identified his voice with the people, yet was not one of them. Much like that of his North American predecessor, the Neruda persona has been enthusiastically yet mistakenly construed by much of his audience as the voice of an Orphic and untutored anti-intellectual, of "a volcanic and torrential intuitive poet, unacquainted with artistic rules," as Rodríguez Monegal describes this misperception, to the extent that "essays even circulate around here as to who counts the syllables for him, or corrects his punctuation or rewrites his lines into prose to help clarify them."[44] Yet Neruda was a careful and consummate craftsman, extensively well read in English and French as well as in his own language, and one of the most sophisticated and indefatigable world travelers of this century. The private man, in fact, was often criticized in his own country for bourgeois tastes inappropriate to a public "poet of the people," including both town and country houses, a cellar of fine wines, and museum-quality collections of rare books and precious shells. Durán identifies the discrepancies between the writer and his persona in this way:

> Ironically, despite his country origins, Neruda, the poetic voice of the people, the working class and the peasants, was never really in his adult life a man *of* the people. On the contrary, his friends were more literary than proletarian, and Neruda's only considerable professional experience outside the literary world was first bureaucratic, as a civil servant in the Foreign Ministry, and then political. Only once in Neruda's adult life did he really come into close contact with the day-to-day life of the working class. That was in the 1940s, when Neruda, like thousands of other members of the newly outlawed Communist Party of Chile, was forced to go into hiding in his own country to avoid arrest. . . . Once safely in exile, Neruda was never again to know firsthand the everyday life and reality of the working man; he could write for this man, he could write of him, he could serve as a symbol and a spokesman, but his own life would be spent in the solitude of his comfortable homes or on the speakers' platform looking at, but not forming part of, the masses he addressed.[45]

Neruda created a persona fused with the causes of freedom, justice, and world peace, yet as an internationally respected member of the Communist party and a frequent and honored guest in Moscow, Beijing, and the Soviet-bloc nations, he did not publicly acknowledge the monumental brutality of the Stalinist era, nor demonstrate any disillusionment with Soviet policy, until a volume of poems published the year after the invasion of Czechoslovakia, appropriately titled *Fin del mundo* (1969). The mask of the Promethean rebel was the creation of an obedient party member. Neruda was such a Stalinist that it is still debated whether, under orders from Stalin, he collaborated with the murderer of Trotsky in Mexico City in 1940, where he was Chilean Consul General. The early Neruda declared himself "an enemy of laws, governments and established institutions" (OC:I:117), in the prologue to *El habitante y su esperanza* (1926), yet during the 1950s he was capable of the blindly ideological insight that "the capitalist world produces cannons, the socialist world produces books."[46] This highly charged rhetoric echoes throughout *Las uvas y el viento* (1954), with its paeans to Stalin and Mao. These were not, however, unusual sentiments to proceed from either side during this dangerously polarized era, especially from a poet of the newly christened Third World caught between the other two. As with Whitman, Neruda the writer was very much a citizen of his historical moment, in his case the Cold War; and the subtext in his poetry is not only broadly political, but is often doctrinaire and propagandistic. Reflecting contemporary history, this subtext is more readily identifiable than Whitman's subtexts of forgotten medical theories or of carefully coded homosexuality, which are, nevertheless, of equal significance.

Many readers of Whitman and Neruda apologetically bracket those seemingly peripheral subtexts of their work that, at the same time, most tellingly indicate the true nature of their personae: sexuality and politics. Both Whitman and Neruda scholars are polemically divided regarding the necessity or relevance of acknowledging that of the two greatest American poets, one was a homosexual, the other a dutiful Communist party member long after it was considered either conscionable or fashionable to be so. To the extent that these controversies are fueled by the confusion of the writers with their personae, they contribute little to our understanding of their work, limiting its universality to the partisan either/or categories of Whitman as a homosexual poet (or not), Neruda as a Marxist poet (or not). Yet the particular sexual or political orientations of Walter Whitman, Jr., and Neftalí Ricardo

Reyes are transfigured in the personae of Walt Whitman and Pablo Neruda into thoroughly inclusive visions of erotic androgyny and universal fraternity, respectively. Whitman dedicates a section of poems in *Leaves of Grass,* "Children of Adam," to the celebration of women and heterosexual love, just as Neruda devotes a book of *Canto general,* "Qué despierte el leñador," to a recognition of those qualities he warmly admires in the United States and its culture. Judging from Whitman's reception among women and Neruda's among North Americans, these converse appreciations were not merely empty gestures to a theoretical universality, but were expressions of a deeply felt connection to the other. The influence of the gay poet, Whitman, on modern women-centered poetry has been crucial, according to the North American feminist poet Alicia Ostriker, who remarks that as women readers, "in him we are freed to be what we actually are . . . not negative pole to positive pole, not adversarial half of some dichotomy, but figures in an energetic dance. His sacralization of sexuality anticipates Audre Lorde's widely read feminist manifesto, 'The Erotic as Power.'"[47] Likewise, nowhere outside of Latin America has the Communist poet, Neruda, found such an enthusiastic audience as in the "belly of the monster," the capitalist United States, where he has become one of the major foreign influences on the present generation of poets.

These inclusive contexts of Whitman's sexuality and of Neruda's politics reveal the same axis around which both their personae revolve: *comradeship. Comrade* is a word used frequently by both poets, be it Whitman's invented "camerado," a corruption of the Spanish *camarada,* which means a "comrade" of either gender, or Neruda's "compañero," which signifies the same. Whitman most often employs the terms "comrade" or "camerado" in the context of what he calls "manly love"; Neruda uses "camarada" or "compañero" to imply a politically working-class connection. Both use the term to address the "common man," to whom poets have seldom spoken, as they use their own sexuality and politics to identify their personae with the proletarian voice of the body and of the body politic.

Along with the poetry and personae that Whitman and Neruda created, they attempted to forge a new American role for the poet, one differing from the antecedent of the European Romantic with an aristocratic yet nostalgic distance from the working class. The North American poet Louis Simpson has commented that in Europe "a taste for poetry was restricted to the aristocracy." The common man has never read poetry, he insists, much less in the United States, where the colonists "had a religious aversion for poetry which they associated with the profligacy of the courts. As the country developed there was a pressing need for men who could use an axe or plough, a need for blacksmiths and shipbuilders, but there was never a need for those who, as Yeats says, 'articulate sweet sounds together.'" Whitman's assertion that poets would replace the hierarchical priests in the New World in establishing a sense of spiritual democracy is curiously ironic, for if the American common man has dismissed his need for anyone more than priests, it must be poets. In the Americas, poets have been acknowledged to the limited extent that poetry is decorously associated with an elevated "culture" representative of the social oligarchy and its European origins, lending prestige to the reader rather than giving voice to the people. This attitude is more prevalent in Latin America, which has traditionally sent its poets "back" to Europe in consular positions, where they might best represent American refinement. Although various nineteenth-century poets such as Longfellow and Darío enjoyed brief eras of popularity, memorized by schoolchildren and recited at civic functions, the traditional role of American poets has never been one that connects them to the daily concerns of ordinary people. In both hemispheres, if listened to at all, poetry has been "overheard" by the common man, not written by or for him. According to Simpson,

> In the New World poets, who had been honored in the Old, would be regarded with contempt, and so they have been regarded ever since, for the character given to a nation at the start is the mould for succeeding generations. In the United States poets have always been regarded as extraneous. . . . To Wordsworth's claim that poets have a greater knowledge of human nature than the common man, the common man replies by tapping his temple with his finger. Poets must be crazy.[48]

The new role that Whitman and Neruda created for the American poet contains a paradox of authenticity: How to identify a voice with the common man yet at the same time be these extraneous, ridiculed, or elevated creatures known in the Americas as poets; that is, how to be at once real "comrades" and true poets? Although both Whitman and Neruda were from working-class backgrounds, as writers they were, as we have seen, no longer the working-class people to and for whom they intended to speak. Yet through the leveling of sexuality and democratic politics, these two writers were able to make their identifications with the working class, incorporating its voice into their personae and locating their poetry within the common life of the tribe they sought to represent.

For Whitman, the love of working-class "camerados" was the liminal experience on which he founded his ideals for a spiritual democracy. The ferment of trade unionism and working-class consciousness in New York City in the 1840s and 1850s was the social background out of which Whitman's politicized sexuality developed. In a letter of 1852, he writes of "the tens of thousands of young men, the mechanics, the writers" whose "divine fire . . . has only waited a chance to leap forward and confound the calculations of tyrants, hunkers, and all their tribe. At this moment, New York is the most radical city in America" (CC:I:40). Eight years later, in the final section of "Starting from Paumanok," this political solidarity is eroticized into what he calls "the pensive ache to be together," the equalizing of status, occupations, social mores, and sexual roles that has always been at the basis of the impulse toward communitas:

> O to be relieved of distinctions! To make as much
> of vices as of virtues!
> O to level occupations and the sexes! To bring all
> to common ground! O adhesiveness!
> O the pensive ache to be together—you know not why,
> and I know not why.
>
> (TV:II:289n)

Whitman's "adhesion" was to working-class young men, of whom he made compulsive lists in his daybooks and notebooks, noting names, ages, occupations, and physical attributes. The homosexual theme in his poetry differs considerably from the English "Uranian" poets of his era, with their neoclassical odes to adolescent perfection, a school that Robert K. Martin describes as "fundamentally elitist and undemocratic; it affirmed the special as opposed to the common."[49] Whitman's concept of adhesion, on the other hand, represented "fervid comradeship" as the democratic common ground between the social classes, which was much the same role that male homosexuality played in the Spartan military or in Athenian education. These "threads of manly friendship" would spiritualize "our materialistic and vulgar American democracy," as he writes in *Democratic Vistas,* "not only giving tone to individual character, and making it unprecedently emotional, muscular, heroic and refined, but having the deepest relations to general politics" (CP:414–15).

Yet nineteenth-century North America was in no sense similar to ancient Greece in its attitudes toward sexuality, and what existed as a clandestine "vice" in the life of the writer was transformed into a social and spiritual "virtue" in the words of his persona. Whitman explained to the homosexual English writer Edward Carpenter that "what lies behind 'Leaves of Grass' is something that few, very few . . . perhaps oftenest women, are at all in a position to seize. It lies behind almost every line; but concealed, studiedly concealed; some passages left purposely obscure."[50] As a subtext in his poetry, Whitman's sexual involvement with working-class youth "goes with his egalitarianism and his common people poetry: the sex, politics and art form one united whole," concludes Shively,[51] in examining the poet's lengthy relationships with Peter Doyle, Harry Stafford, and Bill Duckett, and the body of often semiliterate correspondence sent to Whitman by several other young men. "The unconscious, uncultured, natural types pleased him best, and he would make an effort to approach them," commented Edward Carpenter. "The others he allowed to approach him."[52] In the persona he created, Whitman becomes the "uncultured, natural" man to whom he was attracted, joining the ranks of the common men he celebrates to

> . . . make the continent indissoluble,
> I will make the most splendid race the sun ever
>   shone upon,
> I will make divine magnetic lands,

> With the love of comrades,
>> With the life-long love of comrades.
>>> ("For You O Democracy: 117)

This continent of working-class comrades is made "indissoluble" by the erotic bonding of "lovers, continual lovers," meeting, uniting, and separating in his poems in what is often a sexual manner. The "poor literary man" assumes as his own the "swarthy face" and the "natural and nonchalant" posture of those he loves:

> Yet comes one a Manhattanese and ever at parting
>> kisses me lightly on the lips with robust love,
> And I on the crossing of the street or on the ship's
>> deck give a kiss in return,
> We observe that salute of American comrades land and sea,
> We are those two natural and nonchalant persons.
>>> ("Behold This Swarthy Face": 126)

In *Leaves of Grass,* this homoerotic comradeship becomes the pivotal metaphor for a broader erotic pantheism, or polymorphous androgyny, in which the poet makes everyone and everything his sexually charged comrade, fusing not only with male companions but with women, his own body, nature, animals, and the various elements of the American landscape, as in "Spontaneous Me": "bellies press'd and glued together with love . . . / The body of my love, the body of the woman I love, the body of the man I love, the body of the earth" (104). To limit an understanding of the expansive sexuality in the book to the homoeroticism of the "Calamus" section not only confuses the persona with the writer, but it denies the inclusivity at the heart of the poetry.

In both Whitman and Neruda's poetry, other liminal experiences beside sexuality provide a common ground for the identification of their personae with "American comrades," most notably suffering and sickness, physical labor, war, the ocean, and, of course, death. In Neruda's poetry, death is often associated with the leveling of the political struggle, with images of blood, violence, and martyrdom, as in "La muerte" in *Canto general,* which projects the Marxist class conflict beyond the grave:

Quiero estar en la muerte con los pobres
que no tuvieron tiempo de estudiarla,
mientras los apaleaban los que tienen
el cielo dividido y arreglado.

(XV:21:716)

In death I want to be with the poor
who had no time to study it,
while those who have the sky
divided and deeded beat upon them.

(394)

The subtext in *Canto general* is working-class ideology, yet as with Whitman's subtext of working-class homoeroticism, it is transformed into a parallel definition of spiritual democracy. In "América, no invoco tu nombre en vano," for example, Neruda portrays a moment of comradeship on a ship's deck that recalls the "robust love" in the above passage from Whitman's "Behold This Swarthy Face." Neruda is invited on board by a group of "semi-naked, malnourished" "sea workers" who speak the "language of Spaniards and Chinese, / the language of Baltimore and Kronstadt." Rather than exchange the "parting kisses" on the lips that mark the suggestively erotic relationship between Whitman and his comrade, Neruda experiences an equally tender unity in political solidarity and is "embraced" by his rugged comrades while singing in unison the Communist anthem:

y cuando cantaron 'La Internacional' canté con
* ellos:*
me subía del corazón un himno, quise decirles:
* 'Hermanos,'*
pero no tuve sino ternura que se me hacía canto
y que iba con su canto desde mi boca hasta el mar.
Ellos me reconocían, me abrazaban con sus poderosas
* miradas*
sin decirme nada, mirándome y cantando.

(16:525)

and when they sang 'The Internationale' I sang
  with them:
a hymn rose to my heart, and I tried to tell them:
  "Brothers,"
but I had only tenderness transformed into song
that went with their song from my mouth to the sea.
They acknowledged me, embraced me with their
  powerful stare
without speaking, just staring at me and singing.

                (210)

Clearly, it is to just such a passage that Rodríguez Monegal refers when
he claims that, in certain ways, *Canto general* "is a piece of propaganda,
born under the sign of politics, instigated by a political party. But it
is not only this. Because the story of its real origins is different, more
complex, and does not depend at all on any decision from the Chilean
Communist party, although its visible and invisible support sustained
the poet during its long gestation."[53] In these lines addressed to the
Communist party, Neruda demonstrates how the party represents for
him what Whitman calls, in his own context, the "pensive ache to be
together," and how it serves as a means for the poet to identify his
persona with the common man in order to envision an "indissoluble
continent" of comradeship similar to Whitman's:

> *Me has dado la fraternidad hacia el que no conozco.*
> *Me has agregado la fuerza de todos los que viven.*
> *Me has vuelto a dar la patria como en un nacimiento.*
> *Me has dado la libertad que no tiene el solitario.*
>
> . . . .
>
> *Me enseñaste a dormir en las camas duras de mis*
>   *hermanos.*
>
> . . . .
>
> *Me has hecho indestrutible porque contigo no*
>   *termino en mí mismo.*
>
>   (XV:22:720–21)

You have given me fraternity toward the unknown
man.

You have joined the strength of all the living.
You have given me the country again as in a birth.
You have given me the freedom that the loner
    cannot have.

. . . .

You taught me to sleep in beds hard as my brothers.

. . . .

You have made me indestructible because with you
    I do not end in myself.

(398–99)

Here Neruda's vision transcends the metaphor of the party just as Whitman's expands beyond his concept of adhesion. Their masks of the mythical American comrade are much larger than the dimensions of their own individual faces, although these masks seem molded along the basic contours of the writers' personal affiliations, which were undoubtedly sources of isolation and pain in their own lives. Toward the end of his life, however, Neruda did occupy that place in the common life of his people to which Whitman aspired for his American bard: that "his country absorbs him as affectionately as he has absorbed it" ("Preface 1855":729). "The Chilean people know me well, and I must say I find their love for me very moving," Neruda remarked in the 1970. "They're amazingly responsive, so much that I can hardly get in or out of some places. I have to have a special escort to protect me from the embraces of the crowd, because they rush to meet me. This happens to me everywhere."[54] Yet this later popular renown does not represent the persona in *Canto general,* much of which was written during 1948–49, when Neruda was in hiding from persecution in his own country after President González Videla outlawed the Communist party. As recounted in book VIII, "El fugitivo," Neruda was passed underground from one family to another until, disguised and with falsified documents, he was eventually smuggled into Argentina and a five-year exile, during which his manuscript was published.

Except under the most unusual circumstances, the Communist as well as the homosexual have always been liminal or "threshold people," existing in self-exile at the margins of American societies. Although Walt Whitman and Pablo Neruda were insiders celebrating their belonging to the American common man, the writers who invented them were perpetual outsiders who never did belong. Even during their relatively secure older years, persecution or the fear of it continued: The dying Neruda was poised to board a plane for Mexico to avoid assassination shortly after the military coup that toppled the Allende government in the last month of his life. And in 1890, Whitman felt it necessary to answer with the defensive fabrication of half a dozen grandchildren an admiring letter from the homosexual writer John Addington Symonds pressing him about the true nature of the sexuality in his poetry.[55] Although Whitman's sexual and Neruda's political subtexts were transformed into personae that allowed them to enact a tribal role for the poet, speaking to, for, and as one of the common people, these aspects of the poets' lives were, in reality, often marginal and clandestine, just as effectively isolating the poets from the nations with which they identified. Like the shaman, both paradoxically remained men apart who represent the whole, wearing the often ill-fitting masks that both joined and separated them from the true comradeship they idealized. As Neruda writes in *Aun*, one of his later volumes: "My poetry isolated me / and joined me to everyone."[56] In "Yo soy," the final book of *Canto general*, Neruda recognizes both the features and limitations of his mask, and, in words strongly recalling Whitman's, hopes that it is recognized by those to whom his voice is directed:

> *Escribo para el pueblo, aunque no pueda*
> *leer mi poesía con sus ojos rurales.*
> *Vendrá el instante en que una línea, el aire*
> *que removió mi vida, llegará a sus orejas,*
> *y entonces el labriego levantará los ojos,*
> *el minero sonreirá rompiendo piedras,*
> *el palanquero se limpiará la frente,*
> *el pescador verá mejor el brillo*
> *de un pez que palpitando le quemará las manos,*
> *el mecánico, limpio, recién lavado, lleno*
> *de aroma de jabón mirará mis poemas,*
> *y ellos dirán tal vez: 'Fue un camarada.'*
>
> *Eso es bastante; ésa es la corona que quiero.*
> (20:715)

I write for the people, even though they cannot
read my poetry with their rustic eyes.
The moment will come in which a line, the air
that stirred my life, will reach their ears,
and then the farmer will raise his eyes,
the miner will smile breaking stones,
the brakeman will wipe his brow,
the fisherman will see clearly the glow
of a quivering fish that will burn his hands,
the mechanic, clean, recently washed,
smelling of soap, will see my poems,
and perhaps they will say: "He was a friend."

That's enough, that's the crown that I want.

(393)

III

Jean Franco remembers a public reading that the exiled Neruda gave
in Florence, Italy, in 1950, to "what you probably call hard hats, in
other words, before an audience of thousands, and thousands, and
thousands of Italian trade unionists." She describes the "electric sort of
atmosphere" as the poet read from the recently published *Canto general,*
"rapturously applauded line by line, especially where certain key words,
like *Fascismo,* came up. I, too, found myself applauding madly, particularly at all of the kind of key words, along with the rest of the people."
Franco sensed "that an essential aspect of the poetry reading of Neruda
was evident at this meeting, a kind of communion with the audience."[57]
Such a communion with the collectivity through the word is at the basis
of the poetics of both *Canto general* and *Leaves of Grass*. What Neruda's
audience was so enthusiastically applauding was not the originality or
lyric superiority of his verses, but their own voice returned to them in
the words of the poet. This is the role that Whitman prescribed for the
American poet in his "Preface" of 1855, one that is "more the channel
of thoughts and things" for a writer who "sees health for himself in
being one of the mass" (717, 720). At such meetings, Neruda enacted

"en masse" what the more isolated Whitman was only able to envision. Through their masks of the mythic American comrade, Whitman and Neruda address the collectivity of the common man as its representative individuals, and their role, like that of the American Indian song-poet, is to serve as pronouncer rather than originator of the tribal word. In "Song of Myself," Whitman describes his own poetry in a way that explains the unusual relationship Jean Franco witnessed between Neruda and his audience:

> These are really the thoughts of all men in all
>   ages and lands, they are not original with me,
> If they are not yours as much as mine they are
>   nothing, or next to nothing,
> . . . .
> This is the grass that grows wherever the land is
>   and the water is,
> This is the common air that bathes the globe.
>
> (17:45)

The anonymous American Indian song-poet "sings his place in the tribe and in nature," Kenneth Lincoln observes, "taking no credit, giving thanks that the song has chosen him."[58] In a similar fashion, Whitman and Neruda's personae aspire to a collective authorship on the part of a tribe that Whitman addresses as Democracy and Neruda as The People. The poets do not sing the tribal word as much as it is sung *through* them.

Like the shaman, Whitman and Neruda each serve as a masked medium for the voices of tribe and nature. The shaman often acts as a channel for those ancestral voices that connect the spirit world to that of the living, voices identified as those of the land itself. In "Alturas de Macchu Picchu," Neruda invokes the presence of the Incan laborers who constructed the city:

> *Yo vengo a hablar por vuestra boca muerta.*
> *A tráves de la tierra juntad todos*
> *los silencios labios derramados*
> *y desde el fondo habladme toda esta larga noche*

como si yo estuviera con vosotros anchado,
contadme todo, cadena a cadena,
establón a establón, y paso a paso. . . .

(12:343–44)

I've come to speak through your dead mouths.
Throughout the earth join all
the silent scattered lips,
and from the depths speak to me all night long,
as if I were anchored with you,
tell me everything, chain by chain,
link by link, and step by step. . . .

(41)

These indigenous ancestral voices possess the poet with the spirit of the continent, one of "struggle, iron, volcanoes" absorbed into his own body and language: "Hasten to my veins and to my mouth. / Speak through my words and my blood" (42). Eliade explains the important "role of the souls of the dead in recruiting future shamans. As we saw, the souls of the ancestors often take a sort of 'possession' of a young man and then initiate him. . . . Once he has been consecrated by this first 'possession' and the initiation that follows, the shaman becomes a receptacle that can be entered into indefinitely by other spirits, too."[59] In *Shamanism: The Beginnings of Art,* Andreas Lommel writes that the helping spirits of shamans are often those of ancestors "so that the psychic powers of generations are accumulated in him."[60] Similar to Neruda's vigil at the deserted ruins of Macchu Picchu, where archaeologists have located extensive Incan burial sites,[61] those who seek such a possession often lie by ancestral graves. Whitman's reveries in the grass are granted another meaning when he tells us that it is with the "the beautiful uncut hair of graves" that he communes. As with Neruda's communion, the ancestral spirits in these graves are perceived as disembodied mouths, voices that rise up to speak through the language of the living:

> This grass is very dark to be from the white heads
> of old mothers,

Darker than the colorless beards of old men,
Dark to come from under the faint red roofs of
    mouths.

O I perceive after all so many uttering tongues,
And I perceive that they do not come from the roofs
of mouths for nothing.

                ("Song of Myself":6:34)

These "uttering tongues" of ancestral spirits are received by Whitman, speaking through him in other sections of the poem:

Through me many long dumb voices,
Voices of the interminable generations of prisoners
   and slaves,
Voices of the diseased and despairing and of thieves
and dwarfs. . . .

                (24:52)

The voices are not those of presidents and generals, of the tribal structure, but the liminal voices of those without status, of those "the others are down upon, / Of the deform'd, trivial, flat, foolish, despised." These are also the ancestral voices that Neruda summons, not those of Incan chieftains and priests but of the oppressed, the "laborer, weaver, silent herdsman":

Mostrame vuestra sangre y vuestra surco,
decidme: aquí fui castigado,
porque la joya no brilló o la tierra
no entregó a tiempo la piedra o el grano:
señaladme la piedra en que caísteis
y la madera en que os crucificaron,
encendedme los viejos pedernales,
las viejas lámparas, los látigos pegados
a través de los siglos en las llagas
y las hachas de brillo ensangrentado.

                (12:343)

Show me your blood and your furrow,
tell me: I was punished here,
because the jewel did not shine or the earth
did not surrender the gemstone or kernel on time:
show me the stone on which you fell
and the wood on which you were crucified,
strike the old flintstones,
the old lamps, the whips sticking
throughout the centuries to your wounds
and the warclubs glistening red.

(41)

Many readers have commented on Neruda's discovery of solidarity in "Alturas de Macchu Picchu," but of equal and related importance is the emergence of what Rodríguez Monegal calls "vocalization": "What Neruda does on ending 'Alturas de Macchu Picchu' is acknowledge this gift of vocalization, to give voice to the mute word of the people, which will be his basic vocation from this moment on. Here it is possible to recognize a process similar to the one recorded in Walt Whitman's poetry in *Leaves of Grass.*" Although Rodríguez Monegal does not specifically mention shamanism, he does relate Neruda's vocalization to the process of prophecy that gives voice to the dead word of the pre-Columbian people with whom Neruda identifies, a primal connection with the continent that allows the poet "to be everywhere at once because no longer is he either man or a poet but a voice that rises from the depths of all times and sings today, vocalizing all the mute voices of the New World."[62] Whitman most clearly defines vocalization as the source of his poetry in one of the unpolished manuscript beginnings of "Song of Myself":

I am your voice—It was tied in you—In me it begins
    to talk.
I celebrate myself to celebrate every man and woman
    alive;
I loosen the tongue that was tied in them,
It begins to talk out of my mouth.[63]

This vocalization of mute voices is similar to the process whereby the shaman, as "receptacle," gives voice to the spirits around him: the voice of the sick whom he is healing, of mythic ancestors, of birds and other animals, of landscape and natural forces, and of tribal equilibrium. Eliade cites as typical an example of shamanic vocalization among the Chukchee (Siberian) in which the shaman sings and drums to attract the voices of the "spirits," which "are heard from every direction; they seem to rise out of the ground or to come from very far away. A *ke'let* (spirit) enters the shaman's body, whereupon, moving his head rapidly, the shaman begins to cry out and speak in falsetto, the voice of the spirit. . . . Through the shaman's voice the spirits of the dead converse with the audience."[64] Who is actually speaking in Whitman and Neruda's poetry is an illusion peeled away in successive layers during its performance, as in a shamanic trance: not the writer, but a mask; not the mask, but a voice; not just an individual voice, but a plurality of particular voices contained within the universality of the lyric "I." This is, of course, a virtual performance staged for a virtual audience, based on the oral effects within a written medium, as discussed in the previous chapter. Yet just as the power of speech acts defines the written stylistics in Whitman and Neruda's poetry, the ritual elements of vocalization, or of spirit possession in the shamanic trance, define the dramatic elements of voice in their texts.

The universal solidarity that the American Indian shaman expresses in his songs is a correlate of his own propensity to speak in many voices, which proceeds from his ability to transform himself, by means of trance, dream, meditation, fasting or isolation in nature, into the animal, person, spirit or object to which he seeks to give voice. "In his growing trance he becomes so very much part of the tree, the storm, the thunder, the animal which he contemplates that when finally the song comes to him it is the song of the thunder or of the tree which he is learning to make his own," writes Margot Astrov.[65] The shaman becomes what he sings to the extent that the otherness he approaches sings through him with its own voice. Neither the identity of the "I" nor of the "you" is fixed, nor are the boundaries between subject and object, between genders, or between the human, animal, plant, and mineral worlds. These exist in a state of transformative flux as the shaman passes through various states of identification with the elements of the ritual. The "I" may mark the voice of the shaman, that of a mythical ancestor, of the person seeking a cure in the case of a healing ceremony, or that of the psychopomp or totem animal whose song the shaman sings. This ability for interspecies metamorphosis is based on the shaman's reentry into the *illo tempore* when, as Halifax writes, "the cosmos had total access to itself. There was one language for all creatures and elements, and humankind shared that language. . . . Although the common language was lost, all phenomena in the cosmos are still interrelated."[66] In Whitman's poetry, situated in this *illo tempore,* as we have observed, the poet's solidarity with all life is manifested in repeated transformations of the lyric "I":

> There was a child went forth every day,
> And the first object he look'd upon, that object
>   he became,
> And that object became part of him for the day
>   or for a certain part of the day,
> Or for many years of stretching cycles of years.
>   ("There Was a Child Went Forth":364)

As a result of this ongoing transformation of identity in Whitman's poetry, a range of voices emerges in which the "I" is stretched to include a vast array of characters whose differing voices add to the mosaic structure of the work. In his essay "Who Speaks in Whitman's poems?" Mitchell Robert Breitwieser has commented on "Whitman's boldest proposition, his second "I" independent of any speaker and any specific conversation in which it might be used. Like 'leaf,' this second 'I' . . . floats free, descending into the conversations of Americans, but not captured in those conversations. This would be an 'I' for whom all imaginable speakers of the word *I* would be instances, as each leaf is an instance of the concept denoted by the word *leaf.*"[67]

As leaves, these secondary voices are the sympathetic transformations of the more primary, stemlike "I," based on a recognition of the interrelation of all life, particularly through suffering, as in section 33 of "Song of Myself":

> Agonies are one of my changes of garments,
> I do not ask the wounded person how he feels,
>   I myself become the wounded person,

My hurts turn livid upon me as I lean on a cane
   and observe.

(67)

In this section, the lyric "I" is identified with a whirling kaleidoscope of "changes of garments": "I" is an arctic hunter, a sailor in the crow's nest, a widow with a drowned husband, a hounded slave, an injured fireman, an old artillerist. The "I" of these individual voices is intermittently identified with one that becomes a collective "we" in lines such as these: "All this I swallow, it tastes good, I like it well, it becomes mine, / I am the man, I suffer'd, I was there." Many of these voices are presented with an imagistic shorthand of essential details: "My voice is the wife's voice, the screech by the rail of the stairs, / They fetch my man's body up dripping and drowned." Others involve an extensive elaboration of details with such a chillingly dramatic verisimilitude that they truly suggest a degree of empathy approaching shamanic possession:

> I am the hounded slave, I wince at the bite of
>   the dogs,
> Hell and despair are upon me, crack and again crack
>   the marksmen,
> I clutch the rails of the fence, my gore drips,
>   thinn'd with the ooze of my skin,
> I fall on the weeds and stones,
> The riders spur their unwilling horses, haul close,
> Taunt my dizzy ears and beat me violently over the
>   head with whip-stocks.

(66–67)

The following section of the poem presents another "I," the narrative voice of a young Texan soldier, one more from the multitude of voices melting dreamlike into each other throughout *Leaves of Grass*, voyaging across a country Whitman never crossed, around a world Whitman never circled, engaged in occupations and situations of which the writer had little or no firsthand knowledge, yet identified so closely with the representative persona as if Whitman himself had been "the man [who] suffer'd . . . was there."

In addition to these transformations between voices and places, the categorical distances between subject and object are often fused in Whitman's poetry, as they are in American Indian poetry, in which there is no separation between what we term the subjective and objective realms. "Unscrew the locks from the doors!" Whitman commands in "Song of Myself," and then "Unscrew the doors themselves from their jambs!" (24:52), for all the normal partitions between these linear divisions are swept away by the energy of these transformations. Yet the lyric "I" of the speaker-poet contains all of the various transformative identities populating the poems, as their voices are unified in The Voice that issues from behind the mask of Walt Whitman. The "I" of the voice stands in a shifting relationship to the "you" of a tribal audience created by repeated direct addresses, questions, and imperatives. This "you" is also transformed into the multiple identities of companion, lover, soul, listener, witness, and tribe-at-large, and even exchanges places with the "I" of the speaker himself in "Salut au Monde!" This poem begins with the startling line, "O take my hand Walt Whitman!" (137), which identifies the poet as "you." In the first section, "I" the reader proceed to ask "you," Walt Whitman, questions answered in the following section, structuring a lively example of call-and-response that continues throughout most of the poem: "What do you hear Walt Whitman?" and "What do you see Walt Whitman?" Walt Whitman answers with a series of chants of what "I see" and what "I hear," an extended synesthesia between the visual and aural similar to the one in section 18 of "Starting from Paumanok." This synesthesia is paralleled by a further transformation in sections 11 and 12, in which "I" is again Walt Whitman and "you" are the peoples of the world whom he conjures: "You Roman! Neapolitan! you Greek!" and "You Hottentot with clicking palate! you woolly-haired hordes!" (146–47). What the poem approaches with its I/you transformations is a synesthesia-like fusion between subject and object that effectively invokes the rather dizzying world unity of which it chants: The reader is an "I," "you" are the poet, the poet is "I," and "you" are everyone.

This transformative energy between voices and places, as well as between subject and object, is also reflected in Whitman's poetry in the transformations between genders. It is appropriate that shamans, as the representatives of those specifically matrilinear qualities of communitas that Turner describes, are often women; yet quite frequently they embody the even more liminal qualities of androgyny and are male, or occasionally female, transvestites, identified by most anthropologists as homosexuals. In American Indian cultures, the male shaman is quite often a "berdache," that is, a male who dresses, marries, and lives as a woman. Not all male shamans are berdaches, and not all berdaches are shamans, but as Alberto Cardín explains in *Guerreros, chamanes y travestis,* "what is not in doubt, when we come to making generalizations, is the interrelation between shamanism and homosexuality."[68] In his study of the berdache tradition among North American Indians, *The Spirit and the Flesh,* Walter L. Williams discusses the correlation between spirituality and androgyny in American Indian culture:

> Somewhere between the status of women and men, berdaches
> not only mediate between the sexes but between the psychic and
> the physical—between the spirit and the flesh. Since they mix the
> characteristics of both men and women, they possess the vision
> of both. They have double vision, with the ability to see more
> clearly than a single gender perspective can provide. This is why
> they are often referred to as 'seer,' one whose eyes can see beyond
> the blinders that restrict the average person.[69]

Such an androgynous balancing between polarities is echoed throughout Whitman's poetry, particularly in the manner in which the persona intertwines its expressions of "rough" workingman yet tender "motherly" qualities. This balancing becomes a striking element of the poet's grammar, in which "man" and "woman," "his" and "her" are consistently paired in most contexts that refer to those of unspecified gender, an introduction unique in North American writing until the present day. The first poem in *Leaves of Grass* states the basis for such inclusivity, declaring that "The Female equally with the Male I sing" (1), a double focus running parallel to the assertion in "Song of Myself" that "I am the poet of the Body and I am the poet of the Soul" (21:48). In "I Sing the Body Electric," the male and female are identified as equal if distinct manifestations of the same sexually grounded physicality, which, in turn, is identical to the spiritual: "And if the body

were not the soul, what is the soul?" (1:94). Eliade explains the shamanic transvestite as an attempt to likewise encompass both the male
and female, a form of "ritual androgyny, a well-known archaic formula for the divine biunity and the *coincidencia oppositorum*," [70] that is,
the same coincidence of physical and spiritual planes that Whitman assumes in the poem. The writer's homosexuality no doubt allowed a
empathetic basis for creating an androgynous persona that, like the shamanic berdache, moves beyond "a single gender perspective" toward
the polymorphous assumption of both masculine and feminine qualities, maintaining the ability to transmute consciousness back and forth
between the two.

This transformation between genders is evident in many passages in
Leaves of Grass, not only on those occasions when the poet speaks directly in a woman's voice, such as that of the widow mentioned above,
but when the perspective shifts between the masculine and feminine,
as in the bathers section of "Song of Myself." In this passage, the male
poet becomes identified with the perspective of a lonely woman who
watches from behind blinds twenty-eight men bathing at a beach. Just
as the poet becomes the woman, the woman becomes the twenty-ninth
bather, ostensibly male and unnoticed, who voyeuristically joins the
men. The men "do not know who puffs and declines with pendant and
bending arch" (11:39), nor is the reader certain, for that matter, who
performs this mysteriously suggestive gesture: Is it the male speaker
transposed into the female voyeur, or the lonely woman converted into
the unnoticed male bather? The imagery is drawn in carefully blurred
lines of polymorphous androgyny, which can easily lend itself to both
heterosexual or homosexual readings, yet to translate the essential androgyny into specific sexual narratives of one type or the other, as many
critical readings attempt, only serves to freeze the fluent "changes of
garments" at the heart of the passage. In "The Sleepers," the transposition between male and female is equally subtle and more extensive. The
male speaker identifies himself as both "the actor" and "the actress":

> I am she who adorn'd herself, and folded her hair
>   expectantly,
> My truant lover has come, and it is dark.

Double yourself and receive me darkness,
Receive me and my lover too, he will not let me go
    without him.

(1:426)

The darkness, first awaited as the woman's male lover, is later associated
with the male speaker's mother, "her in whom I lay so long" (8:433).
Hutchinson has identified the shamanic nature of such trance-like transpositions of gender:

> The fact that masculine and feminine identifications are inter-
> changed throughout the poem indicates that the significance of
> the erotic experience exceeds its physical nature in the common
> sense, by which a sexual encounter can be known from one or the
> other, male or female. . . . The narrator is first masculine, them
> feminine, then masculine again. He is not merely 'omni-sexual':
> his identity is fluid. This transformational ability agrees with the
> sexual equivalences of shamanic experience.[71]

At the basis of shamanic androgyny, as it is reflected in Whitman's
poetry, is not the static gender identities of either purely hetero- or
homosexuality, but the fluidity of the "I" to speak with the voices of
varying states of consciousness, including both male and female.

The transpositions in the shamanic trance between voices, places,
subject-object relationships, and genders often include the transformation into other living forms, particularly animals and birds, suggested in
several passages in Whitman's poetry. In this tribal grouping in "Song
of Myself," the poet surveys his evolutionary identity, acknowledging
his atavistic ability to effect temporary returns to mineral, plant, or
animal states:

I find I incorporate gneiss, coal, long-threaded moss,
    fruits, grains, esculent roots,
And am stucco'd with quadrupeds and birds all over,
And have distanced what is behind me for good reasons,
But call any thing back again when I desire it.

(31:59)

A parallel concern in Neruda's poetry is the poet's relationship with stone, and he likewise illustrates his ability to assume and speak from a mineral consciousness, whether it be the subterranean descent "into the genital matrix of the earth" (30), in the first section of "Alturas de Macchu Picchu," or the ascent through the stages of mineral metamorphosis to the celestial light of gems explored in a later work, *Las piedras del cielo* (1970). In this book, Neruda describes "the highway along / which one age passed into another" and his own trancelike return to the "inheritance of fossils," from which he speaks in several sections of the poem:

> *Yo duermo a veces, voy*
> *hacia el origen, retrocelo en vilo*
> *llevado por mi condición intrínseca*
> *de dormilón de la naturaleza,*
> *y en sueños extravago*
> *despertando en el fondo de las piedras.*
>   (OC:III:551–52)

> Sometimes I sleep, I go back
> to the beginning, falling back in mid-air,
> wafted along by my natural state
> as the sleepyhead of nature
> and in dreams I drift on
> waking at the feet of great stones.[72]

Such transformations on the part of the shaman demonstrate not only his powers, but are indicative of a differing view of the nature of personal identity itself. As representative men, Whitman and Neruda depart from the fixed delineations of the individual ego and move toward a more encompassing conception of the communal self, containing all voices, both genders, an atavistic access to other natural beings, as well as a subject "I" constantly redefined by the myriad angles of group interaction.

Such a fluid sense of identity is a central foundation of *Canto general,* in which a mosaic structure similar to that in *Leaves of Grass* allows for voices to be transformed across centuries, languages, genders, and the limits of the poet's ego. Throughout the first four books, voices of the dead Indians that the poet invokes at Macchu Picchu often speak through his mask, weaving in and out of the poet's own lyric "I." Scenes of the Spanish invasion and domination of Latin America are often narrated not from the Spanish but from the native point of view of those identified as "my brothers" or "my people." In "Los libertadores," a group of Araucanian Indians who are preparing to eat the heart of Pedro de Valdivia speak:

> Trajimos tela y cántaro, tejidos
> gruesos como las trenzas conyugales,
> alhajas como almendras de la luna,
> y los tambores que llenaron
> la Araucanía con su luz de cuero.
> Colmamos las vasijas de dulzura
> y bailamos golpeando los terrones
> hechos de nuestra propia estirpe oscura.
> (IV:12:389–90)

We brought cloth and earthen vessels,
fabric thick as conjugal braids,
gemstones like moon almonds,
and drums that filled Araucania
with their leathery light.
We heaped bowls with sweets
and danced, pounding the earth
made of our own dark stock.

(85)

The voices that speak through Whitman's poetry are those of the ill and the outcast, the physically and spiritually unwhole, whereas the voices that speak in *Canto general* are identified with the economically and politically oppressed. When Neruda writes, "I cannot separate my voice from whatever suffers" (IV:40:141), the suffering he means is that endured when struggling for freedom, equality, and the homeland. "There is a constant emotional identification that converts the singer into each of these persecuted and oppressed beings," observes Rodríguez Monegal.[73] The voices of dead Indian warriors are transformed into those of the heroes of colonial liberation, which, in turn, become the voices of working-class comrades aligned in the present struggle against exploitation and imperialism. This, collectively, constitutes the voice of The People vocalized through his mask:

> *sino arrancar de tu silencio*
> *una vez más la voz del pueblo,*
> *elevarla como la pluma*
> *más fulgurante de la selva,*
> *dejarla a mi lado y amarla*
> *hasta que cante por mis labios.*
> (IV:40:452)

> but wrench from your silence
> the people's voice again,
> hold it aloft like the jungle's
> most splendorous feather,
> set it beside me and love it
> until it sings through my lips.
> (142)

"La tierra se llama Juan" is a book devoted almost entirely to a series of dramatic monologues in which Latin American working people speak, structured much in the manner of Edgar Lee Masters' *Spoon River Anthology*. Represented here are the voices of shoemakers, navigators, mothers, children, martyrs, factory workers, and miners, male and female, living and dead, from Chile to Costa Rica. Many of these were the voices that Neruda heard as he visited among the nitrate and copper miners of Tarapacá and Antofogasta, provinces from which he was elected senator in 1945, as well as the voices of the working people who hid him during 1948–49, while underground from the government of González Videla. They tell of poverty and oppression, broken strikes, torture at the hands of police and military, prison and concentration camps, all in the understated, colloquial tones of a testimonial style but with a dramatic verisimilitude of essential details that, like Whitman's "hounded slave" monologue, almost suggests a form of possession. Here Benilda Varela speaks, whose husband is a political prisoner:

This Ecstatic Nation

Arreglé la comida a mis chiquillos y salí.
Quise entrar a Lota a ver a mi marido.
Como se sabe, mandan la policía
y nadie puede entrar sin su permiso.
Les cayó mal mi cara. Eran las órdenes
de González Videla, antes de entrar
a decir sus discursos, para que nuestra gente
tenga miedo. Así pasó: me agarraron,
me desnudaron, me tiraron al suelo a golpes.
Perdí el sentido. Me desperté en el suelo
desnuda, con una sábana mojada sobre
mi cuerpo sangrante.

. . . .

Si no he muerto, es para decirles, camaradas:
tenemos que luchar mucho más, hasta que
     desaparezcan
estos verdugos de la faz de la tierra.
(VIII:14:567–68)

I made lunch for the kiddies and left.
I tried to enter Lota to see my husband.
As you know, the police are in command,
and no one can enter without their permission.
They didn't like the looks of my face. It was
     ordered
by González Videla, before he began
to give his speeches, so that our people
would be afraid. And so it was: they seized me
stripped me, beat me to the ground.
I passed out. I came to on the floor,
naked, with a wet sheet covering
my bleeding body.

. . . .

If I haven't died, it's to be able to tell you,
     comrades:
we must fight much harder, until these butchers
disappear from the face of the earth.
(250–51)

Although Neruda does not engage in the fluid transpositions of gender that characterize the shamanic transvestism of Whitman, several of these monologues are notably spoken by women, lending a recognizable androgyny to the poetic voice. As pronounced as in Whitman's "Salut au Monde!" is the reversal of the normal subject-object relationship that Neruda displays in this book, in which the "I" of the people speak to "you," the poet. Many of the voices in this book directly address Neruda as *señor, camarada,* or *compañero* as they state their names or occupations, and even invite him to return: "Any time, sir, the poor / never shut their doors" (4:241). Juan Figueroa, an iodine factory worker, calls the poet by name and tells his story, answering silent questions in what is one side of an implied dialogue:

> *Usted es Neruda? Pase, camarada.*
> *Sí, de la Case del Yodo, ya no quedan*
> *otros viviendo. Yo me aguanto.*
> *Sé que ya no estoy vivo, que me espera*
> *la tierra de la pampa. Son cuatro horas*
> *al día, en la Casa de Yodo.*
> *Viene por unos tubos, sale como una masa,*
> *como una goma cárdena. La entramos*
> *de batea a batea, la envolvemos*
> *como criatura. Mientras tanto,*
> *el ácido nos roe, nos socava,*
> *entrando por los ojos y la boca,*
> *por la piel, por las uñas.*
> *De la Casa del Yodo no se sale*
> *cantando, compañero.*
>
> (VIII:11:564–65)

> Are you Neruda? Come in, comrade.
> Yes, at the Iodine Works, there are no others
> living now. I'm hanging on.
> I know that I'm no longer alive, that the pampa
> earth awaits me. It's four hours
> a day, at the Iodine Works.
> It comes through some pipes, and emerges like
>   dough,

like purple rubber. We take it
from tub to tub, wrapped
like a baby. Meanwhile,
the acid eats away at us, saps us,
entering our eyes and our mouths,
our skin, our fingernails.
You don't leave the Iodine Works
singing, my friend.

(248)

These voices cut across ages, genders, countries and even, on one
occasion, venture into the spirit world: "I'm dead," states Margarita
Naranjo. "I'm from María Elena / I spent my entire life on the pampa"
(8:245), a voice who recounts her own funeral and burial at the salt-
petre company. As does Whitman, Neruda identifies the agony of these
voices with his own, invoking them to speak through his own lyric "I":

Yo me llamo como ellos, como los que murieron.
Yo soy también Ramírez, Muñoz, Pérez, Fernández.
Me llamo Álvarez, Núñez, Tapia, López, Contreras.
Soy pariente de todos los que mueren, soy pueblo,
y por todo esta sangre que cae estoy de luto.

(VIII:16:570)

My name's the same as theirs, as the ones who died.
I, too, am Ramírez, Muñoz, Pérez and Fernández.
My name's Álvarez, Núñez, Tapia, López, Contreras.
I'm related to all those who die, I'm people,
and I mourn for all the blood that falls.

(253)

Nelson Osorio finds that in *Canto general* the "poet" and the "people"
are no longer the traditional rhetorical figures who sing and tell, "but
rather *are sung* and *are told*. In this work 'poet' and 'people' are not the
polar terms for subjectivity and objectivity, but a symbiosis that creates a dialectical perspective."[74] Who is speaking, particularly in "La
tierra se llama Juan," is neither the poet nor the people, but the land

itself, named Juan or Everyman, testifying in the voice of the people through the mask of the poet. The land represents the continuity between Indian, anticolonial, and working-class heroes who, in Neruda's poetry, speak in much the same voice, not as individuals but as a collectivity that the lyric "I" contains and represents.

Within tribal cultures, the individual is defined by his or her relation to the whole, an identity that exists in a constant state of flux and renewal. The patchwork of diverse voices that speaks through the shaman, as representative tribal member, reinforces this sense of collective identity and individual belonging, unlike the more familiar fragmentation of consciousness depicted by the cacophonous play of voices within works of modernist literature. Even today, according to Ferrandiz, in the possession cults of Venezuela, with their American Indian and African tribal sources, when the shaman "incorporates personalities of science and politics, spirits of the rivers and forests, national heroes and anti-heroes, these symbolically charged fragments of Venezuela, once again in the bodies, the speech and the consciousness of the faithful, powerfully evoke articulated images, 'montages' of dissimilars or subversive 'bricolages' . . which foster a strong sense of definite belonging."[75] In traditional American Indian cultures, such shamanic sessions are ritual expressions of the collective soul of the people, what the Iroquois call *orenda,* or the eternally animating spirit of daily tribal life. In various native cultures this communal spirit is envisioned as a Sacred Tree, which Halifax describes as a "symbol of the place of confluence of the human collective, [which] draws the society together by directing its energy toward the powerful center." The shaman is ritually identified with this tree, since he or she "is the one who is in dynamic relationship to this 'axis of the world.'"[76]

Eliade describes one such initiation ritual among the Mapuche of Neruda's native Araucania, during which the *machi,* a female shaman, climbs a ceremonial tree or *rewe,* which "is also the particular symbol of the shamanic profession, and every *machi* keeps it in front of her hut indefinitely."[77] This tree has seven notched steps by which the shaman symbolically ascends to the world of spirits, as Neruda undoubtedly knew, for in section 6 of "Los libertadores," he writes that during the civil war of the Araucanians against the Spanish "the illustrious shamaness descended / her ladder" (80), using the phrase "la

ilustre Machi" in the original.[78] In the first section of "Los libertadores," Neruda introduces his own version of the Mapuche *rewe*, the
"tree of the people," which serves not only as a symbol of the communal
spirit of the Araucanian natives in numerous references throughout this
book, but emerges as a dominant motif in *Canto general*, representing
the larger tribe of The People that his word unifies as a contemporary
machi. "The entire tribe of red branches" (5:79) of resistant Araucanians in "Los libertadores" becomes the "tree of humanity, / tree of eternity" (18:254) of the oppressed workers in "La tierra se llama Juan,"
a continuing center from which the voices of the collectivity sprout.
This symbol of militant communitas in the fourth book—"the bread
tree, the arrow tree, / the fist tree, the fire tree"—is rooted in the "arbo-
real America" of the virgin continent introduced in the first book: "the
thunder tree, the red tree, / the thorn tree, the mother tree" (1:15).
What speaks through the tree, as through the shaman, is ultimately the
land itself.

Neruda's tree of the people appears as a parallel expression to Whitman's grass, a structurally as well as metaphysically organic metaphor
for the mosaic assemblages of loosely related leaves and branches that
constitute the two books. As a point of cohesion among dissimilar parts
and people, this tree is identified with Neruda's own shamanic voice as
well as with the communal spirit of the American people:

> *Aquí viene el árbol, el árbol*
> *de la tormenta, el árbol del pueblo.*
> *De la tierra suben sus héroes*
> *como las hojas por la savia,*
> *y el viento estrella los follajes*
> *de muchedumbre rumorosa,*
> *hasta que cae la semilla*
> *del pan otra vez a la tierra.*
>
> (IV:1:374)

> Here comes the tree, the tree
> of the storm, the tree of the people.
> Its heroes rise up from the earth
> as leaves from the sap,
> and the wind spangles the whispering

multitude's foliage,
until the seed falls
again from the bread to the earth.

(71)

This tree of the people serves as a ubiquitous and equalizing agent of
tribal continuity, as well as a means of fusing the various secondary "I's"
with the representative "I" of the poet, of uniting the many with the
one, as does Whitman's grass:

> Or I guess it is a uniform hieroglyphic,
> And it means, sprouting alike in broad zones and
> narrow zones,
> Growing among black folks as among white,
> Kanuck, Tuckahoe, Congressman, Cuff, I give them
> the same, I receive them the same.
> ("Song of Myself":6:34)

Both Neruda's tree of the people as well as Whitman's grass grow from
the individual deaths of tribal members:

> *Aquí viene el árbol, el árbol*
> *nutrido por muertos desnudos,*
> *muertos azotados y heridos,*
> *muertos de rostros imposibles,*
> *empalados sobre una lanza. . . .*

> Here comes the tree, the tree
> nourished by naked corpses,
> corpses scourged and wounded,
> corpses with impossible faces,
> impaled on spears. . . .

Just as Neruda assigns a political meaning to these deaths, the colonial
subjugation of the indigenous people that stands as a recurrent metaphor for the current oppression of working-class comrades, Whitman
assumes an erotic significance, an earthy comradeship with those who
resemble his own present "camerados":

Tenderly will I use your curling grass,
It may be you transpire from the breasts of young men,
It may be if I had known them I would have loved them. . . .

Out of the death of the individual, however, grows the perpetuity of
the tribe, its roots claiming the land as American and sending nourish-
ment toward the collective future, lending spiritual coherence to the
present:

> *Aquí viene el árbol, el árbol*
> *cuyas raíces están vivas,*
> *sacó salitre del martirio,*
> *sus raíces comieron sangre*
> *y extrajo lágrimas del suelo:*
> *las elevó por sus ramajes,*
> *las repartió en su arquitectura.*
> *Fueran flores invisibles,*
> *a veces, flores enterradas,*
> *a veces iluminaron*
> *sus pétalos, como planetas.*

> Here comes the tree, the tree
> whose roots are alive,
> it fed on martyrdom's nitrate,
> its roots consumed blood,
> and it extracted tears from the soil:
> raised them through its branches,
> dispersed them in its architecture.
> They were invisible flowers—
> sometimes buried flowers,
> other times they illuminated
> its petals, like planets.

In Whitman's version, there is also a growing "onward and outward"
into spirit, despite—or perhaps because of—the democratically horizontal nature of his foliage:

What do you think has become of the young and old men?
And what do you think has become of the women and
   children?

They are alive and well somewhere,
The smallest sprout shows there really is no death,
And if ever there was it led forward life, and
   does not wait at the end to arrest it,
And ceas'd the moment life appear'd.
All goes onward and outward, nothing collapses,
And to die is different from what any one supposed,
   and luckier.

"As the corpse returns to the earth," Breitwieser writes, "so the individual 'I' returns to this subjectivity bank, but the large 'I' is not
silenced, as the concept 'leaf' does not perish with every leaf."[79] This
larger "I" is, in fact, renewed by the death of the poet, plowed under
into nature and history yet ultimately reborn. In closing *Canto general*,
his "common book of man," Neruda anticipates that

> . . . *una comunidad de labradores*
> *alguna vez recogerá su fuego,*
> *y sembrará sus llamas y sus hojas*
> *otra vez en la nave de la tierra.*
>
> *Y nacerá nuevo esta palabra,*
> *tal vez en otro tiempo sin dolores.* . . .
>   (XV:28:721)

> . . . a community of peasants
> will one day harvest its fire
> and will again sow its flames
> and leaves in the ship of the earth.
>
> And this word will rise again,
> perhaps in another time free of sorrow. . . .
>   (399)

Whitman, in his conclusion to "Song of Myself," imagines a similar yet more personal resurrection by the side of a companion who stops somewhere waiting for him: "I bequeath myself to the dirt to grow from the grass I love, / If you want me again look for me under your boot-soles" (52:89).

It is appropriate that both Whitman and Neruda chose such simple yet pervasive forms of botanical life as grass or trees as their fundamental symbols of communitas and continuity, as well as that both enumerate in such abundant detail the American names, often of American Indian origin, of plants, trees, and flowers throughout their work. This motif is present even in Whitman's cover design for the first edition of *Leaves of Grass,* which features, against a dark green background, the title in a gold tendril-like script sprouting downward into a web of roots and upward into a profusion of leaves;[80] the 1860 edition also introduces a group of poems clustered around the symbol of the calamus lily. In many American Indian cultures, the shaman is closely identified with vegetable life, in part because of his or her extensive knowledge of the medicinal and psychotropic qualities of herbs used both in curing and visions. Among mestizo populations in large areas of South America today, shamans are known as *vegetalistas* and shamanism as *vegetalismo.* [81] The relation between trees, plant life, and the origins of poetry is elaborated in detail by Robert Graves in *The White Goddess,* in which he traces the source of British poetry to the shamanic bards of the tree cults in the pre-Christian tribes of Wales, Ireland, and Scotland, particularly to the Druid worship of the oak and the "tree alphabet" that became the basis of Gaelic script.[82] Graves laments the decay of modern poetry, the lost connection to its primitive identity with nature, as does Emerson in "The Poet," where he calls for the American reinvention both of poetry and the poet's role, for a "genius" who "repairs the decay of things." [83] Whitman and Neruda's reinvention both of poetry and the poet in the Americas parallels the tribal model that is the point of origin of all poetry, revitalizing the link between modern and primitive that Graves finds broken in his own literature, and recalling once again the atavistic process that Matthiessen finds at the basis of Whitman's poetics. "It is likewise probable," explains Eliade of the shamanic trance, "that the pre-ecstatic euphoria constituted one of the universal sources of lyric poetry. In preparing his trance, the shaman drums, summons his spirit helpers, speaks a 'secret language' or the 'animal language,' imitating the cries of beasts and especially the songs of birds. He ends by obtaining a 'second state' that provides the impetus for linguistic creation and the rhythms of lyric poetry."[84] The Araucanian *machi* ascending the Sacred Tree is one of the many forms of this ritual present in the New World, one given renewed meaning by the personae we encounter in *Leaves of Grass* and *Canto general*. In North America, on the Third Sacred Day of the Lakota Sun Dance, bundles of sweet grass and sage are tied to a raised pole that symbolizes, for these plains people, what Neruda calls "the tree / that grows in the middle of the earth" (IV:1:73). The Lakota shaman climbs to the top to sing these words, enacting a ceremony that Whitman and Neruda echo in the tribal role they created for the American poet and in their own ritual use of trees and grass:

> At the center of the earth
> Stand looking around you.
> Recognizing the tribe
> Stand looking around you.[85]

The Vertical Voyage:
"The Sleepers" and
"Alturas de Macchu Picchu"

I rise extatic through all, and
    sweep with the true gravitation,
The whirling and whirling
    is elemental within me.
—*"Song of Myself": 37 (1855)*

Whitman and Neruda are both known as poets "of the open road," their rooted Americanness inevitably expressed in terms of the expansive and restless mobility of a recently immigrant culture, their regionalism framed by a global perspective. Between them, the two poets undoubtedly celebrate the name not only of every geographic location in the American hemisphere but of the world at large, far beyond Mannahatta and Araucania. Whitman, who traveled relatively little, issued his various "salutes au monde" with the buoyant universality that accompanied the nineteenth-century interconnection of the world through railroad, telegraph, and steamship lines. Although early poems, such as "Song of the Open Road," emphasize the loose clothing, fresh air, and rustic exercise prescribed by various health enthusiasms of his day, his later poems of the 1870s, such as "Passage to India" and "Prayer of Columbus," demonstrate the incorporation into his persona of the Columbus-like role of the world voyager. From an early age, on the other hand, Neruda lived out this myth of the later Whitman, that of a world citizen well acquainted with India, Burma, Indonesia, Argentina, France, Spain, Mexico, the Soviet Union, and China, a poet who confessed, in *Extravagaria* (1958), "that when I explain myself, / I'll be talking geography."[1] Yet both poets are less concerned with the act of travel, the details of movement and location, than with the metaphor of the journey itself, around which much of their major work is structured. Whitman's "Passage to India" is a "passage to more than India!" (9:420), a correlate of the flight of the "soul to primal thought" (7:418). The motionless traveler is the unifying image at the basis of Rodríguez Monegal's study of Neruda, *El viajero inmóvil*, of which the poet approvingly remarked that the critic "perceived at once that I like to travel without stepping out of my house or leaving my country or even going out of myself."[2] In *Cantos ceremoniales* (1961) Neruda characterizes his voyage as having little to do with travel in the conventional sense:

> *Qué podía decir sin tocar tierra?*
> *A quién me dirigía sin la lluvia?*
> *Por eso nunca estuve donde estuve*
> *y no navegué más que de regreso*
> *y de las catedrales no guardé*
> *retrato ni cabellos. . . .*
>   (OC;II·969)

> What could I say without touching the earth?
> To whom should I speak but the rain?
> Wherever I was, I was never truly there,
> I never traveled anywhere but the way here
> and from the grand cathedrals I treasured
> no post cards or souvenirs. . . .[3]

Exterior movement through the world is only a secondary means of expressing the nature of an immobile interior journey.

In Whitman and Neruda's poetry, this journey is a perpetual state of being, independent of both time and place: "I tramp a perpetual journey," Whitman announces in "Song of Myself" (46:83). The journey of the motionless traveler is intimately connected with death, in which the soul also undergoes a separation from the limitations of time and place. In "Song of the Open Road," Whitman describes the "universe itself as a road, as many roads, as roads for traveling souls" (13:157), a migratory form of consciousness seldom experienced in the waking lives of most individuals. Within the limits of this ordinary mentality, Whitman senses "a secret silent loathing and despair" in which a true knowledge of death remains repressed, parceled out into the "little death," that "daily ration of death" (3:32) Neruda identifies as the lot of the individual in "Alturas de Macchu Picchu." Whitman's "open road" leads not only to the public thoroughfare but to a larger experience of psychic migration, what he calls "the delicious near-by freedom of death" (12:156), the bodiless flight of "traveling souls" through a realm generally experienced only after dying. This is a state unexplored and unexpressed in daily life, stifled in

> . . . the houses of men and women, at the table,
>   in the bedroom, everywhere,
> Smartly attired, countenance smiling, form upright,
>   death under the breast-bones, hell under
>   the skull-bones,
> Under the broadcloth and gloves, under the ribbons
>   and artificial flowers,
> Keeping fair with the customs, speaking not a syllable
>   of itself,
> Speaking of any thing but never of itself.
>   ("Song of the Open Road":13:158)

This realm of "traveling souls" well acquainted with death is the domain of the tribal shaman, who, during his initiation, "dies" in a prolonged voyage to an Underworld of suffering and unwholeness, returning with a mastery that allows him to heal, making whole not only the individual tribal members but the tribe itself. "The journeys of the shaman into the beyond, his diving down into psychic depths," writes Andreas Lommel, "the real result of which, the pacification of the group psyche, the increase in certainty and confidence, remains incomprehensible to us, are generally experienced and reported as a journey to the dead, to the underworld, the beyond."[4] At the basis of his roles as chanter, namer, spirit-guardian, word-conjurer, healer, and tribal unifier is the shaman's primary experience as a psychic voyager. The initiatory voyage, during which the neophyte suffers the near-fatal consequences of actual privations, is repeated as the model of a "perpetual journey," in which the shaman travels back and forth between the spirit and human realms in the trance that gives birth to lyric flights of rhythmic song. The purpose of this vertical voyage is to exorcise the same "hell under the skull-bones" that Whitman finds within the tribal psyche. In the terms of Western psychiatry, Géza Róheim defines shamans as "the lightning conductors of common anxiety. They fight the demons so that others can hunt the prey and in general fight reality."[5]

There are myriad cultural modifications upon the basic pattern of the shamanic journey, yet Joan Halifax points out that "from Lapland to Patagonia, from the Paleolithic to today, the archetypes activated during shamanic ordeals and exaltations are astonishingly similar."[6] Although Eliade devotes most of his volume on shamanism to describing the variations between Siberian, American, and Oceanic shamanic practices, his preliminary definition is a universal yet exacting one: "A shaman specializes in a trance during which his soul is believed to leave his body and ascend to the sky or descend to the underworld."[7] This journey occurs along the coordinates of the *axis mundi* of the World Tree, with its roots drawing sustenance from the Underworld of the dead, its trunk marking the Middle World of ordinary tribal life, and its branches reaching up into the spirits of the Sky World. The vertical voyage is often represented in world mythology in terms of a horizontal correlate, that of travel across land and water. As a narrative, this journey in many ways resembles what Joseph Campbell has described in *The Hero with a Thousand Faces* as the basic comparative unit, or monomyth, of world mythology, in which a hero suffers "a separation from the world, a penetration to some source of power, and a life-enhancing return."[8] Although many of these mythologies may have developed from the shamanic rituals of earlier tribal cultures as animistic beliefs were translated into the mythic frameworks of deistic religions, the essential difference remains in the non-epic nature of the shamanic journey, in which there is no mythic hero, only the shifting identity of the masked voice of the shaman, and no historical time, only the dreamtime of the trance. The shamanic journey is therefore not a story *about* an idealized past event performed by a legendary figure mythologized as an example of vicarious individuation, as are most religious mythologies and vision-quest narratives, but the ritual enactment on the part of the representative tribal individual of the process of dying and rebirth for the concrete purpose of healing the collective being. Significantly, Halifax has suggested how the shamanic journey parallels the processes of schizophrenic disintegration and reintegration,[9] and Holger Kalweit has demonstrated, in *Dreamtime and Inner Space: The World of the Shaman,* how the shamanic journey follows the most common motifs reported in modern research on what is called the Near-Death Experience, or that universal experience recounted by those returned from a state of clinical death.[10] In Lévi-Strauss's terms, the shamanic journey is a "raw" and mythology a "cooked" version of the same human phenomenon, the voyage through death to rebirth.

This journey is, on one level, the "content" of the native forms of language, persona, and voice that have been located in the poetics of *Leaves of Grass* and *Canto general.* The journey represents the unifying function of these other elements, the chant, mask, and ventriloquial use of voice each contributing to the ecstatic state that propels the shaman through his descent and flight. The rhythmic repetitions of Whitman and Neruda's lines, the equivalent of the shaman's drum, are essential to the trance, in which words are brought back from the "other side" in the absence of the writer's control or direction. Matthiessen relates that Whitman "tried later to describe the sensation he had when first composing 'Song of Myself,' how it had seemed to him afterwards as though the poem had risen from a kind of trance, how 'in contemplating it, he felt, in regard to his own agency in it, like a somnambulist who is shown, during his waking hours, the giddy heights and impossible situations over which he has passed safely in his sleep.'"[11] Whitman was conscious of the nature of this mental state and that it formed the genesis of his creative work, which he describes in another notebook entry as growing out of "a trance, yet with all the senses alert—only a state of high exalted musing—the tangible and material with all its shows, the objective world suspended or surmounted for a while, and the powers in exaltation, freedom, vision—yet the senses not lost or counteracted."[12] Although this trance state sustains major portions of *Leaves of Grass* and *Canto general* in a hypnotic suspension that prevents sudden falls from the "giddy heights" to which they often soar, the books, as such, do not follow in a precise pattern the consecutive stages of the shamanic journey. Given the works' mosaic structures, this pattern occurs episodically throughout, with varying points of emphasis. The stages of the shamanic "call," descent, and ascent are best represented in Whitman's "The Sleepers" (1855 edition) and Neruda's "Alturas de Macchu Picchu." Like the initiatory journey, these two poems form the archetypal experiences repeated and augmented in subsequent journeys. Whitman's "Song of Myself," "Crossing Brooklyn Ferry," and "When Lilacs Last in the Dooryard Bloomed" are extensions of the experiences represented in "The Sleepers," and Juan Villegas has observed that the structure of "Alturas de Macchu Picchu" "is the same as the whole of *Canto general:* the symbolic journey from vital chaos to luminosity."[13] These poems, as representatives of a structure so basic to the work of both poets, merit a close analysis as American expressions of the shamanic journey.

II

Stories of a voyage to the Underworld and ascent to the sky abound in the American Indian cultural tradition, from the oral myths and legends of the preliterate North American tribes to the written version present in the Mayan *Popul Vuh*. In *The North American Indian Orpheus Tradition*, Ake Hultkrantz examines the extensive presence of a parallel to the Orpheus myth in North American Indian mythology, generated over the centuries from shamanic healing and funerary practices. He notes that "in certain cases living persons who have visited the realm of the dead have gone there with their guardian spirits. We do not need to be in any doubt, however, as to the category of persons here in question: they are, of course, the medicine-men, the shamans, who, accompanied by their assistant spirits, have tried to fetch the souls of sick persons from the realm of the dead."[14] Myths of such a quest for the soul of a beloved woman, as in the Orpheus parallel, are but one manifestation of the pervasive pattern of this journey, which Halifax has distilled into these most common elements: "descent to the Realm of the Dead, confrontations with demonic forces, dismemberment, trial by fire, communion with the world of spirits and creatures, assimilation of the elemental forces, ascension via the World Tree and/or the Cosmic Bird, realization of a solar identity, and return to the Middle World, the world of human affairs."[15] Both "The Sleepers" and "Alturas de Macchu Picchu" complete this voyage in its major phases, presenting in the most concise, unified forms within the poets' works the ritual journeys that initiated the poets in taking on their shamanic personae.

Although Whitman was in his mid-thirties and Neruda in his early forties when these poems were written, they both seem to be based on previous adolescent rites of passage. Edwin H. Miller has commented on the Whitman poem as "a reenactment of ancient puberty rites,"[16] an appropriate interpretation of the anxious adolescent sexuality that it displays, from its concern with "onanists," gender roles, and sexual embarrassment to its preoccupation with a separation from and reunification with the mother. The first five sections of "Alturas de Macchu Picchu" are not situated on the Andean mountain but, according to John Felstiner, "essentially recapitulate the experience of Neruda's twenties,"[17] when, like the shamanic neophyte undergoing severe isolation and privation far from the tribe, Neruda suffered both the isolation and penury of serving at obscure Chilean consular posts in Rangoon, Sri Lanka, and Java, a condition reflected in the anguished persona of the first two books of *Residencia en la tierra*. The complex syntax and densely interior imagery in the first half of "Alturas de Macchu Picchu" do recall the voice of *Residencia,* in contrast to the more immediate and direct incantational forms that mark the second half of the poem as a heightened expression of the voice of *Canto general*. Both "The Sleepers" and "Alturas de Macchu Picchu" begin with the voices of unfinished adolescents notably suffering in the very areas later emphasized in their reborn personae. Just as the shaman is best able to heal the sickness from which he ritually "died," Whitman's sexual and Neruda's social alienations are not only self-cured in these poems, but become the sources of their self-definitions, the means by which they identify their individuality within the interdependency of all life.

This interconnection between all beings is known to the shaman as "the net of power," one that grants him mastery over the transformations of being. "The net of power animates the cosmos," Halifax explains. "The shaman plays into that net and is able to go far beyond the normal boundaries of human action and interaction."[18] In the first sections of both "The Sleepers" and "Alturas de Macchu Picchu," the speakers are presented as wandering in an unhealthy vapor of loss and confusion, "like an empty net," as Neruda describes himself, moving from "air to air." Neruda moves restlessly through what appears to be a summer night, straying "between the streets and atmosphere, arriving and departing" (29). Whitman is also walking "all night in my vision . . . Wandering and confused, lost to myself, ill-assorted, contradictory, / Pausing and gazing and bending and stopping" (424). Both poets are like an empty "net of power," disconnected from the life around them. Yet this net has another meaning, as Eliade notes: "The shamans likewise possessed laces and nooses to serve the same purpose—capturing vagabond souls that have left their bodies. The gods and the demons of death capture the souls of the dead with a net."[19] As if snared in such a net, Whitman is drawn along the threshold between various states of consciousness, between sleep and wakefulness, the serene and tortured, the living and dead. Although he takes benign note of "the little children in their cradles" and "the married couple sleep[ing] calmly in their bed," he wonders how the murdered sleep, and is propelled toward "the worstsuffering and restless," those disembodied "vagabond souls" that he encounters in this demonic tableau:

> The wretched features of ennuyés, the white
>   features of corpses, the livid faces of drunkards,
>   the sick-gray faces of onanists,
> The gash'd bodies on battle-fields, the insane in
>   their strong-door'd rooms, the sacred idiots,
>   the newborn emerging from gates and the dying
>   emerging from gates,
> The night pervades them and enfolds them.

Neruda is also wandering along the same threshold, conveyed toward a sulfuric Underworld, past "days of vivid splendor in the inclemency / of corpses," magnetized into a spiraling descent:

> *Alguien que me esperó entre los violines*
> *encontró un mundo como una torre enterrada*
> *hundiendo su espiral más abajo de todas*
> *las hojas de color de ronco azufre:*
> *más abajo, en el oro de la geología,*
> *como una espada envuelta en meteoros,*

hundí la mano turbulenta y dulce
en lo más genital de lo terrestre.

(331)

Someone awaiting me among the violins
discovered a world like an entombed tower
spiraling down beneath all
the harsh sulphur-colored leaves:
further down, in the gold of geology,
like a sword enveloped in meteors,
I plunged my turbulent and tender hand
into the genital matrix of the earth.

(29-3-0)

At distinct moments in each poem, this descent is realized as both poets finally are seduced by the "laces and nooses" of the dead. Neruda's mysterious "someone awaiting me" draws the poet's hand toward the "genital matrix of the earth." Neruda literally dives into this rendezvous with his own death at the end of his first section: "I put my brow amid the deep waves, / descended like a drop amid the sulphurous peace." One tale of Eskimo initiation recounts an identically unlikely posture: "To their astonishment they discovered that [the initiate] was in the act of diving down into the earth. He had already gone down so far that only the soles of his feet were visible."[20] Whitman's seduction is more extended, his descent more graduated throughout the first section, which dramatizes the sexual preoccupation of the poem. He lingers with growing distance along the horizon between being and nonbeing: "The earth recedes from me into the night, / I saw that it was beautiful, and I see that what is not the earth is beautiful" (425). Yet as his trance increases ("the fit is whirling me fast!"), he begins to "see nimble ghosts whichever way I look, / Cache and cache again deep in the ground and sea, and where it is neither ground nor sea" (426). As in Neruda's approach, the Underworld is characterized as both land and water, both fluid and substantial. Whitman is escorted farther by a "gay gang of blackguards," as the sleepers with whom he lay suddenly throw back their covers like the dead rising on Judgment Day to act as spirit guides, or "journeymen divine . . . [who] surround me, and lead me and run ahead when I walk." The curious introduction of "blackguards" as "divine" may be in reference to the traditional Christian Hell, peopled with the souls of scoundrels and sinners, as well as to the increasing darkness through which the poet is escorted, in a literal sense, by blackened guards. The derivation of the word, from those lowly servants smudged black by the cleaning of pots and pans, suggests an association with the infernal elements of metal, darkness, smoke, and fire. Kalweit characterizes such spirit guides as essential elements in the shamanic journey, whether they appear in animal or human forms, comparing them to teachers in the guise of the "imaginary friends" with whom children converse.[21] Although in shamanic ascent these spirit guides are most often birds, horses, or other animals that carry the shaman into flight, the spirit guides of the descent into the Underworld are generally the souls of the dead, here represented by the spectral ushers whom Whitman calls "blackguards" and Neruda merely "someone."

Once descended, Whitman approaches his disembodiment in sexual terms as Neruda describes his own in terms of human relationship. Both poets use metaphors of clothing and nakedness to describe the relationship between body and soul, and present dying as an undressing, which takes on sexual connotations in the Whitman version. "Amid clothing and mist," writes Neruda in section II, "upon the sunken table, / like a jumbled quantity, lies the soul." This soul is tormented "under the habitual rug," lacerated "in the hostile vestments of wire" of the body. In Neruda's frustrated relationships with his fellow man, he "could grasp nothing but a clump of faces or precipitous / masks, like rings of empty gold, / like scattered clothes." In this journey to the Underworld, he sheds the clothes and masks that separate him from himself and others in search of "the indestructible, the imperishable, life."

> Cuántas veces en las calles de invierno de una
>   cuidad o en
> un autobús o un barco en el crepúsculo, o en
>   la soledad
> más espesa, la de la noche de fiesta, bajo el sonido
> de sombras y campanas, en la misma gruta del placer
>   humano,

me quise detener a buscar la eterna veta insondable
que antes toqué en la piedra o en el relámpago que
el beso desprendía.

(II:332)

How many times in the wintry streets of a city or in
a bus or a boat at dusk, or in the deepest
loneliness, a night of revery beneath the sound
of shadows and bells, in the very grotto of human
    pleasure,
I've tried to stop and seek the eternal unfathomable
    lode
that I touched before on a stone or in the lightning
    unleashed by a kiss.

(30–31)

Neruda finds nothing to return "the warmth or cold of my outstretched hand," and under the clothing and masks no one to receive his naked being. His descent is a long undressing or disembodiment of that being, as is Whitman's, who presents his clothed being in the guise of a woman who "adorn'd herself" and waits for her lover. Darkness, however, takes the place of that mortal lover, whose "flesh was sweaty and panting," and she, in a somnambulist trance, pursues her lover-darkness into death: "My hands are spread forth, I pass them in all directions, / I would sound up the shadowy shore to which you are journeying" (427). The moment of this erotic death ("I hear the heart-beat, I follow, I fade away") is succeeded in the 1855 version by the acute confusion of the recently dead or disembodied soul, which Whitman likens to an awkward adolescent sexual embarrassment:

O hotcheeked and blushing! O foolish hectic!
O for pity's sake, no one must see me now! . . . .
    my clothes were stolen while I was abed,
Now I am thrust forth, where shall I run?

.   .   .   .

. . . I feel ashamed to go naked about the world,
And am curious to know where my feet stand . . . .

and what is this flooding me, childhood or manhood
. . . . and the hunger that crosses the bridge between.
(TV:I:112n)

This transitory panic of the soul suddenly naked and invisible ("no one must see me now!"), between life and death, is compared to another change of skin, the initiatory passage between childhood and manhood. Between these two skins, only a constant hunger remains. The hunger of "the cloth" or the body for food and drink, as the final lines of this first section of the 1855 version suggest, is transposed in the disembodied state into a chillingly spectral image of the "hungry ghost." Like a skull in the growing darkness, only "the white teeth stay" or are visible, "and the boss-tooth advances in darkness," a macabre phallus sensually toasting the other dead with a liquor "spilled on lips and bosoms by touching glasses, and the best liquor afterward." This image recalls the familiar carousing skeleton of medieval carnival representations, a figure incorporated into Christian iconography from earlier tribal religions. The intertwining of the morbid and erotic is a major motif in shamanic visual art, in which what Lommel calls an "X-ray style" provides a skeletal view of animals and humans who are often in a state of sexual arousal.[22]

"The shaman is the classic investigator of the realm of death," Kalweit explains, one who "explores the routes of travel to and in the Beyond and thereby produces a map of the postmortem terrain."[23] The first six sections of the Whitman poem, together with the middle sections of "Song of Myself," constitute such a map, while the first five sections of Neruda's poem primarily refer to the extensive map already present in *Residencia en la tierra,* books I and II. Whitman's poem represents an initiatory descent, while Neruda's is a ritual recurrence of the more vivid descent presented in the *Residencias,* although in its final sections it does mark an initiatory flight or rebirth. Neruda begins section IV of "Alturas de Macchu Picchu" by recounting how "mighty death invited me many times" (32), a death that he contrasts in the previous section to the "little death" of daily living on the part of those who have never undertaken such a descent to the Underworld. This "daily ration of death" is the dying inherent in living, "a black glass from which they drank trembling." This is distinguished from the "entombed tower" or vertical voyage to death permeating the *Residencias,* in which (as in "The Sleepers") "there are beds sailing to a port" where death waits, "dressed as an admiral." In this poem, "Sólo la muerte," Neruda provides a present-tense account filled with all the ghastliness of Whitman's imagery concerning his own solitary journey:

> *Yo veo, solo, a veces*
> *ataúdes a vela*
> *zarpar con difuntos pálidos, con mujeres de trenzas*
> *   muertas,*
> *con panaderos blancos como ángeles,*
> *con niñas pensativas casadas con notarios,*
> *ataúdes subiendo el río vertical de los muertos,*
> *el río morado,*
> *hacia arriba, con las velas hinchadas por el sonido*
> *   de la muerte,*
> *hinchadas por el sonido silencioso de la muerte.*
>
> (OC:I:209)

> I see alone, at times,
> coffins with sails
> weighing anchor with pale corpses, with dead-tressed
>   women,
> with bakers white as angels,
> with pensive girls married to notaries,
> coffins going up the vertical river of the dead,
> the dark purple river,
> upstream, with the sails swollen by the sound
>   of death,
> swollen by the silent sound of death.[24]

In "Alturas de Macchu Picchu," Neruda narrates this initiatory confrontation with demons and his own dismemberment with greater distance and in the past tense:

> *Yo al férreo filo vine, a la angostura*
> *del aire, a la mortaja de agricultura y piedra,*
> *al estelar vacío de los pasos finales*

y a la vertiginosa carretera espiral:
pero, ancho mar, oh muerte!, de la ola en ola no
vienes,
sino como un galope de claridad nocturna
o como los totales números de la noche.

(4:334)

I came to the cutting edge, to the narrows
of the air, to the shroud of agriculture and stone,
to the stellar void of the final steps
and the vertiginous spiraling road:
but, wide sea, O death! you do not come in waves
but in a galloping nocturnal clarity
or like the total numbers of the night.

(32)

The image in the penultimate line, of death arriving in "un galope de claridad nocturna," echoes the opening poem in *Residencia*, "Galope muerto," in which Neruda introduces the chaos that animates the entire book with a vision of material disintegration. "The "narrows / of the air" of the first line of this section of "Macchu Picchu," while literally referring to the steep terraces mounting toward the Incan citadel, suggest the narrow or dangerous passage that Eliade finds is a "common motif in both funerary and initiatory mythologies." The "férreo filo" (the "iron" and/or "severe" cutting edge of a blade) brings to mind the "ladder of knives" to the beyond that Eliade discovers in several Asian shamanic initiation rites.[25]

This ladder of knives is one manifestation of the more universal phenomenon of the ritual dismemberment and scattering of his own body that the disembodied soul of the initiate must witness. A central aspect of Neruda's horror at the material universe in *Residencia* is the radically disconnected manner in which he views the human body in general and his own in particular. This book is filled with a whirl of isolated anatomical parts, as in "Ritual de mis piernas," in which the speaker observes his legs as if they were severed, androgynous, alien:

Bueno, mis rodillas, como nudos,
particulares, funcionarios, evidentes,

separan las mitades de mis piernas en forma seca:
y en realidad dos mundos diferentes, dos sexos
  diferentes
no son tan diferentes como las dos mitades de mis
  piernas.

(OC:I:196)

Well, my knees, like knots
private, functional, evident,
separate neatly the halves of my legs:
and really two different worlds, two different sexes
are not so different as the two halves of my legs.[26]

In this poem, Neruda observes his own body from the disassociated perspective of a disembodied soul, the same one that watches in horror and disgust the "huge flowers like mouths and teeth" floating in "Caballero Solo" and the "horrible intestines / hanging from the doors of the houses that I hate" in "Walking Around," images characterizing a world in which the body is disassembled and strewn about like "dentures left forgotten in a coffee pot."[27]

The demonic apparitions and lugubrious density of the first two *Residencias* clearly mark the psychological contours of a netherworld that is, for Neruda, the polar opposite of Sartre's revelation in *No Exit* that "hell is—other people." For Neruda, hell is human isolation, a terrain resembling the violent, corpse-bearing waters of "El sur del océano," with eyes that "have already died of dead water:"

Es una región sola, ya he hablado,
de esta región tan sola,
donde la tierra está llena de océano,
y no hay nadie sino unas huellas de caballo,
no hay nadie sino el viento, no hay nadie
sino la lluvia que cae sobre las aguas del mar,
nadie sino la lluvia que crece sobre el mar.

(OC:I:214)

It is a solitary region, I have already spoken
of this so solitary region,

where the earth is covered with ocean,
and there is no one but some hoofprints,
there is no one but the wind, there is no one
but the rain that falls upon the waters of the sea,
no one but the rain that grows upon the sea.[28]

The Underworld is often portrayed in various American Indian cultures, particularly among the Eskimo and the Chilean Guisende tribe from Tierra del Fuego, as a submarine rather than subterranean world. Lommel describes the call of the Guisende shaman in a manner that, in part, could serve as a prose paraphrase of "El sur de océano": "A man is walking alone along the shore, as though lost in a dream world, without any particular mental images. Suddenly he finds himself translated into a state of spiritual horror known as *asikaku*: 'before him crowds an endless swarm of herrings, whales, swordfish, vultures, cormorants, stormy petrels and other creatures.'"[29] The image of the Underworld swimmer, elaborated in the Whitman poem as a ritual dismemberment, becomes in "Alturas de Macchu Picchu" an image of the frustrations of the incarnate soul: "I've tried to swim in the most expansive lives, / in the most free-flowing estuaries" (32). This swimmer is alienated from the tribal axis or World Tree, conscripted to an individual life and death like that of a thousand separate trees with their thousand inevitable deaths:

> *No pude amar en cada ser un árbol*
> *con su pequeño otoño a cuestas (la muerte de mil*
> *   hojas),*
> *todas las falsas muertes y las resurrecciones*
> *sin tierra, sin abismo. . . .*
>   (4:334)

> I could not love in each being a tree
> with a little autumn on its back (the death of a
>   thousand leaves),
> all the false deaths and resurrections
> without land, without abyss. . . .
>   (32)

The Vertical Voyage

Suffering the austere isolation and deprivation of his initiating descent, the disembodied soul of the poet in the conclusion to section IV wanders in a dislocated haze that is reminiscent of the more immediate "Walking Around":

> *entonces fui por calle y calle y río y río,*
> *y ciudad y cuidad y cama y cama,*
> *y atravesó el desierto mi máscara salobre,*
> *y en las últimas casas humilladas, sin lámpara, sin*
> *   fuego,*
> *sin pan, sin piedra, sin silencio, solo,*
> *rodé muriendo de mi propia muerte.*
>
> (334)

> then I went from street to street and river to river,
> city to city and bed to bed,
> my brackish mask traversed the desert,
> and in the last humiliated homes, without light or
>   fire,
> without bread, without stone, without silence, alone,
> I rolled on dying of my own death.
>
> (33)

In such a state, the wounded healer "dies" in order to cure himself: "I raised the bandages dressed in iodine, sank my hands / into the pitiful sorrows killed by death."

The shamanic "dying" presented in sections 2 through 6 of "The Sleepers" proves to be more of a parallel to the primary experiences of Neruda's *Residencias* than to the distillation reenacted in "Alturas de Macchu Picchu." "The Sleepers" displays the subtly variated hues of soft gray to pitch black that are present in the *Residencias*, as opposed to the monochrome of memory elicited in the first sections of the Neruda poem. Hutchinson notes that the "deepening shades of darkness . . . correspond to the descent of the poet by degrees through the graded levels of his trance, leading to the 'blank' darkness of the ritual death in which his visions of loss arise."[30] Section 2 completes this descent: The poet is the "wake," in several senses, of the "perfume and youth" of his mortal self. Whitman begins section 2 with "I de-

194

scend my western course," the traditional direction of death. No longer the adorned, amorous woman of the previous section, yet remaining female, he is transformed into an old woman, a grandmother darning socks, a "sleepless widow," his "sinews are flaccid" and his "face yellow and wrinkled":

> A shroud I see and I am the shroud, I wrap a body
>   and lie in the coffin,
> It is dark here under ground, it is not evil or pain
>   here, it is blank here, for reasons.
>
> (It seems that every thing in the light and air
>   ought to be happy,
> Whoever is not in his coffin and the dark grave
>   let him know he has enough.)
>   (427–28)

From this blankness he witnesses, in the following section, the violent dismemberment of his body represented as a "beautiful gigantic swimmer swimming naked," one whose form strikingly resembles in its masculine magnitude the one idealized in Whitman's persona "in the prime of his middle age." As his body is dashed by waves against the rocks, Whitman watches first with alarm, then with a growing dispassion as this body is "baffled and banged and bruised" and finally disappears out to sea:

> The slapping eddies are spotted with his blood,
>   they bear him away, they roll him, swing him,
>   turn him,
> His beautiful body is borne in the circling eddies,
>   it is continually bruis'd on rocks,
> Swiftly and out of sight is borne the brave corpse.
>   (428)

The "circling eddies" correspond to the whirl of the poet's trance and recall the "vertiginous spiraling road" of Neruda's descent. The whirlpool or whirlwind, reflecting the nature of the shamanic trance itself, are common images of descent and ascent during the vertical voyage.

The following three sections of the Whitman poem complete the ceremony of personal disintegration, building upon the loss of the body to include the loss of father and country as well as of mother and land, and continue the shifting subject-object perspective and the transformative identity of the shamanic voice. Whitman is still journeying within the blank darkness of the coffin: "I turn but do not extricate myself, / Confused, a past-reading, another, but with darkness yet" (4:428). At the same time, his disembodied vision remains hovering about his mortal remains, as Kalweit insists is universally reported as an integral part of dying in the Near-Death Experience,[31] witnessing the recovery of his sea-bashed corpse, a funereal good-bye from a father and a ghostlike visit with his mother. Undergoing a series of fluid transformations, the floating soul of the speaker incarnates as a burier of the dead, a revolutionary soldier, and an American Indian woman. In section 4, the suggestion of dismemberment persists along a beach "cut by the razory ice-wind," where a ship, like the swimmer's body, is crushed by the sea. This vignette portrays the poet as among a group of the living retrieving the bodies of the dead from a shipwreck, and relates to what Eliade calls the "Boat of the Dead," a shamanic practice that "would carry the dead man's soul back to the original homeland from which the ancestors set forth"[32] Yet here, we must bear in mind, the dead are not setting forth but arriving: The mutilated corpse that disappears out to sea at the end of the previous section is discovered and welcomed home, laid among the others "in rows in a barn." This is the shore of the ancestral home to which the dead return, and significantly, the American poet's body is not washed up along the coasts of Europe. Yet, as we witness in the following two sections, both the fatherland and the motherland, George Washington and Pocahontas, are also lost, as even the geographical, paternal, and maternal extensions of the self "die." Section 5 approaches one aspect of the ancestral home of the poet's soul by narrating a brief "pastreading" of Washington's defeat at Brooklyn. By situating George Washington in Brooklyn, where Whitman was born and raised, the poet forges a strongly composite image of father, country, and home, at once national and deeply personal. Yet, in this vignette, the father is described in a state of mourning and leave-taking, as if, like Huck Finn, Whitman were attending his own funeral and observing the paternal grief at the loss of a son. The young soldiers have been slaughtered, "the southern braves confided to him by their parents." The father-president bears the aspect of someone attending a funeral: "His face is cold and damp, he cannot repress the weeping drops, / He lifts the glass perpetually to his eyes, the color is blanch'd from his cheeks . . . ." The mourning suitably is followed by a leave-taking between father and son: "The chief encircles their necks with his arm and kisses them on the cheek, / He kisses lightly the wet cheeks one after another, he shakes hands and bids good-bye to the army" (5:429).

This leave-taking is carried over into section 6, in which the dis-embodied presence of the poet, in the form of a "red squaw," pays a ghostly visit to his mother. This section has previously been quoted in Chapter 2 as representative of Whitman's relationship with Pocahontas as "the mother of us all," demonstrating an appropriate twinship with the previous section that portrays the "father of our country." As in Neruda's poetry, the American Indian woman represents the maternal ancestral lineage identified with the spirit of the land. The identification between this "squaw" and the body of the poet, as described in section 3, is clearly suggested, further testifying to the assumption of shamanic androgyny and American Indian roots in Whitman's persona. The appearances of the squaw and swimmer are both celebrated in physically parallel terms of a natural dignity and strength, emphasizing hair, statue, and dexterity:

> Her hair, straight, shiny, coarse, black, profuse
>   half-envelop'd her face,
> Her step was free and elastic. . . .
>
> My mother look'd in delight and amazement at the
>   stranger,
> She look'd at the beauty of her tall-borne face
>   and full and pliant limbs. . . .
>   (6:430)
>
> His brown hair lies close and even to his head,
>   he strikes out with courageous arms, he urges
>   himself with his legs,
> I see his white body, I see his undaunted eyes. . . .
>   (3:428)

Both descriptions recount grievous disappearances as singular aspects of a more general personal disintegration. The first line ("Now what my mother told me one day as we sat at dinner together") establishes a correspondence between Whitman's *tête-à-tête* with his mother and her previous visit with the Indian squaw. Within the context of disappearance, return, leave-taking, and grief established in the previous three sections, this vignette portrays a disappearance as well as a more protracted grief in relation to the poet's "dying," as this simple pronoun substitution might suggest:

> O my mother was loth to have [me] go away,
> All the week she thought of [me], she watch'd
> for [me] many a month,
> She remember'd [me] many a winter and many
> a summer. . . .
>
> (6:430)

The following three stanzas of the 1855 version of the poem, excised in 1876, are troublesome because, as Hutchinson points out, a climactic narration associating slavery with the destructive power of the whale was never incorporated into the final manuscript.[33] Draft notes show that the transformation into an American Indian woman was to be followed by a further metamorphosis into a slave named "Black Lucifer," which would have situated the voice in a historical context, as granted it in the previous two sections. Following as it does, without benefit of section break, the vignette of the Indian woman one might well identify the fiery vengeance of "Lucifer's heir" as the voice of the disappearing American Indian, as perhaps Whitman later intended: "I have been wronged . . . . I am oppressed . . . . I hate him that oppresses me, / I will either destroy him, or he shall release me" (TV:6:116n). As it stands, the source of this "I" is unclear, and therefore the import of its emotion remains confused. What is essential is the dual identification with Lucifer and with the whale. Lucifer, the fallen angel of light associated with the planet Venus, is not only identified with the Underworld but with fire, and represents the devil as Promethean fire-bringer. During the shamanic journey, notes Halifax, after the surrender to death "apotheosis is attained by means of a mystical identification with fire."[34]

" 'Fire,' of whatever kind, transforms man into 'spirit';" Eliade explains, "this is why shamans are held to be 'masters over fire.' "[35] In many North American Indian cultures, the shaman is also believed to be a "devil" or "trickster," capable of changing his form at will, because of his role as fire-bringer from the Underworld. Whitman's assumption of the rebellious voice of Lucifer at this point in his journey indicates, even in the vague context in which it exists, the moment of final disintegration of the former self as well as his transformation into spirit through a "mastery over fire," and ultimately foreshadows his imminent ascent and return as a fire-bringer. The final two lines of this section identify the poet with the dormant bulk of a whale, as if the body lost to the sea has been transformed in its depths and the reincarnated spirit has assumed the whale's powerful, almost menacing potential to surge from the submarine shadows of the Underworld in which it remains rooted: "though I lie so sleepy and sluggish, my tap is death."

III

In section 6 of "The Sleepers," as in the "wild gander" (14) and "stallion" (32) sections of "Song of Myself," Whitman prefigures his bursts of flight by identifying with an animal that carries him into the heights of full incantational song. The ascent of the shaman from the Underworld to the Sky World is realized, in most instances, either through flight in the form of an animal, mounting a ritual ladder, or climbing the World Tree. "Siberian, Eskimo, and North American shamans fly," states Eliade.[36] Just as the symbol of their ecstatic trance experience is often the feather, the shamanic totem or psychopomp is usually a bird or other animal identified with rapid movement, into which the shaman transforms himself to accomplish his feats of "magical flight" as a psychic voyager. Like the chants of these bird-poets, both Whitman and Neruda's often come from air-borne altitudes. In section 33 of "Song of Myself," Whitman "outgallops" the stallion that he mounts at the end of the previous section: "I but use you a minute, then resign you, stallion, / Why do I need your paces when I myself out-gallop them? / Even as I stand or sit passing faster than you" (32:61). According to Eliade, "the 'horse' is employed by the shaman, in various contexts, as a means of achieving ecstasy, that is, the 'coming out of oneself' that makes the mystical journey possible. This mystical journey—to repeat—is not necessarily in the infernal direction. The 'horse' enables the shaman to fly through the air, to reach the heavens,"[37] as Whitman does in the section that follows his horse:

> My ties and ballasts leave me, my elbows rest in sea-gaps,
> I skirt sierras, my palms cover continents,
> I am afoot with my vision.
>
> (33:61)

The extensive panoramic vistas in which Whitman proclaims from an exalted perspective all that he sees approximate this imaginative flight. The passing phenomena are linked and chanted with a rapidity suggesting both height and forward motion, as though seen through the window of an airplane taking off:

> Over the western persimmon, over the long-leav'd
>   corn, over the delicate blue-flower flax,
> Over the white and brown buckwheat, a hummer and
>   buzzer there with the rest,
> Over the dusky green of the rye as it ripples and
>   shades in the breeze. . . .
>
> (33:62)

Later in this section, the poet ascends even higher, taking the form of a meteor:

> Speeding through space, speeding through heaven
>   and the stars,
> Speeding amid the seven satellites and the broad
>   ring, and the diameter of eighty thousand miles,
> Speeding with tail'd meteors, throwing fire-balls
>   like the rest. . . .
>
> (64)

Often Whitman's flights are accompanied by the "spirit helper" of a bird, or the poet transforms himself into one to attain his elevated perspective. In "When Lilacs Last in the Dooryard Bloom'd," Whitman first changes himself into the "solitary thrush" isolated like an initiate in nature ("the hermit withdrawn to himself, avoiding the settlements,") before he carries the perspective of the poem, in the next section, on a soaring imaginative flight to accompany Lincoln's coffin:

> Over the breast of the spring, the land, amid cities,
> Amid lanes and through old woods . . .
> Amid the grass in the fields each side of the lanes,
>   passing the endless grass,
> Passing the yellow-speared wheat . . .
> Passing the apple-tree blows of white and pink
>   in the orchards. . . .
>
>   (5:330)

In the same fashion, the "wild gander" in section 14 of "Song of Myself" invites the poet into a transformation that transports him through the aerial panoramas of the "pure contralto sings" chant of the following section. According to Joseph Campbell, in *The Flight of the Wild Gander,* the most common paleolithic emblem of shamanic flight is the wild gander.[38] This wild gander, which beckons to the poet from the winter sky, is an archaic symbol of the shaman who leads his flock in trancelike flights of ecstatic vision. As a symbol, it was most powerful among the paleolithic hunters who first wandered across the land bridge from what Whitman calls, in "Facing West from California's Shores," the "house of maternity, the land of migrations" (111), from Siberia into North America. These ancestors of the American Indians, as a migratory people, chose a migratory bird as a totem for spiritual flight.

The importance of the bird, and of the bird's-eye perspective, in Neruda's poetry is grounded in his pervasive dichotomy of stone and bird, that is, of descent, permanency, and the material as opposed to ascent, transformation, and the spirit. As a stone city located on an Andean mountaintop aligned with the flight of eagles and condors, the city of Macchu Picchu serves as a *coincidencia oppositorum* of these two sets of qualities, and therefore is a central moment in his poetry, marking the birth of his shamanic persona. This initiatory flight reverberates through other sections of *Canto general,* as in "América, no invoco tu nombre en vano," in which Neruda approaches his continent "Desde arriba (1942)," as the first section is titled, with a staccato incantation of detail that carries the lines forward into aerial motion:

> Lo recorrido, el aire
> indefinible, la luna de los cráters,
> la seca luna derramada
> sobre las cicatrices,
> el calcáreo agujero de la túnica rota,
> el ramaje de venas congeladas, el pánico del cuarzo,
> del trigo, de la aurora,
> las llaves extendidas en las rocas secretas,
> la aterradora línea
> del Sur despedazado. . . .
>
> (518)

> The journey's end, the indefinable
> air, the moon of craters,
> dry moon poured
> upon scars,
> the torn tunic's calcareous hole,
> frozen veins of foliage, the panic
> of quartz, wheat, the dawn,
> keys spread out in secret rocks,
> the terrifying line
> of the dismembered South. . . .
>
> (203)

In "Qué despierte el leñador," Neruda also views the North American continent from above, describing it as "stretched out like a buffalo skin." In these introductory lines, the poet, jumping from Wisconsin to Florida to the Northwest, is clearly suspended in an "aerial and clear night of the gallop, / there toward the starry heights. . . ." (IX:1:255–56). Neruda's descents and ascents are woven throughout his language, occurring almost with the frequency with which he mentions stones and birds, although not always signaled by these two images. The flying stones of *Las piedras del cielo* (1970), for instance, represent another reconciliation of this dichotomy, in which the vertical voyage of "Alturas de Macchu Picchu" echoes throughout the long poem, from section IV ("When everything was high, / height, / height") to section XXVI, which begins "Leave me an underground," as the poet descends in search of the mineral body resurrected as a star in the final lines.[39]

In his magazine *The Seventies,* Robert Bly called attention to the "leaping" quality of Neruda's poetry, which causes the reader to "leap from the conscious to the unconscious and back again, a leap from the known part of the mind to the unknown part and back to the known."[40] On a stylistic level, these associative jumps represent a form of short-distance flying, an instantaneous, line-to-line correlate of the broader vertical voyage in which the shaman-poet moves ritually back and forth between the Underworld, Middle World, and Sky World, fusing them in the energy of his descent and flight. Bly's approximation of the three realms represented by the World Tree are what he calls "the three brains," the reptile brain, mammal brain, and "new" brain, all three of which, the neurologist Paul MacLean has concluded, co-exist independently and simultaneously within the human cranium.[41] A poet such as Neruda, Bly argues, "leaps" from one brain to another in an associative brilliance. Bly's theory bears an interesting relationship to the shamanic voyage, although when the effect of such movement is mechanically reproduced as a self-conscious style, as in much contemporary "deep image" and surrealist poetry, the results are often only superficially entertaining or shocking. Yet when this "leaping" is rooted within the traditional trajectory of the vertical voyage, as in Neruda's "Alberto Rojas Jiménez viene volando," an elegy for a dead friend from the second *Residencia,* the effect is one of a compressed journey up and down the spine of the World Tree, as in these two stanzas:

> *Bajo las tumbas, bajo las cenizas,*
> *bajo los caracoles congelados,*
> *bajo las últimas aguas terrestres,*
> > *vienes volando.*

> *Más abajo, entre niñas sumergidas,*
> *y plantas ciegas, y pescados rotos,*
> *más abajo, entre nubes otra vez,*
> > *vienes volando.*
> > > (OC:I:239–40)

Beneath the tombs, beneath the ashes,
beneath the frozen snails,
beneath the last terrestrial waters,
    you come flying.

Farther down, among submerged girls,
and blind plants, and broken fish,
farther down, among clouds again,
    you come flying.[42]

The velocity of the "flying" movement here between descent and, in the penultimate line, sudden ascent, is maintained throughout the poem, in which the elements of the shamanic voyage serve as a basis for the short-distance associations.

Neruda's lifelong fascination with flight is best represented in his *Arte de pájaros* (1966), a later work devoted to birds and their significance: "A plant dies and is buried again, / man's feet return to the terrain, / only wings evade death."[43] In "El pájaro yo," Neruda introduces us to the "Pablo bird," engaged in a larger metaphysical flight:

ave de una sola pluma,
volador de sombre clara,
y de claridad confusa,
las alas no se me ven,
los oídos me retumban
cuando paso entre los árboles
o debajo de las tumbas. . . .
        (OC:III:53)

bird of a single feather,
a flier in the clear shadow
and obscure clarity,
my wings are unseen,
my ears resound
when I walk among the trees
or beneath the tombstones. . . .[44]

The bird as totem animal appears at a significant moment in "Alturas de Macchu Picchu." Just as in "The Sleepers," Whitman prefigures his ascent from the Underworld by transforming himself into a whale, in section V, before he ascends the mountain, Neruda addresses his "spirit guide" as "you, solemn death, iron-plumed bird." This address not only foreshadows the imminent nature of his ascent in the following section, but the "iron-plumed" nature of the bird suggests Neruda's own "mastery over fire." Eliade devotes considerable attention to the relation between shamanism and metalworking, insisting "that metallurgical magic, by the 'power over fire' that it involved, assimilated a number of shamanic exploits." The address to a bird with iron feathers recalls Whitman's assumption of the role of "Lucifer's heir" at a parallel moment, as well as the costume of the Yakut shaman which, according to Elaide, "displays a complete bird skeleton of iron,"[45] which attests both to his ability to fly as well as to his mastery of fire in the Underworld. This clanging, Hadean association of bird and iron with the Underworld, with its significance to the transformative role of the shamanic firebringer, resurfaces several times in *Arte de pájaros*. In "Flamenco," Neruda confides that

> *Abandoné aquellas regiones,*
> *me vestí de frac y de hierro,*
> *cambié de idioma y de estatura,*
> *rescuité de muchas muertes. . . .*
> (OC:III:25)

> I abandoned those regions,
> dressed in tails and iron,
> changed languages and stature,
> resurrected from many deaths. . . .[46]

Throughout successive sections of "Alturas de Macchu Picchu," Neruda's ferrous, subterranean bird reappears in the metamorphic vision of the ascended poet as the lofty eagle and condor, as well as the bird released like "the aged heart of the forsaken" after a thousand years of captivity in the "stone night" (11:40).

In the ascent represented in sections 7 and 8 of "The Sleepers" and in sections VI–XII of "Alturas de Macchu Picchu," the dead speaker is reborn from the womb of the Underworld as the "collective soul" who both heals and unites the tribe with his shamanic powers. Whitman abruptly ascends from the sluggish lair of the whale into the Sky World, into "an amour of the light and air" through which he will "gallivant with the light and air" on a summer day (7:430). Neruda also mysteriously ascends what could be the traditional *rewe*, or laddered tree, of the Mapuche shaman: "And so I scaled the ladder of the earth / amid the atrocious maze of lost jungles / up to you, Macchu Picchu" (VI:33). Yet this *axis mundi* is not the World Tree of "Los libertadores," but another shamanic symbol of the Sky World, the mountain that rises above the earthly Middle Realm. Here Neruda is also gallivanting in air, which "flowed with orange-blossom / fingers over all the sleeping: / a thousand years of air, months, weeks of air, / of blue wind. . . ." These heights represent a spiritual home, and this "myth of heaven," as Whitman calls it, offers a homecoming, for "the wildest and bloodiest is over and all is peace." Whitman chants this homecoming from an elevated perspective, in which he can see that

> . . . the exile returns home,
> The fugitive returns unharm'd, the immigrant is
>   back beyond months and years,
> The poor Irishman lives in the simple house of his
>   childhood, with the well-known neighbors
>   and faces,
> They warmly welcome him, he is barefoot again,
>   he forgets he is well off,
> The Dutchman voyages home, and the Scotchman and
>   Welshman voyage home, and the native of the
>   Mediterranean voyages home. . . .

(431)

This homecoming of the European immigrant to his ancestral origins is paralleled in Neruda's Indianist version in the return of the nativized American to the "house of his childhood," the Incan citadel of Macchu Picchu, an American Parthenon where the indigenous race once walked beside the gods:

The Vertical Voyage

Aquí los pies del hombre descansaron de noche
junto a los pies del águila, en las altas guaridas
carniceras, y en la aurora
pisaron con los pies del trueno la niebla enrarecida. . . .

(6:336)

Here man's feet rested at night
beside the eagle's feet, in the high gory
retreats, and at dawn
they trod the rarefied mist with feet of thunder. . . .

(34)

At these heights all that marks the temporal life "is gone, fallen to earth," as Neruda observes, "clothing, skin, vessels, / words, wine, bread," leaving an innocently primordial "towering reef of the human dawn." Whitman likewise perceives the renewed perfection of *in illo tempore:* "The universe is duly in order, everything is in its place." Those mortal elements, which Neruda sees as fallen to earth, are for Whitman suspended, present but waiting: "The twisted skull waits, the watery or rotten blood waits." What the initiated shaman reestablishes is "this myth of a paradisal period brutally abolished by the 'fall' of man," as Eliade explains.[47] The ascended shaman renews the bridge between earth and heaven, between now and that dreamtime when genitals, womb, head, bowels, and joints, as Whitman emphasizes, were "perfect and clean" and "proportion'd and plumb." The exile who returns home is man, restored to his original perfection.

From these heights, the experience of death is recapitulated and integrated in both poems into a vision of renewal and unity. "Psychologically speaking, the whole structure of the [shaman's] personality is thereby altered," as Lommel comments on the initiation process. "The original individuality is suppressed . . . . Then the conscious ego is extinguished; the spirits, representatives of the super-ego, are incorporated into the personality and identified with the shaman."[48] The chant in section 7 of "the homeward bound and the outward bound" accomplishes precisely such an act of incorporation. Whitman reintroduces the larval personalities of his dying experience by regrouping most of the figures previously engaged in an exhaustive roll call of collective unity. We again greet the demons who haunted his descent, "the en-nuyee, the onanist, the female that loves unrequited," as well as the audience, the actor and actress, the dancer, "the criminal that stood in the box," a review that seems, considering its theatrical emphasis, a curtain call of the death ritual. At this height, the tragedy becomes a comedy as many of the major protagonists reappear to join hands: the swimmer, the midnight widow, the red squaw, "those through with their parts and those waiting to commence" (431), all are averaged, likened, restored, and take their bows. When the masks are removed, we learn that all the roles have been played by the same actor, the re-born tribal representative, in a one-man show projected by a possessed shaman who "contains multitudes." "I swear they are all beautiful," Whitman exclaims, admiring his many masks, as he assumes the perma-nent identity of an inclusively collective soul. In a less theatrical mode, Neruda reintroduces, in section VII, the larval stages of his own ritual death, now immortalized at Macchu Picchu in "a life of stone after so many lives." His own death is identified with that of the Incas, who pre-viously inhabited the mountainous features of his tribal persona. The black cup that man drinks in his "little death," in section III, becomes the city itself, "raised like a chalice in the hands / of all, the living, the dead, the silent, sustained / by so much death" (35). The "empty air" of section I "no longer weeps" at these heights. Macchu Picchu is no longer the "spider hands, fragile / filaments, spun web" of the "empty net" of power that propelled the poet toward the Underworld. As with Whitman, the theatrical masks, or the clothes of the soul represented in section II, have fallen away and what remains is a naked and aerial "per-manence of stone and word." The reiteration of the dying experience, in these two sections, seems to form an essential aspect of the rebirth, a means for the recently initiated shaman to reaffirm his tribal identity atop what Neruda calls "this high site of the human dawn."

Sections VIII–XII of "Alturas de Macchu Picchu," together with the final section of "The Sleepers," begin the work of tribal unification and healing to which the initiated shaman is dedicated. "The diverse shall be no less diverse, but they shall flow and unite—they unite now" (7:432), as Whitman ends the penultimate section of his poem. The ascended shaman is not a hermit enlightened on his mountaintop but, like the Buddhist bodhisattva motivated by compassion, returns to ele-vate the whole tribe with him to the Sky World. In the final section of the poem, Whitman describes the sleepers as "unclothed," that is, not compromised by the mortal vestments that caused him such pain and confusion during his descent. As if viewing the entire globe from the aerial perspective of the Sky World, in an extended chant Whitman sees the sleepers

> . . . flow hand in hand over the whole earth from east
>   to west as they lie unclothed,
> The Asiatic and African are hand in hand, the European
>   and American are hand in hand,
> Learned and unlearned are hand in hand, and male and
>   female are hand in hand. . . .
>
> (8:432)

The family members, separated during his "death" in sections 5 and 6, are reunited: the son with his father, the elderly mother with a daughter. Pairs of opposites are resolved, that of the boy and man, the student and teacher, the slave and master. In this trance vision, Whitman chants not only as a tribal unifier but as a healer, his words assuming the illocutionary power to act as they are pronounced, as if his language itself were effecting the cures he describes:

> The sweatings and fevers stop, the throat that was
>   unsound is sound, the lungs of the consumptive
>   are resumed, the poor distress'd head is free,
> The joints of the rheumatic move as smoothly as ever,
>   and smoother than ever,
> Stiflings and passages open, the paralyzed become
>   supple,
> The swell'd and convuls'd and congested awake to
>   themselves in condition,
> They pass the invigoration of the night and the
>   chemistry of the night, and awake.
>
> (433)

The shaman's return to the tribe from his vertical voyage of death and rebirth is intended to raise its members to the level of unity and health that he has witnessed in his vision. "Through the encounter with death and the knowledge of the pairs of opposites," Halifax writes, "the shaman has attained the wisdom of the 'two-worlds'. . . . Huichol shaman Ramón Medina Silva once said, 'It is one, it is unity, it is ourselves.' The shaman, through sacred action, reveals this unity. It is the way of compassion that opens in the course of this revelation."[49]

This compassion is also what motivates the final sections of "Alturas de Macchu Picchu" in its vision of human solidarity. In addition to the city itself, there are two "you's" whom Neruda addresses, the reader and the dead Incan laborers who constructed the citadel, both of whom are fused toward the end of the poem into an exalted, mythic, yet living tribe of *americanos*. Neruda directs two addresses to the reader as "americano" and "brother," inviting him to ascend to the heights of his perspective: "Rise up with me, American love" (VIII:36) and, more climactically in the final section, "Rise up to be born with me, my brother" (41). These direct addresses identify the living reader as a member of the tribe of dead Incan city-builders with whom Neruda communicates like a shaman with the souls of his ancestors:

> veo el antiguo ser, servidor, el dormido
> en los campos, veo un cuerpo, mil cuerpos,
>   un hombre, mil mujeres,
> bajo la racha negra, negros de lluvia y noche,
> con la piedra pesada de la estatua:
> Juan Cortapiedras, hijo de Wiracocha,
> Juan Comefrío, hijo de estrella verde,
> Juan Piedescalzos, nieto de la turquesa,
> sube a nacer conmigo, hermano.
>   (11:342–43)

> I see the man of old, the servant, asleep in the
>   fields,
> I see a body, a thousand bodies, a man, a thousand
>   women,
> black with rain and night, beneath the black squall,
> with the heavy stone of the statue:
> Juan Stonecutter, son of Wiracocha,
> Juan Coldeater, son of a green star,

The Vertical Voyage

> Juan Barefoot, grandson of turquoise,
> rise up to be born with me, my brother.
> (40–41)

The final line, addressed to the ancestors, is repeated as the first line of the following section, where it assumes a more compelling universality. Neruda's revelation is that "the dead kingdom is still alive" (VIII:37), and that "entombed America" or the "Ancient America, sunken bride" (X:39) lives reincarnate in the hunger and sufferings of present workers. Neruda's resolution, unlike Whitman's, is not a vision of resolved polarities embracing, asleep in one eternal, androgynous bed, but of the indigenous past re-empowered in the present through the agent of his shamanic voice. It is not surprising that the differing visions to which these initiated shamans wish to raise their tribes correspond to the divergent North and Latin American views of the American Indian, as discussed in Chapter 2: Whitman's vision is of the renewal of innocence, Neruda's of the restoration of power. The greatest gulf that separates Whitman's vision from Neruda's, even more so than those visions determined by their differing historical or geographic circumstances, involves Neruda's solemn anger at the recognition of social evil, which Whitman attempts to dissolve in an optimistically cosmic resolution of opposites: a sexual healing. In Whitman's trance, he sees that "the call of the slave is one with the master's call" in a return to a social equilibrium in which political and social differences are equalized by "kissing," that is, like the girl lying chastely next to her bare-breasted lover, virginally and "without lust." Neruda, on the other hand, passionately demands the rectification of Oedipal wrongs, the rape of the American Indian mother by the European father. In an illocutionary chant that parallels Whitman's healing of the sick in section 8, he employs the power of the ascended shaman to command that the "stone mother," *la chingada,* Macchu Picchu, raise her mistreated son, Neruda's dark brother, from the dead:

> *Devuélveme el esclavo que enterraste!*
> *Sacude de las tierras el pan duro*
> *del miserable, muéstrame los vestidos*
> *del siervo y su ventana.*

Dime cómo durmió cuando vivía.
Dime si fue su sueño
ronco, entreabierto, como un hoyo negro
hecho por la fatiga sobre el muro.

(X:341)

Bring me back the slave that you buried!
Shake from the earth the hard bread
of the poor wretch, show me the slave's
clothing and his window.
Tell me how he slept when he lived.
Tell me if his sleep was
harsh, gaping, like a black chasm
worn by fatigue upon the wall.

(39)

Whitman's resolution is a lullaby for sleeping children, Neruda's a war cry preparing the gathered tribe for battle. Neruda's extended incantation in section IX, which augments the trance state culminating in his final solar ascension, is not one of the nostalgic sleep of ruins but of stone waking violently inside, as if the citadel were a volcano poised to erupt:

Ramos de espejo, bases de tormenta.
Tronos volcados por la enredadera.
Régimen de la garra encarnizada.
Vendaval sostendio en la vertiente.
Inmóvil catarata de turquesa.

. . . .

Volcán de manos, catarata oscura.
Ola de plata, dirección del tiempo.

(340)

Mirror bouquets, stormy foundations.
Thrones toppled by the vine.
Regime of the enraged claw.

Hurricane sustained on the slopes.
Immobile cataract of turquoise.

.   .   .   .

Volcano of hands, obscure cataract.
Silver wave, pointer of time.

(38)

These differences in tone and resolution between the two poems point
to the seeming contrast in their endings, in which Whitman concludes
with another descent into darkness and Neruda with the resurrection
of buried darkness into the full light. In reality, however, both poems
end with the same identification of the initiated shaman with the sun,
yet at differing times of day, or at distinct stages in the circular path
of the "perpetual journey." Halifax explains that "the journey's mythic
end is the sun. . . . The shaman's transformation via fire into a master of fire allows for a parallel transformation of the neophyte shaman
into soaring bird—Sun Bird—and a return to the source—the sun or
Sun Father."[50] Whitman's identification is with the setting sun and is
sexual in nature, whereas Neruda's is with the sun positioned at the
high noon of a militant solidarity. Neruda's exhortation to the living
and dead members of his tribe to "rise up to be born with me" is based
not only on the metaphor of his own solar ascent, but on the more than
one hundred flights of stone steps that lead to the mountaintop ruins.
The arduous act of mounting is reflected in his command to "tell me
everything, chain by chain, / link by link, and step by step" (12:41).
The city of Macchu Picchu serves not merely as a dramatic backdrop,
but as a principal protagonist in the poem, and its architecture and culture are fundamental to Neruda's meaning. Neruda visited the city on
October 22, 1943, although it is not certain how much he knew of
the mysterious Incan monument at the time that the poem was composed. Yet only five years later, Hiram Bingham, who discovered the
ruins in 1914, published his popular *Lost City of the Incas,* which com-
piled detailed information widely available in South America during
the decades of excavation, much of which would have been explained
to the distinguished poet during his visit. Incan religion was centered
around the sun, which as a symbol permeated their culture, and thus

the highest buildings at Macchu Picchu form a group called the Temple of the Sun. The Incan emperors were believed to embody the sun, and Macchu Picchu was where the last of these emperors, Tupac Amaru—quoted in "Los conquistadores"—last displayed the sacred golden sun disc. Its theft by the Spanish Viceroy, Francisco de Toledo, symbolically marked the end of the Incan empire. The interplay of the images of light and shadow, together with the return of the sun god to Macchu Picchu in the concluding section, contain the broadest political implications in terms of the Latin American Indianism prevalently espoused during the era in which the poem was written. In the final section, Neruda's address to the Incan souls in the Underworld mirrors the Incan fear that the sun itself would not return from its descent, a concern so pronounced that a major religious ceremony involved "tying up" the sun to the *Intihuatanna,* or stone sun dial, at Macchu Picchu on the winter solstice to prevent its departure.[51]

> *No volverás del fondo de las rocas.*
> *No volverás del tiempo subterráneo.*
> *No volverá tu voz endurecida.*
> *No volverán tus ojos taladrados.*
> (XII:343)

> You'll not return from the bottom of the rocks.
> You'll not return from subterranean time.
> Your stiff voice will not return.
> Your drilled eyes will not return.
> (41)

The sun, of course, does return, here in the form of the ascended shaman whose former nature is simultaneously crucified in the manner of Saint Sebastian as his reborn solar nature is crowned by his Incan ancestors in a nimbus of yellow rays:

> *afilad los cuchillos que guardasteis,*
> *ponedlos en mi pecho y en mi mano,*
> *como un río de rayos amarillos . . . .*
> (344)

> sharpen the knives that you've kept,
> put them in my breast and in my hand,
> like a river of yellow lightning. . . .
>
> (41–42)

The subsequent references to measures of time ("and let me weep hours, days, years, / blind ages, stellar centures") is perhaps associated with the ceremonial sun dial and the mourning of a dark millennium during which the Incan sun did not return. The metallurgical images in the concluding lines indicate the fire-bringing role by which Neruda makes his identification with the Incan sun. Not only the knives from the Underworld that form his emanating rays above, but the iron and magnets in the final lines demonstrate his "mastery over fire." Neruda's vertical voyage has been completed, from the "entombed tower" of his shamanic death, in the first section, to the "high suspended towers" of Macchu Picchu that mark, in the tenth, the prelude to his solarization. Rodríguez Monegal observes that "in the short space of the poem the complete metamorphosis of Neruda has been effected: from the poet of anguish and solitude to the poet of human solidarity; from the surrealist rhetoric of *Residencia en la tierra* to the exhortatory simplicity of his social poetry."[52]

Whitman chooses not to conclude with the transcendent solidarity expressed in the chant opening section 8, a more innocent parallel to Neruda's confrontational, high-noon ending, but rather continues several steps farther in the tonal direction of a universal lullaby for sleepers, toward the sun's return to the sexual folds of darkness, the mother and death:

> I stay awhile away O night, but I return to you
> and I love you.
>
> Why should I be afraid to trust myself to you?
> I am not afraid, I have been well brought forward
> by you,
> I love the rich running day, but I do not desert her
> in whom I lay so long. . . .
>
> (8:433)

The identification of "I" here is not only with the sun, but with the fully circular path of the sun. Just as Neruda rises self-cured of the social alienation that ensnared him as a "vagabond soul" in the Underworld, Whitman is reborn in his relationship to the sexual source of life and death. The adorned lover's awkward insecurities in the first section are overcome: "Be careful, darkness," the nervous adolescent lover protests, "already what was it touch'd me?" (1:427). The multiple gender guises adopted throughout the narrative of his death are replaced not only by the androgynous innocence of his final vision, but by a recognition of the shamanic two-world nature of his being, one which involves, like the path of the sun, both descent and ascent. Like the sun, Whitman can predict at the end of the poem that "I will stop only a time with the night, and rise betimes . . . ." The imagery of rebirth from the womb of the Underworld is carefully developed in both poems. Neruda emerges from that "mother of stone," the "genital matrix of the earth," to assume the vengeful splendor of the rebellious slave and fire-bringer, the Incan sun god, almost identical to the rebellious slave Black Lucifer, whom Whitman partially deleted from the 1855 version of his poem. Yet this is a journey both poets repeat many times in the course of their poetry. Rodríguez Monegal has commented on this essential circularity of Neruda's writing in reference to that of his "grandfather's": "Like the poets of prophecy (Blake, Hugo, Whitman, Lautréamont), Neruda will have to return tirelessly, again and again, to the same motives, the same landscapes, the same persons. In this circularity of his writing is located a central characteristic of his prophetic vocation."[53]Whitman's final revelation in "The Sleepers" is the inevitability of this circularity to his shamanic vocation, in which he must ceremonially reenact the solar descent and ascent of the vertical voyage: "I will duly pass the day O my mother and duly return to you." This eternal return is not limited to his own lifetime but, as Eliade has demonstrated,[54] is related to the central mythology of all tribal religions. In "Song of Myself," Whitman perceives the eternal nature of this voyage, invoking a distant return not as the "poor literary man" whom Borges recognized, but as an American Indian shaman performing the actual rituals celebrated at the remove of print in his poetry:

> Believing I shall come again upon the earth after
> five thousand years,

The Vertical Voyage

Waiting responses from oracles, honoring the gods,
    saluting the sun,
Making a fetich of the first rock or stump, powowing
    with sticks in the circle of obis, . . .

(43:78)

Epilogue
Ghost Dance

*I*n a letter of 1883, near the beginning of the Gilded Age, Whitman makes an observation almost heartbreaking in the stubborn optimism it displays and the inverse prophecy it foreshadows: "The seething materialistic and business vortices of the United States, in their present devouring relations, controlling and belittling everything else, are, in my opinion, but a vast and indispensable stage in the new world's development, and are certainly to be followed by something entirely different . . ." (CP:553). These sentiments extend in tone the critique of North American democracy begun twelve years earlier in *Democratic Vistas*, in which Whitman expounds in prose on the shamanic role he intended for the American bard, yet appears to question that if the "divine literatus" has arrived, where is the nation that should greet him? In *The Imperial Self*, Quentin Anderson writes that Whitman "was an amazing man, a shaman without a tribe to follow him, who nonetheless believed that he could, by using words, communicate a sense of the world, a mode of consciousness, that would create a tribe for him."[1] Anderson myopically adds that Whitman "turned out to be right" in this belief, yet to the contrary, even Whitman in his final years, ignored amid "the seething materialistic and business vortices" of a nation already rehearsing its twentieth-century identity, recognized that he had been wrong. The tribe to and for whom he spoke, Democracy, never gathered around his voice. North American poets have granted Whitman a place of fluctuating honor and disregard in their literary history, and the "camerados" whom he was to imbue with a spiritual democracy have named a rest stop on the New Jersey turnpike in his memory. "Whitman was wrong about the People," Louis Simpson concludes *At the End of the Open Road,* "But right about himself."[2]

In *Incitación al Nixonicidio y alabanza de la revolución chilena,* the last of Neruda's volumes published during his lifetime, the first poem "begins by invoking Walt Whitman" as a "necessary brother" to lend his "extraordinary support" in killing Nixon, "verse by verse."[3] Copies of this book, written in three days in a satiric doggerel based on the metaphor of poetry-as-bullets in the just fight, were distributed free in the streets of Santiago months before the brutal military coup that ended Salvador Allende's life and Chile's democracy on September 11, 1973. This book represents Neruda's final attempt, before his own death twelve days later, to speak to and for The People, to inspire his tribe with the unity, identity, and militant spirit that characterize the shamanic persona he assumed in *Canto general.* Neruda's Chile, the "Chile of the poets" as it was known during the Allende years, was betrayed not only by the extensive complicity of the United States in efforts to destablize its government, but as Neruda tragically recognizes in the last pages of his memoirs, by many of The People themselves. The memoir's final words, written only a few days before the poet's own death, describe how Allende's body, "that corpse, followed to its grave only by a woman who carried with her the grief of the world, that glorious dead figure, was riddled and ripped to pieces by the machine guns of Chile's soldiers, who had betrayed Chile once more."[4]

American Indian shamans, as we have observed, are not "artists" remembered for the esthetic quality of their chants, but singers and healers treasured for the power of their visions and their effect upon the tribe. It is hardly necessary to point out that neither Whitman's aboriginal vision of a renewal of innocence nor Neruda's of a restoration of power has been realized. The fates of their not entirely imaginary tribes have been decidedly the opposite: the cynicism and pollution of the corporate culture dominating the United States, the continuing subjugation of most of Latin America by its harsh dictatorships. During the 1960s, however, both continents were jarred by the impact of both Whitman and Neruda's Indianist children: the North American flower children who adopted various attributes of tribal cultures in a search for what many of them believed was an androgynous, communal return "back to the earth" and the young Latin American revolutionaries who took up American Indian *noms de guerre* and musical instruments in "la lucha" for social justice. Those who doubt the ability of poetry to enter history need only study the Beats' relationship with *Leaves of Grass* and their own enormous influence upon the subsequent generation of utopian rebels, or understand the significance of Che Guevara's decision to carry only one book with him into the Bolivian mountains, a copy of *Canto general*. Yet as Pound realized during his final years in Italy, when poetry does enter history it is not always in triumph.

The chants of the American Indian, Whitman, and Neruda share an essential tone that sharply distinguishes them from the European mode of poetry prevalent during the past several centuries: Theirs is a poetry of affirmation, in which little place is granted the irony or tragedy of historical circumstances. In their vision, history is not an interminable, irreversible line but a revolving circle, continually renewed. As a twentieth-century poet, Neruda is the most focused of the three in a recognition of social evil, yet as *Canto general* concludes with the image of his word redisseminated "perhaps in another time free of sorrow" (XV:28:399), his work is dominated by the same affirmation of an "eternal return" on which Whitman's and the American Indian's poetry are based.

Among North American tribal cultures, the most dramatic manifestation of this view of history, as well as of the importance of affirmation-in-defeat, was the Ghost Dance religion that spread from 1870 until the massacre at Wounded Knee in 1890. This movement was based on prolonged rituals of ecstatic dancing that culminated in communication with the spirits of the dead, who were to return during the "Indian millennium," when the American lands would once again belong to their native tribes and the white people would disappear. As such, it represented the last stand of the North American shamanic cultures and of the power of their medicine men against alien domination. The thousands of songs produced during this movement were, according to

Michael Castro, "composed in response to an unbearable situation—the destruction of Plains culture by military defeat, and eradication of the buffalo, and reservation life's subsequent dependency on the American government—[and they are] visionary charms that attempt to restore harmony and coherence to a broken world by affirmative poetic assertion."[5] A Comanche Ghost Dance chant asserts that "We shall live again, / We shall live again,"[6] the haunting reply of indigenous America.

For contemporary readers, the poems of Whitman, Neruda, and the American Indian share one final aspect that, in the end, must determine our relationship to them as a whole: The America they sing of is presently a defeated one, and we cannot pretend otherwise. In spite of whatever hopes we might share at the moment about the revival of American tribal cultures, ours is an era marked by extermination policies against Amazonian and Guatemalan indigenous peoples—in the name of "progress" or "anti-communism"—on a scale that rivals the Manifest Destiny of the Indian-hunting Wild West. They, too, may soon be gone. And Whitman's comment in the same letter of 1883 could have been made yesterday by a Brazilian or Guatemalan writer: "As to our Aboriginal or Indian population . . . I know it seems agreed that they must gradually dwindle as time rolls on, and in a few generations more leave only a reminiscence, a blank. But I am not at all clear about that" (CP:553). This defeat is not only historical but—whether considering North American "business vortices," Latin American dictatorships, or native genocide—ongoing. Despite the historical ironies that inevitably frame the words of these poets, as Julio Cortázar writes about Neruda, "One would have to be blind and dumb not to feel that these pages of *Canto general* were written in the last two months, or last night, or at this very moment."[7] The words of Whitman and Neruda rise like the songs of a life-affirming Ghost Dance amid the incongruous realities that continue to claim the Americas, generation after generation. Today we read their chants to Democracy and The People, tribes that once were or could have been, with the same sense of reverent loss with which Whitman and Neruda heard the last echo of American Indian song-poets on the shores of Paumanok and in the forests of Araucania.

Note on Texts
Used and Abbreviations

References to Walt Whitman's *Leaves of Grass* and selected prose are to the Comprehensive Reader's Edition from the New York University Press (1965). Quotations from the poetry are cited by poem title, section, and page number, and from the selected prose by title and page number. Other references to Whitman's poetry and prose are to the following New York University Press editions, as indicated by these abbreviations:

TV. *Leaves of Grass: A Textual Variorum of the Printed Poems.*
CP. *The Collected Writing of Walt Whitman: Prose.*
CC. *The Collected Writing of Walt Whitman: The Correspondence.*

In addition, AP indicates a reference to *An American Primer,* the facsimile edition.

Pablo Neruda's poetry is quoted in both Spanish original and English translation in all extracts. Bilingualism is regretfully sacrificed to readability, however, in the body of the text, where the poetry is quoted only in English translation and the titles of books and poems appear only in Spanish. Quotations from the original of *Canto general* are from *Obras completas,* volume I, the fourth Losada edition, and are indicated by book, section, and page number. *Canto General* is quoted in English from the University of California Press translation by Jack Schmitt, which is cited in the same manner. Quotations from the Spanish of Neruda's other poems are also from the fourth edition of the *Obras completas,* indicated by the abbreviation OC plus volume and page number. Sources of published translations are included in notes; otherwise, translations are previously unpublished and my own.

Notes

Introduction

1. Oscar Williams, ed., *A Little Treasury of American Poetry: The Chief Poets from Colonial Times to the Present Day* (New York: Charles Scribner's Sons, 1948), p. xvi.

2. Anne Waldman, *Fast Speaking Woman* (San Francisco: City Lights Books, 1975), p. 12. For transcriptions of the chants of María Sabina, see Alvaro Estarada, *María Sabina: Her Life and Chants,* trans. Henry Munn (Santa Barbara: Ross-Erikson, 1981), pp. 105–90.

3. N. Scott Momaday, *Angle of Geese and Other Poems* (New York: David R. Godine, 1974), p. 22.

4. Antler, *Last Words* (New York: Ballantine Books, 1986), p. 80. The quotation from Allen Ginsberg appears on the front cover of this volume, and on the back cover appear these words from the Whitman biographer Gay Wilson Allen: "I think Walt passed on his humanity to you, and now you are passing it on to this and future generations."

5. Robert Bly, ed., introduction to *Neruda and Vallejo: Selected Poems,* trans. Robert Bly et al. (Boston: Beacon Press, 1971), p. 10.

6. James E. Miller, Jr., *The American Quest for a Supreme Fiction: Whitman's Legacy in the Personal Epic* (Chicago: University of Chicago Press, 1979), p. 19. See p. 36 for Miller's definition of the "personal epic."

7. For example, see the substantial chapters devoted to "Las literaturas precolombinas" (pp. 5–47) and "La voz de los nativos" (pp. 77–98) in Giuseppe Bellini, *Historia de la literatura Hispanoamericana* (Madrid: Editorial Castalia, 1985).

8. Louis Simpson, "American Poetry," in *At the End of the Open Road* (Middletown, Conn.: Wesleyan University Press, 1963), p. 55.

9. Ralph Waldo Emerson, "Cockayne," in *The Complete Works of Ralph Waldo Emerson* (New York: Sully and Kleinteich, 1883), V: 148.

10. Martin Waldseemüller, as quoted in Gianni Granzotto, *Christopher Columbus,* trans. Stephen Sartarelli (Norman: University of Oklahoma Press, 1987), p. 278.

Notes

11. Bell Gale Chevigny and Gari Laguardia, the editors of *Reinventing the Americas: Comparative Studies of the Literature of the United States and Spanish America* (Cambridge: Cambridge University Press, 1986), chose the adjectives *Spanish American, U.S.* and *Amerindian* as terms for their collection of hemispheric critical studies.

12. As quoted in Thomas Donaldson, *Walt Whitman the Man* (New York: Francis P. Harper, 1896), p. 264.

Chapter 1

1. Emir Rodríguez Monegal, *Neruda: El viajero inmóvil* (Caracas: Monte Avila Editores, C.A., 1977), p. 204. The photograph of Neruda's house in Isla Negra appears in Margarita Aguirre, *Las vidas de Pablo Neruda* (Buenos Aires: Grijalbro, S.A., 1973), p. 65.

2. Pablo Neruda, "The Murdered Albatross" (1972), in *Passions and Impressions,* trans. Margaret Sayers Peden (New York: Farrar, Straus and Giroux, 1983), pp. 376–77.

3. See introduction, *Pablo Neruda: Modern Critical Views,* ed. Harold Bloom (New York: Chelsea House Publishers, 1989), pp. 2–3. Bloom claims that Neruda felt no "anxiety of influence" about Whitman because Quevedo, not Whitman, was his "true ancestor." Bloom traces Neruda's poetry back to the Spanish Baroque, arguing that real influences "must come out of the poetic traditions of one's own language." Yet even inheritance, as defined in this chapter, must begin with a cross-cultural influence at some point. Bloom's assumption, which would have us reading Cervantes rather than Faulkner to find García Márquez's roots, is one of the erroneous foundations of the exclusively European approach to American literatures, orthodox in English and Spanish departments, which has hampered comparative hemispheric studies for so long.

4. Walt Whitman, "Pasto de llamas," trans. Pablo Neruda, in *El aviso de escarmentados del año que acaba y escaramiento para el que empieza de 1935* (Madrid: Cruz y Raya, 1935), pp. 61–64. This translation does not appear in *Obras completas.* For fragments, see John Felstiner, *Translating Neruda: The Way to Macchu Picchu* (Stanford, Calif.: Stanford University Press, 1980), pp. 29–30 and 104–6.

5. The photograph appears *en face* of "El locomóvil" in Pablo Neruda, *Una casa en la arena,* with photographs by Sergio Larrain (Barcelona: Editorial Lumen, 1966), no page number.

Notes

6. Pablo Neruda (interview), in Rita Guibert, *Seven Voices,* trans. Frances Partridge (New York: Alfred A. Knopf, 1973), p. 43.

7. Fernando Alegría, *Walt Whitman en Hispanoamérica* (México: Colección Studium, 1954), p. 315; all quotations appear in my translation.

8. Pablo Neruda, *Memoirs (Confieso que he vivido),* trans. Hardie St. Martin (New York: Farrar, Straus and Giroux, 1977), p. 262.

9. See Fernando Alegría, "The Whitman Myth," *Americas* (February 1954), 10.

10. José Martí, "The Poet Walt Whitman" (1887), trans. Arnold Chapman, in *Walt Whitman Abroad,* ed. Gay Wilson Allen, (Syracuse, N.Y.: Syracuse University Press, 1955), pp. 210–11.

11. Ibid., p. 210.

12. Walt Whitman, "An English and an American Poet," an unsigned review in *The American Phrenological Journal* (1856), in *Walt Whitman: The Critical Heritage,* ed. Milton Hindus (London: Routledge and Kegan Paul, 1971), p. 44.

13. Whitman, an unsigned review in *Brooklyn Daily Times* (1856), in Hindus, *Walt Whitman,* p. 46.

14. Alegría, *Walt Whitman en Hispanoamérica,* p. 247.

15. Martí, "Poet Walt Whitman," p. 201.

16. Alegría, "Whitman Myth," p. 10.

17. Rubén Darío, *Obras desconocidas,* as quoted by Alegría, *Walt Whitman en Hispanoamérica,* p. 254.

18. Rubén Darío, "Walt Whitman," trans. Didier Tisdel Jaen, in *Walt Whitman: The Measure of His Song,* ed. Jim Perlman et al. (Minneapolis: Holy Cow! Press, 1981), p. 18.

19. Rubén Darío, *Prosas profanas* in *Poesías completas* (Madrid: Aguilar, 1968), p. 546; my translation.

20. Cf. Hernán Vidal, *Literatura Hispanoamericana e ideología liberal: surgimiento y crisis* (Buenos Aires: Ediciones Hispamerica, 1976). In his polemic on Latin American cultural dependency, Vidal draws a valid parallel between the *modernistas* and the "Boom" novelists of the 1950s and 1960s in regard to the rise of new economic classes, the cultural return to Europe, and the spirit/ body dichotomy between Europe and America. In the same sense, the new technocratic class of the United States during the prosperous 1980s sought its cultural validation not in Europeanized poets or novelists, but in French literary theory.

21. Randall Jarrell, "Reflections on Wallace Stevens" (1953), in *Wallace Stevens: A Critical Anthology,* ed. Irvin Ehrenpreis (Middlesex: Penguin, 1972), p. 200.

Notes

22. William Carlos Williams, "The American Idiom" (1961), in Perlman, *Walt Whitman,* p. 118.

23. Darío, *Prosas profanas,* p. 546.

24. Wallace Stevens, "Explanation," in *Collected Poems* (New York: Vintage Books, 1954), p. 72.

25. Jorge Luis Borges, as quoted in Selden Rodman, *Tongues of Fallen Angels* (New York: New Directions, 1974), p. 31.

26. Armando Vasseur, "Prólogo," *Walt Whitman: Poemas,* as quoted in Jaime Alazraki, *Poética y poesía de Pablo Neruda* (New York: Las Americas Publishing Company, 1965), p. 86; my translation. Alazraki's book contains a brief consideration of Whitman's influence on Neruda, pp. 86–92.

27. Alegría, *Walt Whitman en Hispanoamérica,* p. 282.

28. José Santos Chocano, "Blasón," in *La poesía Hispanoamericana desde el modernismo,* ed. Eugenio Florit and José Olivio Jiménez (New York: Meredith Corporation, 1968), p. 135; my translation.

29. Carlos Sabat Ercasty, *Poemas del hombre: Libro del mar* (Montevideo, 1922), pp. 18–19; my translation.

30. Volodia Teitelboim, *Neruda* (Madrid: Ediciones Michay, S.A., 1984), p. 98.

31. Neruda, *Memoirs,* p. 51.

32. Gabriela Mistral, as quoted in *Antología de la poesía Hispanoamericana contemporánea 1914–1970,* ed. José Olivio Jiménez (Madrid: Editorial Alianza, 1984), p. 66; my translation.

33. Enrique González Martínez, "Tuércele el cuello al cisne," in Florit and Jiménez, *Antología,* p. 145; my translation.

34. Gabriel García Márquez and Mario Vargas Llosa, *La novela en América Latina: Diálogo* (Lima: Universidad Nacional de Ingeniera, 1967), p. 53.

35. Gordon Brotherston, *Latin American Poetry: Origins and Presence* (Cambridge: Cambridge University Press, 1975), p. 13. The terms *maternal* and *paternal,* introduced by Brotherston to indicate the sources of two differing poetic traditions, are consistent with the American myths of the North American "Mother Pocahontas" and the Latin American "La Chingada" (see chapter 2), which assume the indigenous as the maternal branch of our cultural lineage, as opposed to that of our colonial "forefathers." Although these terms are seemingly rooted in the politics of the family metaphor, *maternal* and *paternal* are specifically used here to refer to cultural origins, not to gender-defined poetic voices, either the matriarchal or patriarchal. Most male poets of the maternal tradition speak with what could be considered a patriarchal authority on behalf of what Whitman calls "the eloquent dumb great mother" ("Rolling Earth":1:221).

36. June Jordan, "For the Sake of a People's Poetry: Walt Whitman and the Rest of Us" (1980), in Perlman, *Walt Whitman*, p. 348.

37. Esperanza Figueroa, "Pablo Neruda en inglés," in *Revista Iberoamericana*, nos. 82–83 (enero-junio 1973), 321; my translation.

38. James Wright, "The Delicacy of Walt Whitman" (1962), in Perlman, *Walt Whitman*, pp. 173–74.

39. Fernando Alegría, "¿Cuál Whitman?: Borges, Lorca y Neruda," in *Texto crítico*, 7, nos. 222–23 (July–December, 1981), 3–12.

40. Walt Whitman, "Home Literature" (from the *Brooklyn Daily Eagle*, July 11, 1846), in *The Uncollected Poetry and Prose of Walt Whitman*, ed. Emory Holloway, (Garden City, N.Y.: Doubleday, Page and Company, 1921), II:121.

41. Neruda (interview), in Guibert, *Seven Voices*, p. 62.

42. Neruda, "The Murdered Albatross," p. 377.

Chapter 2

1. Octavio Paz, *Children of the Mire: Modern Poetry from Romanticism to the Avant Garde*, trans. Rachel Phillips (Cambridge, Mass.: Harvard University Press, 1974), p. 137.

2. D. H. Lawrence, *Studies in Classic American Literature* (Middlesex: Penguin Books, 1961), pp. 1 and 26.

3. Alberto Busigani, as quoted in Jamake Highwater, *The Primal Mind: Vision and Reality in Indian America* (New York: Harper and Row, 1981), p. 121.

4. Martha Graham, as quoted in Highwater, *Primal Mind*, p. 138.

5. Jerome and Diane Rothenberg, eds. *Symposium of the Whole: A Range of Discourse toward an Ethnopoetics* (Berkeley: University of California Press, 1983), p. xi.

6. Roy Harvey Pearce, *Savagism and Civilization: A Study of the Indian and the American Mind* (Baltimore: Johns Hopkins Press, 1967), p. 178.

7. Gordon Brotherston, *Latin American Poetry: Origins and Presence* (Cambridge: Cambridge University Press, 1975), p. 7.

8. Ibid., p. 3.

9. Jack Weatherford, *Native Roots: How the Indians Enriched America* (New York: Fawcett Columbine, 1991), p. 16.

10. Mary Austin, *The American Rhythm: Studies and Re-expressions of Amerindian Songs* (New York: Cooper Square Publishers, Inc., 1970), pp. 43–44.

11. Emir Rodríguez Monegal, *Neruda: El viajero inmóvil* (Caracas: Monte

Notes

Avila Editores, C.A., 1977), p. 322; all quotations appear in my translation.

12. Gary Snyder, as quoted in *Alcheringa,* 1 (Fall 1970), 4.

13. See Philip Young, "Pocahontas, the Mother of Us All," *Kenyon Review* 24, no. 3 (Summer 1962), 391–415, for an account of the development of the Pocahontas myth in North American literature and culture. Young writes of this romance between male colonialists and Pocahontas: "Americans must see the Indian girl in one last way: as a progenitress of all the 'Dark Ladies' of our culture—all the erotic and joyous temptresses, the sensual, brunette heroines, whom our civilization (particularly our literature: Hawthorne, Cooper, Melville, and many others) has summoned up only to repress" (p. 415).

14. Vachel Lindsay, *Selected Poems* (New York: Macmillan and Co., 1963), pp. 115–17.

15. Leslie A. Fiedler, *The Return of the Vanishing American* (New York: Stein and Day, 1968), p. 87.

16. William Carlos Williams, *In the American Grain* (Norfolk, Conn.: New Directions, 1925), p. 74.

17. Michael Castro, *Interpreting the Indian: Twentieth-Century Poets and the Native American* (Albuquerque: University of New Mexico Press, 1983), pp. xviii and 69. Although Castro claims Whitman as the "grandfather" of the poets he considers, he but briefly mentions Whitman's poetics and persona in relation to the American Indian influences he finds in twentieth-century poets.

18. Octavio Paz (interview), in Rita Guibert, *Seven Voices,* trans. Frances Partridge (New York: Alfred A. Knopf, 1973), p. 243.

19. Richard Slotkin, *Regeneration through Violence: The Mythology of the American Frontier, 1600–1860* (Middletown, Conn.: Wesleyan University Press, 1973), pp. 358 and 564.

20. Robert F. Sayre, *Thoreau and the American Indians* (Princeton, N.J.: Princeton University Press, 1977), pp. 18 and 213.

21. Harold Beaver, "The Transcendental Savage," *Times Literary Supplement,* 6 October 1978.

22. Slotkin, *Regeneration through Violence,* p. 534.

23. Thoreau, as quoted in Sayre, *Thoreau,* p. 23.

24. For a treatment of nineteenth-century protest poetry concerning the American Indian, see Aaron Kramer, *The Prophetic Tradition in American Poetry, 1835–1900* (Rutherford, N.J.: Fairleigh Dickinson University Press, 1968), pp. 216–72. Maurice Kenny, in "Whitman's Indifference to Indians" (*The Continuing Presence of Walt Whitman: The Life and After,* ed. Robert K. Martin [Iowa City: University of Iowa Press, 1992]), regrets that "the American Indian did not prove a fit subject for Whitman's powerful poetics" (p. 38), in-

terpreting this as indifference. Although Kenny ignores the instances in which the American Indian does figure strongly as a theme in Whitman's work, perhaps it was precisely Whitman's original poetics that prevented him from embracing a subject so closely identified at the time with the sentimental parlor verse of the Indian protest genre, with its dominant motif of "sad inevitability."

25. As quoted in *Alcheringa* 4 (Fall 1972), 112.

26. Pearce, *Savagism and Civilization,* p. 224.

27. Lawrence, *Studies,* pp. 181–82.

28. As quoted in Harold Aspiz, *Walt Whitman and the Body Beautiful* (Urbana, Ill.: University of Chicago Press, 1980), p. 20.

29. Philip Rahv, "Paleface and Redskin," in *Essays on Literature and Politics* (1932–1972), ed. Arabel J. Porter and Andrew J. Duosin (Boston: Houghton Mifflin Co., 1978), pp. 3–7.

30. See Edwin Haviland Miller, ed., *A Century of Whitman Criticism* (Bloomington: Indiana University Press, 1969): George Santayana, "The Poetry of Barbarism" (1911) p. 127; Gerard Manley Hopkins, "Letter to Robert Bridges" (1882), p. 80; Ezra Pound, "What I Feel About Walt Whitman" (1909), p. 125.

31. Walt Whitman, Item 54 of "Preparatory Reading and Thought," in *The Complete Writings of Walt Whitman,* ed. Richard M. Bucke, Thomas B. Harned, and Horace L. Traubel (New York: G. P. Putnam's Sons, 1902), IX:96.

32. F. O. Matthiessen, *American Renaissance: Art and Expression in the Age of Emerson and Whitman* (New York: Oxford University Press, 1941), p. 544.

33. Ernesto Cardenal, *Homage to the American Indians,* trans. Monique and Carlos Altschul (Baltimore: Johns Hopkins University Press, 1973), pp. 61–62.

34. Brotherston, *Latin American Poetry,* p. 8.

35. Andrés Bello, *América,* in Brotherston, *Latin American Poetry,* p. 31; my translation.

36. Brotherston, *Latin American Poetry,* p. 31.

37. José Martí, "Nuestra América," in *Obras completas,* (La Havana: Editorial Trópico, 1939), I:12; my translation.

38. Rubén Darío, "A Roosevelt," in *Poesías completas* (Madrid: Aguilar, 1968), p. 640; my translation.

39. See John M. Baines, *Revolution in Peru: Mariátegui and the Myth* (University: University of Alabama Press, 1972). Baines notes that "Mariátegui's essays are an effort to orient the mestizo (whom he represents) toward the Indian rather than the Iberian heritage. 'The problem of our time,' he wrote, 'is not knowing what Peru has been . . . but what Peru is. The past interests us as

a means of explaining the present. The only thing that survives of Twantinsuyo is the Indian'" (p. 103).

40. Octavio Paz, *The Labyrinth of Solitude: Life and Thought in Mexico,* trans. Lysander Kemp (New York: Grove Press, 1961), p. 177.

41. Pablo Neruda, "We Indians," in *Passions and Impressions,* trans. Margaret Sayers Peden (New York: Farrar, Straus and Giroux, 1983), p. 250.

42. Pablo Neruda, "Algo sobre mi poesía y mi vida," *Aurora* (Santiago), 1 (July 1954), 12; as translated in John Felstiner, *Translating Neruda: The Way To Macchu Picchu* (Stanford, Calif.: Stanford University Press, 1980), p. 132.

43. Paz, *Labyrinth of Solitude,* p. 86. It is significant, in contrasting North and Latin American attitudes toward their origins, that while Pocahontas is represented as a naively seductive yet repentant convert to Christianity who dies in London, doña Malinche is a virtuous native woman who is raped and defiled by Europeans, yet retains her native integrity and place.

44. Brotherston, *Latin American Poetry,* p. 204n.

45. Thoreau, as quoted in Albert Keiser, *The Indian in American Literature* (New York: Oxford University Press, 1933), pp. 221–22.

46. Rodríguez Monegal, *Neruda,* p. 318.

47. Hernán Loyola, "Pablo Neruda: Itinerario de una poesía," in *Pablo Neruda: Antología esencial,* ed. Hernán Loyola, 3d ed. (Buenos Aires: Losada, 1978), p. 25.

48. Jack Weatherford, *Indian Givers: How the Indians of the Americas Transformed the World* (New York: Fawcett Columbine, 1988), pp. 161–62.

49. Pearce, *Savagism and Civilization,* p. 147.

50. Weatherford, *Indian Givers,* pp. 192–93.

51. Margarita Aguirre, *Las vidas de Pablo Neruda* (Buenos Aires: Grijalbro, S.A., 1973), p. 71; my translation.

52. Manuel Durán and Margery Safir, *Earth Tones: The Poetry of Pablo Neruda* (Bloomington: Indiana University Press, 1986), p. xiv.

53. Sergio Bocoz-Moraga, as quoted by William O'Daly in the introduction to Pablo Neruda, *Still Another Day,* trans. William O'Daly (Port Townsend, Wash.: Copper Canyon Press, 1984), p. 8.

54. Matthiessen, *American Renaissance,* p. 564.

55. Austin, *American Rhythm,* p. 42. A useful survey of Mary Austin's background and work appears in Richard Drinnon, *Facing West: The Metaphysics of Indian-Hating and Empire-Building* (Minneapolis: University of Minnesota Press, 1980), pp. 219–31.

56. Austin, *American Rhythm,* p. 19.

57. Ibid., p. 9.

58. Williams, *In the American Grain,* p. 137.

Notes

59. Austin, *American Rhythm*, p. 10.

60. Duane Niatum, ed., *Harper's Anthology of 20th Century Native American Poetry* (San Francisco: Harper and Row, 1988), p. xi.

61. Snyder, as quoted in *Alcheringa* 1 (Fall 1970), 4.

Chapter 3

1. Justin Kaplan, *Walt Whitman: A Life* (New York: Bantam Books, 1980), p. 298.

2. Ruth Finnegan, *Oral Poetry: Its Nature, Significance and Social Context* (Cambridge: Cambridge University Press, 1977), p. 107.

3. C. Carroll Hollis, *Language and Style in Leaves of Grass* (Baton Rouge: Louisiana State University Press, 1983), p. 66.

4. "The Tree of the Great Peace" (Iroquois), in *The Magic World: American Indian Songs and Poems,* ed. William Brandon (New York: William Morrow and Company, 1971), p. 102.

5. Jean Franco, "Orfeo en utopía: El poeta y la colectividad en el *Canto general,*" in *Simpósio Pablo Neruda,* ed. I. J. Lévy and Juan Loveluck (Long Island City, N.Y.: University of South Carolina-Las Americas, 1975), pp. 284–85; all quotations appear in my translation.

6. Hollis, *Language and Style,* p. 102.

7. William Grimes, "On Tape, Scholars Think They Hear Walt Whitman Reading," *The New York Times,* 16 March 1992, Sec. B, pp. 1–2. Traubel is quoted by the discoverer of this recording, Larry D. Grimes, in his discussion of "Walt Whitman's Voice," *Walt Whitman Quarterly Review* 9, no. 3 (Winter 1992), 129.

8. Pablo Neruda, "Ode to the Book (I)," trans. Nathaniel Tarn, in *Pablo Neruda: Selected Poems,* ed. Nathaniel Tarn (New York: Dell Publishing Co., 1972), pp. 285–87.

9. "Translator's Note," in Pablo Neruda, *Isla Negra: A Notebook,* trans. Alastair Reid (New York: Farrar, Straus and Giroux, 1981), p. xvi.

10. Franco, "Orfeo en utopía," p. 274.

11. Pablo Neruda, "The Word," in *Fully Empowered,* trans. Alastair Reid (New York: Farrar, Straus and Giroux, 1975), pp. 5–7.

12. Pablo Neruda, as quoted in Franco, "Orfeo en utopía," pp. 286–87.

13. Federico García Lorca, "Presentación de Pablo Neruda," in *Obras completas,* 14th ed. (Madrid: Aguilar, 1968), p. 147; my translation.

14. José Santos Chocano, "Panorama lírico (a través de un recital poético),"

La Prensa (Buenos Aires), 12 March 1933; as translated in René de Costa, *The Poetry of Pablo Neruda* (Cambridge, Mass.: Harvard University Press, 1979), pp. 74–75.

15. Pablo Neruda, "Algo sobre mi poesía y vida," 12–13; as translated in John Felstiner, *Translating Neruda: The Way to Macchu Picchu* (Stanford, Calif.: Stanford University Press, 1980), p. 125.

16. Kenneth Lincoln, "Native American Literatures," in *Smoothing the Ground: Essays on Native American Literature,* ed. Brian Swann (Berkeley: University of California Press, 1983), p. 21.

17. Ralph Waldo Emerson, "The Poet" in *Selections from Ralph Waldo Emerson,* ed. Stephen E. Whicher (Boston: Houghton Mifflin Company, 1957), pp. 238 and 231.

18. Walt Whitman, unsigned review, *Brooklyn Daily Times* 1856, in *Walt Whitman: The Critical Heritage,* ed. Milton Hindus (London: Routledge and Kegan Paul, 1971), p. 46.

19. See Pablo Neruda, "Some Thoughts on Impure Poetry," in *Passions and Impressions,* trans. Margaret Sayers Peden (New York: Farrar, Straus and Giroux, 1983), pp. 128–29.

20. Volodia Teitelboim, *Neruda* (Madrid: Ediciones Michay, S.A., 1984), p. 276; all quotations appear in my translation.

21. Emir Rodríguez Monegal, *Neruda: El viajero inmóvil* (Caracas: Monte Avila Editores, C.A., 1977), p. 12; all quotations appear in my translation.

22. Pablo Neruda, as quoted in Rodríguez Monegal, *Neruda,* p. 13.

23. Pablo Neruda, as quoted in *Revista Hoy* (Santiago, Chile), November 1979; my translation.

24. Friedrich von Schiller, *Naive and Sentimental Poetry,* trans. Julius A. Elias (New York: Friedrick Ungar Publishing Co., 1966), p. 98.

25. Ralph Waldo Emerson, "Nature," in Whicher, *Selections,* p. 33.

26. F. O. Matthiessen, *American Renaissance: Art and Expression in the Age of Emerson and Whitman* (New York: Oxford University Press, 1941), p. 33.

27. Neruda, "The Word," p. 9.

28. Schiller, *Naive and Sentimental Poetry,* p. 106.

29. Emerson, "Nature," p. 34.

30. Ralph Waldo Emerson, as quoted in *The Life of Henry Wadsworth Longfellow,* ed. Samuel Longfellow (Boston: Houghton, Mifflin and Company, 1886), II:266.

31. Swann, *Smoothing the Ground,* p. xii.

32. Lincoln, "Native American Literatures, p. 20.

33. As quoted in Margot Astrov, *The Winged Serpent: American Indian Prose and Poetry,* (Boston: Beacon Books, 1992), p. 20.

Notes

34. Matthiessen, *American Renaissance,* p. 556.

35. R. W. B. Lewis, "The New Adam: Whitman," in *Whitman: A Collection of Critical Essays,* ed. Roy Harvey Pearce (Englewood Cliffs, N.J.: Prentice Hall, 1962), pp. 110–16.

36. "Translator's Introduction," in Pablo Neruda, *Art of Birds,* trans. Jack Schmitt (Austin: University of Texas Press, 1985), p. 9.

37. Pablo Neruda, "The Lamb and the Pinecone," an interview with Robert Bly in *Neruda and Vallejo: Selected Poems,* ed. Robert Bly (Boston: Beacon Press, 1971), pp. 156–57.

38. Manuel Durán and Margery Safir, *Earth Tones: The Poetry of Pablo Neruda* (Bloomington: Indiana University Press, 1981), p. 86.

39. Jerome Rothenberg, ed., *Technicians of the Sacred: A Range of Poetries from Africa, America, Asia, Europe and Oceania* (Berkeley: University of California Press, 1985), pp. xxvii–xxx.

40. Richard Bridgman, *The Colloquial Style in America* (New York: Oxford University Press, 1966), p. 13.

41. Dennis Tedlock, "The Spoken Word and the Work of Interpretation in American Indian Religion," in *Traditional Literatures of the American Indian: Text and Interpretations,* ed. Karl Kroeber (Lincoln: University of Nebraska Press, 1981), p. 45.

42. Finnegan, *Oral Poetry,* pp. 130–31.

43. "The Night Chant," in Rothenberg, *Technicians of the Sacred,* p. 83.

44. Joan Halifax, *Shaman: The Wounded Healer* (New York: Crossroad, 1982), p. 10.

45. "Magic Words for Hunting Caribou," in *Shaking the Pumpkin: Traditional Poetry of the Indian North Americas,* ed. Jerome Rothenberg (Albuquerque: University of New Mexico Press, 1991), p. 43.

46. John Fire/Lame Deer, "The Meaning of Everyday Objects," in Jerome and Diane Rothenberg, eds., *Symposium of the Whole: A Range of Discourse toward an Ethnopoetics* (Berkeley: University of California Press, 1983), p. 172.

47. Neruda, "Some Thoughts on Impure Poetry," p. 128.

48. Hollis, *Language and Style,* pp. 89–90.

49. John Bierhorst, ed. *The Sacred Path: Spells, Prayers and Power Songs of the American Indians* (New York: William Morrow and Company, 1983), p. 5. Also see Rothenberg on "events" in *Shaking the Pumpkin,* pp. 432–33.

50. "Invoking the Powers" (Pawnee, Osage, Omaha), in Brandon, *Magic World,* p. 69.

51. Joel Sherzer, "Poetic Structuring of Kuna Discourse: The Line," in *Native American Discourse: Poetics and Rhetoric,* ed. Joel Sherzer and Anthony Woodbury (Cambridge: Cambridge University Press, 1987), p. 118.

52. Hollis, *Language and Style,* pp. 119–20.

53. Alvaro Estrada, *María Sabina: Her Life and Chants,* trans. Henry Munn (Santa Barbara: Ross-Erickson, 1981), p. 145.

54. "The Killer" (Cherokee), in Rothenberg, *Technicians of the Sacred,* p. 70.

55. Sherzer, "Poetic Structuring of Kuna Discourse," p. 119.

56. Textual variation: In the final line of this quotation, "hear" appears as "here" both in the original 1860 edition and in the Comprehensive Reader's Edition. In the manuscript edition, however, the word is clearly "hear": See *Whitman's Manuscripts: Leaves of Grass* (1860), ed. Fredson Bowers (Chicago: University of Chicago Press, 1955), p. 34. This typographical error has been corrected in both the Modern Library (ed. Lawrence Buell, 1981) and the Funk and Wagnalls (ed. Malcolm Cowley, 1968) editions of *Leaves of Grass.*

57. Michael Castro, *Interpreting the Indian: Twentieth-Century Poets and the Native American* (Albuquerque: University of New Mexico Press, 1983), p. 23.

58. Rothenberg, *Technicians of the Sacred,* p. xxix.

59. Astrov, *Winged Serpent,* p. 3.

60. Lincoln, "Native American Literatures," p. 20.

61. Herbert Read, as quoted in Jamake Highwater, *The Primal Mind: Vision and Reality in Indian America* (New York: Harper and Row, 1981), p. 88.

62. Lincoln, "Native American Literatures," p. 22.

63. Carl Sandburg, "Aboriginal Poetry," *Poetry: A Magazine of Verse* 9, no. 5 (February 1917), 255.

64. F. S. Flint, *"Imagisme," Poetry: A Magazine of Verse* 1 (March 1913), 198.

65. See Michael Bernstein, *The Tale of the Tribe: Ezra Pound and the Modern Verse Epic* (Princeton, N.J.: Princeton University Press, 1980), p. 43, for a discussion of Pound's use of the "ideogrammic technique," a form of metaphor-by-juxtaposition based on partly mistaken ideas about the poetic nature of the Chinese ideogram. This technique approximates the imagistic construction of Whitman's chants and suggests that Pound sought a foreign equivalent for a poetics first learned from his "pig-headed father."

66. "Dawn Song" (Mescalero Apache), in Brandon, *Magic World,* p. 58.

67. John Felstiner, "A Feminist Reading of Neruda," in Lévy and Loveluck, *Simpósio Pablo Neruda,* p. 336.

68. "Magic Spell to Turn a Woman's Heart" (Arekuna) in Bierhorst, *Sacred Path,* p. 52.

69. Lincoln, "Native American Literatures," p. 23.

70. "Song of Black Bear" (Navajo), in Astrov, *Winged Serpent,* p. 187.

71. Astrov, *Winged Serpent,* p. 11.

72. "Eagle Song" (Papago), in Bierhorst, *Sacred Path,* p. 133.

73. See James J. Y. Liu, *The Art of Chinese Poetry* (Chicago: University of

Chicago Press, 1962), p. 149, for an explanation of antithesis. Liu presents this poem by Tu Fu as a classic couplet of antithesis: "The stars drooping, the wild plain [is] vast / The moon rushing, the great river flows."

74. Textual variation: The line "era la noche de los caimanes" does not appear in fourth edition of the *Obras completas,* but this deletion has been restored in subsequent editions of *Canto general,* such as the one edited by Fernando Alegría (Caracas: Biblioteca Ayacucho, 1981) and the Seix Barral edition (Barcelona: 1983). The University of California Press translation also includes the deleted line.

75. Leo Spitzer, *La enumeración caótica en la poesía moderna,* trans. Raimundo Lida (Buenos Aires: Colección de Estudios Estilísticos, 1945), pp. 25 and 9; my translation.

76. Pablo Neruda, "The Destroyed Street," in *Residence on Earth,* trans. Donald D. Walsh (New York: New Directions, 1973), pp. 128–29.

77. Emile Durkheim and Marcel Mauss, *Primitive Classification,* trans. Rodney Needham (Chicago: University of Chicago Press, 1963), pp. 81 and 6.

78. Durkheim and Mauss, *Primitive Classification,* p. 43.

79. Claude Lévi-Strauss, *The Savage Mind* (Chicago: University of Chicago Press, 1962), p. 147.

80. Osage song, as quoted in Lévi-Strauss, *Savage Mind,* p. 147.

81. Lincoln, "Native American Literature," p. 29.

82. From "Navaho Correspondences," in Rothenberg, *Shaking the Pumpkin,* p. 255.

83. Lévi-Strauss, *Savage Mind,* pp. 58–59.

84. Harold Aspiz, *Walt Whitman and the Body Beautiful* (Urbana: University of Illinois Press, 1980), p. 72.

85. See Frank Riess, *The Word and the Stone: Language and Imagery in Neruda's Canto General* (London: Oxford University Press, 1972), for a structuralist analysis of the interlocking patterns of meaning between these key words. Reiss makes use of Lévi-Strauss and structural anthropology to develop "sets" of connections, often in detailed diagrams, without indicating the larger significance of such a means of primitive classification in Neruda's language. Cf. Reiss's diagrams, pp. 37–42, with the table of Zuñi clan relationships that Durkheim presents, p. 45.

86. Russell Salmon and Julia Lesage, "Stones and Birds: Consistency and Change in Pablo Neruda," *Hispania,* 60 (May 1977), 224–40. The authors trace the significance of birds and stones from their central meanings in Neruda's later books back through their appearances in his earlier work, illustrating the process by which single words generate their individual complexity in his poetry.

87. Felstiner, "A Feminist Reading of Neruda," p. 336.

88. Rothenberg, *Technicians of the Sacred*, p. xxxix. In *Translating Neruda*, Felstiner comments on the interchangeability of many of the poet's compound elements. Of section IX of "Alturas de Macchu Picchu," he notes that "a few of Neruda's paired epithets could even be scrambled in translation without much damage: *Serpiente andina, frente de amaranto*, could come out 'Serpent of amaranth, Andean brow,' and go unnoticed" (p. 181).

89. Bridgman, *Colloquial Style in America*, p. 31.

90. Hollis, *Language and Style*, p. 85.

91. George Wright, "The Lyric Present: Simple Present Verbs in English Poems," *Publications of the Modern Language Association* 89 (1974), 565.

92. Ibid., p. 568.

93. Joseph Epes Brown, "The Roots of Renewal," in *Seeing with a Native Eye: Essays on Native American Religion*, ed. Walter Holden Capps (New York: Harper and Row, 1976), p. 28.

94. Mircea Eliade, *The Sacred and the Profane: The Nature of Religion*, trans. Willard R. Trask (New York: Harper and Row, 1959), p. 70.

95. Ibid., pp. 72 and 94.

96. Julio Cortázar, "Neruda among Us," trans. Frank Menchaca, in *Neruda: Modern Critical Views*, ed. Harold Bloom (New York, Chelsea House, 1989), pp. 86–87.

97. See Josefina Ludmer, *Cien años de Soledad: Una interpretación* (Buenos Aires: Editorial Tiempo Contemporáneo, 1972), for an analysis of the interpenetration of circular and linear time in the novel. The same dialectic between a mythic and historical perspective appears to be operating in *Canto general*. In both works, history seems to become submerged in its own repetitions. Both writers share a sense of the timelessness and namelessness of a primordial America, and use structures in which the second half of the work mirrors the first: In Neruda's book the creation of America in the first half is reflected by the creation of the poet in the second.

98. Saúl Yurkievich, "Mito e historia, dos generadores del *Canto general*," in *Fundadores de la nueva poesía Latinoamericana* (Barcelona: Barral Editores, 1978), pp. 226–27; all quotations appear in my translation.

99. Ibid., p. 235.

100. Gabriel Celaya, "Pablo Neruda, poeta del Tercer Día de la creación," in *Pablo Neruda*, ed. Emir Rodríguez Monegal and Enrico Mario Santi (Madrid: Taurus Ediciones, 1985), p. 17; my translation.

101. Yurkievich, "Mito e historia," p. 234.

102. Kenneth M. Roemer, "Native American Oral Narratives: Context and Continuity," in Swann, *Smoothing the Ground*, p. 40.

Notes

103. Brown, "Roots of Renewal," p. 29.

104. Francisco Ferrandiz, "Dimensions of Nationalism in a Venezuelan Possession Cult: The Crystallization of an Oral Tradition," *Kroeber Anthropological Society Papers* (University of California at Berkeley), nos. 75–76 (1992), p. 38.

105. Yurkievich, "Mito e historia," p. 240.

106. A term introduced by Mary Austin in "Medicine Songs: Translated from Indian originals," *Everybody's Magazine* 31 (September 1914), 413.

107. Kroeber, *Traditional Literature*, 47.

Chapter 4

1. Frank Menchaca, "'A Language Full of Wars and Songs,'" in *Pablo Neruda: Modern Critical Views,* ed. Harold Bloom (New York: Chelsea House Publishers, 1989), p. 307.

2. Kenneth Lincoln, "Native American Literatures," in *Smoothing the Ground: Essays on Native American Literature,* ed. Brian Swann (Berkeley: University of California Press, 1983), pp. 32 and 20–21.

3. Joan Halifax, *Shaman: The Wounded Healer* (New York: Crossroad, 1982), p. 10.

4. Victor Turner, *The Ritual Process: Structure and Anti-Structure* (Chicago: Aldine Publishing Company, 1969), pp. 96–97.

5. Ibid., p. 114.

6. Henry Alonzo Myers, "Whitman's Conception of the Spiritual Democracy, 1855–1856" (1934), in *On Whitman: The Best from American Literature,* ed. Edwin H. Cady and Louis J. Budd (Durham, N.C.: Duke University Press, 1987), p. 40.

7. Turner, *Ritual Process*, p. 96.

8. Mitchell Robert Breitwieser, "Who Speaks in Whitman's Poems?" in *The American Renaissance: New Dimensions,* ed. Harry R. Garvin and Peter C. Carafiol (Lewisburg: Bucknell University Press, 1983), p. 122.

9. George B. Hutchinson, *The Ecstatic Whitman: Literary Shamanism and the Crisis of the Union* (Columbus: Ohio State University Press, 1986), pp. xxiv–xxv. This is the first book-length study of Whitman as a shamanic figure, structured as an analysis of those individual poems that conform to a shamanic motif. Hutchinson exclusively uses the model of classic Siberian shamanism, which is productive yet ignores the cultural logic of linking Whitman to American Indian forms.

10. Mircea Eliade, *Shamanism: Archaic Techniques of Ecstasy,* trans. Willard R. Trask (New York: Bolligen Foundation, 1964), pp. 508–9.

Notes

11. Pablo Neruda, "I Explain a Few Things," in *Residence on Earth,* trans. Donald D. Walsh (New York: New Directions, 1973), p. 261.

12. Neruda, "Meeting under New Flags," in *Residence,* pp. 245–47.

13. Hutchinson, *Ecstatic Whitman,* p. xxiv.

14. In Latin America, the Catholic church has always represented the colonial bond to the oligarchic past, from the wars for independence through the Marxist movements of this century. Yet in the past two decades the theology of liberation has introduced a new chapter of the revolutionary priest involved with ideas of spiritual democracy, the best example of which is Ernesto Cardenal, a priest who was the poet-chief of the Sandinista government in Nicaragua, where he was Minister of Culture.

15. Turner, *Ritual Process,* pp. 116–17.

16. Paula Gunn Allen, "The Sacred Hoop: A Contemporary Indian Perspective on American Indian Literature," in *Symposium of the Whole: A Range of Discourses Toward an Ethnopoetics,* ed. Jerome and Diane Rothenberg (Berkeley: University of California Press, 1983), p. 176.

17. Joan Halifax, *Shamanic Voices: A Survey of Visionary Narratives* (New York: E. P. Dutton, 1979), p. 21.

18. Ralph Waldo Emerson, "The Poet," in *Selections from Ralph Waldo Emerson,* ed. Stephen E. Whicher (Boston: Houghton Mifflin Company, 1957), p. 223.

19. Nelson Osorio, "El problema del hablante poético en *Canto general,*" in *Simpósio Pablo Neruda,* eds. I. J. Lévy and Juan Loveluck (Long Island City, N.Y.: University of South Carolina-Las Americas, 1975), pp. 185–86; all quotations appear in my translation.

20. Justin Kaplan, *Walt Whitman: A Life* (New York: Bantam Books, 1980), p. 300.

21. Ernst Cassirer, *An Essay on Man: An Introduction to a Philosophy of Human Culture* (New Haven: Yale University Press, 1944), p. 82.

22. Joseph Epes Brown, "The Roots of Renewal," in *Seeing with a Native Eye: Essays on Native American Religion,* ed. Walter Holden Capps (New York: Harper and Row, 1976), p. 32.

23. An example of such a misreading, see Doris Sommer, "Supplying Demand: Walt Whitman as the Liberal Self," in *Reinventing the Americas: Comparative Studies of the United States and Spanish America,* ed. Bell Gale Chevigny and Gari Laguardia (Cambridge: Cambridge University Press, 1986), pp. 69–91. Sommer confuses Whitman's rough persona with a "sloppiness," "a rawness and dissonance" in the poetry (p. 70). In her Lacanian reading, she portrays Whitman as a narcissistic megalomaniac who "rapes" the reader through the mirror act of reading in order to stamp out democratic clones of himself.

Gratefully, she concedes that "Whitman could not have known Lacan's theory" (p. 85), which is undoubtedly why he remained such a raw American poet.

24. Jorge Luis Borges, "Nota sobre Walt Whitman," in *Inquisiciones* (Buenos Aires: Emecé, 1960), pp. 98–99; my translation.

25. Eliade, *Shamanism,* pp. 167–68.

26. Joseph Campbell, *The Masks of the Gods: Primitive Mythology* (New York: Viking Press, 1969), p. 21. Cf. the early poetry of Yeats, in which the mythic mask is used to dramatize the collective identity of a nation.

27. Hutchinson, *Ecstatic Whitman,* p. 206n.

28. Henry Miller, "Walt Whitman" (1957), in *Walt Whitman: The Measure of His Song,* ed. Jim Perlman et al. (Minneapolis: Holy Cow! Press, 1981), p. 117.

29. Eliade, *Shamanism,* p. 14.

30. A classic example of the Freudian interpretation of Whitman's neurosis is Gustav Bychowski, "Walt Whitman—A Study in Sublimation" (1951), in *A Century of Whitman Criticism,* ed. Edwin Haviland Miller (Bloomington: Indiana University Press, 1969), pp. 203–15.

31. Harold Aspiz, *Walt Whitman and the Body Beautiful* (Urbana: University of Illinois Press, 1980), p. 20.

32. Whitman, as quoted in Aspiz, *Walt Whitman,* p. 51. Aspiz relates the persona of the healer-hero to the poet's involvement with the health theories of his era, explaining the source and significance of images of bathing, water, loose clothing, fresh air, animal magnetism, and so on.

33. Charley Shively, ed., *Calamus Lovers: Walt Whitman's Working Class Lovers* (San Francisco: Gay Sunshine Press, 1987), p. 17. This is the most complete compilation to date of the notebook and daybook fragments, unpublished correspondence, and other material detailing Whitman's homosexual relationships. The editor, however, interprets the poet's life in the terms of contemporary gay argot, often bordering on pure fantasy.

34. Edward Carpenter, *Days with Walt Whitman: With Some Notes on His Life and Works* (London: George Allen and Unwin, 1906), p. 43.

35. Harold Jaffe, "Bucke's *Walt Whitman:* A Collaboration," *Walt Whitman Review* 15 (1969), 190–94.

36. Aspiz, *Walt Whitman,* p. 7.

37. Walt Whitman, unsigned review in *United States Review* (1855), in *Walt Whitman: The Critical Heritage,* ed. Milton Hindus (London: Routledge and Kegan Paul, 1971), p. 34.

38. Leadie M. Clark, *Walt Whitman's Concept of the American Common Man* (New York: Philosophical Library, 1955), (pp. 113 and 166).

39. Maurice Kenny, "Whitman's Indifference to Indians," in *The Continuing*

Notes

Presence of Walt Whitman: The Life after the Life, ed. Robert K. Martin (Iowa City: Iowa University Press, 1992), p. 30.

40. Jorge Luis Borges (interview) in Rita Guibert, *Seven Voices,* trans. Frances Partridge (New York: Alfred A. Knopf, 1973), p. 97.

41. Pablo Neruda, as quoted in Margarita Aguirre, *Las vidas de Pablo Neruda* (Buenos Aires: Grijalbro, S.A., 1973), p. 277; my translation.

42. Emir Rodríguez Monegal, *Neruda: El viajero inmóvil* (Caracas: Monte Avila Editores, C. A., 1970), pp. 21–22. All quotations appear in my translation.

43. J. M. Alonso, "Neftalí Ricardo Reyes Invents Pablo Neruda," *Review of the Center for Inter-American Relations* (Winter 1971-Spring 1972), 36–38.

44. Rodríguez Monegal, *Neruda,* p. 448.

45. Manuel Durán and Margery Safir, *Earth Tones: The Poetry of Pablo Neruda* (Bloomington: Indiana University Press, 1981), pp. xxvi–xxvii.

46. Pablo Neruda, *Viajes* (1955), as cited in Raúl Silva Castro, *Pablo Neruda* (Santiago: Editorial Universitaria, S.A., 1964), p. 208; my translation. This section of *Viajes* is not included in *Obras completas.* Silva Castro discusses the contradictions within the Marxist background of the poet, pp. 190–213.

47. Alicia Ostriker, "Loving Whitman and the Problem of America," in Martin, *Continuing Presence of Walt Whitman,* p. 228.

48. Louis Simpson, "Poetry in a Cold Climate," in *The Character of the Poet* (Ann Arbor: University of Michigan Press, 1986), p. 196.

49. Robert K. Martin, *The Homosexual Tradition in American Poetry* (Austin: University of Texas Press, 1979), p. 46. For a discussion of Whitman's concept of adhesion, see pp. 33–47.

50. Carpenter, *Days with Walt Whitman,* p. 43.

51. Shively, *Calamus Lovers,* p. 17.

52. Carpenter, *Days with Walt Whitman,* p. 67.

53. Rodríguez Monegal, *Neruda,* p. 311.

54. Neruda (interview) in Guibert, *Seven Voices,* p. 9.

55. For an account of Neruda's last days, see Salvatore Bizzaro, "Pablo's Death: Conversations with Matilde Urrutia," in *All Poets the Poet* (Metuchen, N.J.: Scarecrow Press, 1979), pp. 149– 64. For a discussion of the Symonds response and Whitman's "children of psychology," see Gay Wilson Allen, *The Solitary Singer: A Critical Biography of Walt Whitman* (Chicago: University of Chicago Press, 1985), pp. 535–36.

56. Pablo Neruda, *Still Another Day (Aun,* 1969), section XVII, trans. William O'Daly (Port Townsend, Wash.: Copper Canyon Press, 1984), p. 47.

57. Jean Franco, "Orfeo en utopia: El poeta y la colectividad en el *Canto general,*" in Lévy and Loveluck, *Simpósio Pablo Neruda,* p. 269; this quota-

Notes

tion is from the transcription of an oral introduction in English to a seminar presentation.

58. Lincoln, "Native American Literatures," p. 20.

59. Eliade, *Shamanism*, p. 82.

60. Andreas Lommel, *Shamanism: The Beginnings of Art*, trans. Michael Bullock (New York: McGraw-Hill, 1967), p. 27.

61. See Hiram Bingham, *Lost City of the Incas: The Story of Machu Picchu and Its Builders* (New York: Atheneum, 1973), for an account of Bingham's discovery and excavation of the city. One archaeological theory of the city's origin is that, never populated, it served as a ceremonial necropolis for the priestly class of Incas fleeing the Spanish invasion of nearby Cuzco.

62. Rodríguez Monegal, *Neruda*, p. 458.

63. The Whitman manuscript is quoted in F. O. Matthiessen, *American Renaissance: Art and Expression in the Age of Emerson and Whitman* (New York: Oxford University Press, 1941), p. 555.

64. Eliade, *Shamanism*, p. 255.

65. Margot Astrov, ed., *The Winged Serpent: American Indian Prose and Poetry* (Boston: Beacon Books, 1992), p. 46.

66. Halifax, *Shaman*, p. 11.

67. Breitwieser, "Who Speaks in Whitman's Poems?" p. 129.

68. Alberto Cardín, *Guerreros, chamanes y travestis: indicios de homosexualidad entre los exóticos* (Barcelona: Tusquets Editores, 1984), p. 41; my translation.

69. Walter L. Williams, *The Spirit and the Flesh: Sexual Diversity in American Indian Culture* (Boston: Beacon Press, 1986), pp. 41–42.

70. Eliade, *Shamanism*, p. 352.

71. Hutchinson, *Ecstatic Whitman*, pp. 61–62.

72. Pablo Neruda, *Stones of the Sky*, section VIII, trans. James Nolan (Port Townsend, Wash.: Copper Canyon Press, 1987), p. 24.

73. Rodríguez Monegal, *Neruda*, p. 314.

74. Osorio, "El problema," p. 183.

75. Francisco Ferrandiz, "Dimensions of Nationalism in a Venezuelan Possession Cult: The Crystallization of an Oral Tradition," *Kroeber Anthropological Society Papers* (University of California at Berkeley), nos. 75–76 (1992), pp. 36–37.

76. Halifax, *Shamanic Voices*, p. 15.

77. Eliade, *Shamanism*, p. 123.

78. According to Alfred Métraux, *Religions et magies indiennes d'Amérique du Sud* (Paris: Gallimard, 1967), p. 233, the Araucanian *machis* at the time of Chief Caupolicán (1520), the era in which Neruda sets this narrative, would have been berdaches. Although women *machis* presently predominate, they first

Notes

24. Pablo Neruda, "Only Death," in *Residence on Earth*, trans. Donald D. Walsh (New York: New Directions, 1973), p. 103.

25. Eliade, *Shamanism*, pp. 442–43.

26. Neruda, "Ritual of My Legs," in *Residence*, p. 75.

27. Neruda, "Single Gentlemen," p. 71, and "Walking Around," p. 121, in *Residence*.

28. Neruda, "The Southern Ocean," in *Residence*, p. 117.

29. Lommel, *Shamanism*, pp. 49–50.

30. George B. Hutchinson, *The Ecstatic Whitman: Literary Shamanism and the Crisis of the Union* (Columbus: Ohio State University Press, 1986), p. 60.

31. Kalweit, *Dreamtime and Inner Space*, p. 4. "Dying persons, after various acoustic sensations, suddenly find themselves in a strange situation: They are able to see their bodies from the outside, as it were; they feel themselves separate from their bodies, weightless, perhaps even floating just under the ceiling, gliding along and sometimes even passing through solid objects. They hear and see everything that happens around their bodies. . . . With lightning speed they move from one place to another and feel themselves transposed into a state in which time and space no longer have any meaning."

32. Eliade, *Shamanism*, p. 355. This ritual was prevalent among several North American Indian tribes, and remains among the few authentic myths incorporated into Longfellow's "Hiawatha," in which the dead body of the protagonist is set out upon the river in a funerary canoe.

33. Hutchinson, *Ecstatic Whitman*, pp. 63–65. Hutchinson here cites Dr. Bucke's edition of Whitman's "Notes and Fragments," Items 38 and 40. One must agree with Hutchinson's assessment of Whitman's deletions, that "the image of the enslaved demon who will either be released or will destroy his oppressor makes for an interesting premonition of the Civil War" and that the exclusion of the whale and its preceding destructive, fire-bringing context "leaves a gap at the very climax of the poem; it is as if Dante had cut the fourth round of Cocytus—Canto 34—out of his Inferno."

34. Halifax, *Shaman*, p. 7.

35. Eliade, *Shamanism*, p. 206.

36. Ibid., p. 477.

37. Ibid., p. 467.

38. Joseph Campbell, *The Flight of the Wild Gander* (South Bend, In: Regnery/Gateway, 1979), p. 165-66.

39. Pablo Neruda, *Stones of the Sky*, trans. James Nolan (Port Townsend, Wash.: Copper Canyon Press, 1987).

40. Robert Bly, "Looking for Dragon Smoke," *The Seventies* 1 (Spring 1972), p. 3.

41. Bly, "The Three Brains," *The Seventies* 1 (Spring 1972), pp. 61-6.

were introduced during the eighteenth century due to the growing influence of Christian morality.

79. Breitwieser, "Who Speaks in Whitman's Poems?" p. 130.

80. See Richard Bridgman, introduction to Walt Whitman, *Leaves of Grass,* facsimile of the first edition (San Francisco: Chandler Publishing Company, 1968). Based on its unity of content and appearance, Bridgman calls the first edition "the green book *par excellence*" (p. xxx). In the notes to his translation of *Canto general,* Jack Schmitt emphasizes Neruda's concern with botanical life by identifying the scientific names of many of the numerous trees and plants to which Neruda refers in the text.

81. See Luis Eduardo Luna, *Vegetalismo: Shamanism among the Mestizo Population of the Peruvian Amazon,* Stockholm Studies in Comparative Religion no. 27 (Stockholm: Acta Universitatis Stockholmienis, n.d.).

82. Robert Graves, *The White Goddess: A Historical Grammar of Poetic Myth* (New York: Farrar, Straus and Giroux, 1948). See particularly the two chapters on the tree alphabet, pp. 165–204.

83. Emerson, "Poet," p. 231.

84. Eliade, *Shamanism,* p. 510.

85. Halifax, *Shaman,* p. 88; photographs *en face* of both the Mapuche and Lakota ceremonies.

Chapter 5

1. Pablo Neruda, "We Are Many" ("Somos muchos"), in *Extravagaria,* trans. Alastair Reid (New York: Farrar, Straus and Giroux, 1974), p. 101.

2. Pablo Neruda, *Memoirs,* trans. Hardie St. Martin (New York: Farrar, Straus and Giroux, 1977), p. 293.

3. Pablo Neruda, "End of the Party" ("Fin de fiesta"), an imitation by James Nolan, *New Orleans Review* 14, no. 3 (Fall 1987), 89.

4. Andreas Lommel, *Shamanism: The Beginnings of Art,* trans. Michael Bullock (New York: McGraw Hill Book Company, 1967), p. 84.

5. Géza Róheim, as quoted in Joseph Campbell, *The Hero with a Thousand Faces* (Princeton, N.J.: Princeton University Press, 1968), p. 101. For a discussion of the parallels between magical and schizophrenic thinking, see Géza Róheim, *Magic and Schizophrenia* (New York: International University Press, 1955). Cf. note 9, below.

6. Joan Halifax, *Shaman: The Wounded Healer* (New York: Crossroad, 1982), p. 6.

7. Mircea Eliade, *Shamanism: Archaic Techniques of Ecstasy,* trans. Willard Trask (New York: Harper and Row, 1959), p. 5.

8. Campbell, *Hero,* p. 35.

9. Halifax, *Shaman,* p. 7. Halifax cites John Weir Perry's *The Far Side of Madness,* drawing a parallel between the stages of what Perry calls "the renewal of the self" and the shamanic voyage. R. D. Laing proposes the classic interpretation of schizophrenia as a psychic journey through the death and rebirth of the ego, a journey that contains detailed correspondences to the shamanic voyage, in *The Politics of Experience* (New York: Pantheon Books, 1967).

10. Holger Kalweit, *Dreamtime and Inner Space: The World of the Shaman,* trans. Werner Wunsche (Boston: Shambala, 1988), pp. 3–20. Kalweit argues that the shaman's rigorous training and almost fatal deprivations "enable him to intentionally enduce in himself a state of death, during which his soul leaves his body" (p. 11). He then compares the stages of the shamanic voyage to the Near-Death Experiences studied by such thanatologists as Kenneth Ring writing in *Life at Death* (New York 1980) and in the journal *Anabiosis: The Journal of Near-Death.* His argument is convincing that the patterns of experience reported by revived survivors of clinical death resemble the patterns that anthropologists attribute to the shamanic voyage.

11. F. O. Matthiessen, *American Renaissance: Art and Expression in the Age of Emerson and Whitman* (New York: Oxford University Press, 1941), pp. 573–74.

12. Whitman, as quoted in Matthiessen, *American Renaissance,* p. 539–40.

13. Juan Villegas, *Estructuras míticas y arquetipos en el Canto general de Neruda* (Barcelona: Editorial Planeta, 1976), p. 54; my translation. Villegas presents a mythic interpretation of *Canto general* following the model of Campbell's monomyth.

14. Ake Hultkrantz, *The North American Indian Orpheus Tradition* (Stockholm: Ethnographical Museum of Sweden Monograph Series, 1957), p. 85. For variations of the shamanic descent and ascent in Latin American Indian literature, see *First Fire: Central and South American Indian Poetry,* ed. Hugh Fox (New York: Anchor Press/Doubleday, 1978).

15. Halifax, *Shaman,* p. 7.

16. Edwin H. Miller, *Walt Whitman's Poetry* (New York: New York University Press, 1968), p. 72.

17. John Felstiner, *Translating Neruda: The Way to Macchu Picchu* (Stanford, Calif.: Stanford University Press, 1980), p. 159.

18. Halifax, *Shaman,* p. 9.

19. Eliade, *Shamanism,* p. 419.

20. Lommel, *Shamanism,* p. 31.

21. Kalweit, *Dreamtime and Inner Space,* pp. 112–26.

22. Lommel, *Shamanism,* pp. 129–33.

23. Kalweit, *Dreamtime and Inner Space,* p. 11.

Notes

42. Neruda, "Alberto Rojas Jiménez Comes Flying," in *Residence,* p. 181.

43. Pablo Neruda, *Art of Birds,* trans. Jack Schmitt (Austin: University of Texas Press, 1985), p. 50.

44. Neruda, "The Pablo Bird," in *Art of Birds,* p. 84.

45. Eliade, *Shamanism,* pp. 474 and 156. Eliade's section on "Shamans and Smiths" (pp. 470–74) lays an important foundation in terms of Iron Age anthropology for understanding the Prometheus myth as well as the Vulcanic imagery incorporated into the Christian concept of Hell.

46. Neruda, "Flamingo," in *Art of Birds,* p. 38.

47. Eliade, *Shamanism,* p. 133.

48. Lommel, *Shamanism,* p. 137. In this section (pp. 137–40), Lommel examines "Shamanism and the primeval forms of the theatre," pointing out that the shaman's "histrionic achievement lies in his almost complete identification with the 'images' in and through his trance," elucidating Whitman's theatrical presentation of his vertical voyage: "I am the actor, the actress . . ." (1:426).

49. Halifax, *Shaman,* p. 26.

50. Ibid., p. 24.

51. See Hiram Bingham, *Lost City of the Andes: The Story of Macchu Picchu and Its Builders* (New York: Atheneum, 1973), pp. 181–84 and p. 116, plate. The bellicose chant of the Incan sun priests, upon welcoming their Great Divinity at dawn, was in part: "O Sun! Thou who has said let there be Cuzco and Tampu, grant that these children may conquer all other people. We beseech thee that thy children the Incas may always be conquerors, since it is for this that thou has created them" (p. 120). Neruda's identification with the Incan sun is not inconsistent with the militancy of his tone.

52. Emir Rodríguez Monegal, *Neruda: El viajero inmóvil* (Caracas: Monte Avila Editores, C.A., 1977), p. 332; all quotations appear in my translation.

53. Ibid., p. 465.

54. See Mircea Eliade, *Cosmos and History: The Myth of the Eternal Return,* trans. Willard R. Trask (New York: Harper and Row Torchbooks, 1960).

Epilogue

1. Quentin Anderson, *The Imperial Self: An Essay in American Literary and Cultural History* (New York: Alfred A. Knopf, 1971), p. 136.

2. Louis Simpson, "Lines Written near San Francisco," in *At the End of the Open Road* (Middletown, Conn.: Wesleyan University Press, 1963), p. 69.

3. Pablo Neruda, *Incitación al Nixonicidio y alabanza de la revolución Chilena* (Lima: Editorial Causachun, 1973), p. 11; my translation.

4. Pablo Neruda, *Memoirs,* trans. Hardie St. Martin (New York: Farrar, Straus and Giroux, 1977), p. 350.

5. Michael Castro, *Interpreting the Indian: Twentieth Century Poets and the Native American* (Albuquerque: University of New Mexico Press, 1983), p. 33.

6. As quoted in James Mooney, *The Ghost-Dance Religion and the Sioux Outbreak of 1890* (Chicago: University of Chicago Press, 1965), p. 284. Mooney was an ethnologist present on the reservations during the Ghost Dance era, and his book contains an extensive selection of the songs, both in the original languages and in his translations.

7. Julio Cortázar, "Neruda among Us," trans. Frank Menchaca, in *Pablo Neruda: Modern Critical Views,* ed. Harold Bloom (New York: Chelsea House, 1989), p. 89.

Bibliography

I

Whitman and the North American Background

Allen, Gay Wilson. *The Solitary Singer: A Critical Biography of Walt Whitman*. Chicago: University of Chicago Press, 1985.

Anderson, Quentin. *The Imperial Self: An Essay in American Literary and Cultural History*. New York: Alfred A. Knopf, 1971.

Antler. *Last Words*. New York: Ballantine Books, 1986.

Aspiz, Harold. *Walt Whitman and the Body Beautiful*. Urbana: University of Illinois Press, 1980.

Beaver, Harold. "The Transcendental Savage." *Times Literary Supplement*, 6 October, 1978.

Bernstein, Michael. *The Tale of the Tribe: Ezra Pound and the Modern Verse Epic*. Princeton, N.J.: Princeton University Press, 1980.

Breitwieser, Robert Mitchell. "Who Speaks in Whitman's Poems?" In *The American Renaissance: New Dimensions,* ed. Harry R. Garvin and Peter C. Carafiol, pp. 121–43. Lewisburg: Bucknell University Press, 1983.

Bridgman, Richard. *The Colloquial Style in America*. New York: Oxford University Press, 1966.

Cady, Edwin H., and Louis J. Budd, eds. *On Whitman: The Best from American Literature*. Durham: Duke University Press, 1987.

Callow, Philip. *From Noon to Starry Night: A Life of Walt Whitman*. Chicago: Ivan R. Dee, 1992.

Carpenter, Edward. *Days with Walt Whitman: With Some Notes on His Life and Works*. London: George Allen & Unwin, 1906.

Castro, Michael. *Interpreting the Indian: Twentieth Century Poets and the Native American*. Albuquerque: University of New Mexico Press, 1983.

Clark, Leadie M. *Walt Whitman's Concept of the Common Man*. New York: Philosophical Library, 1955.

Dickinson, Emily. *The Complete Poems,* ed. Thomas H. Johnson. Cambridge: Harvard University Press, 1955.

Bibliography

Donaldson, Thomas. *Walt Whitman the Man*. New York: Francis P. Harper, 1896.

Drinnon, Richard. *Facing West: The Metaphysics of Indian-Hating and Empire-Building*. Minneapolis: University of Minnesota Press, 1980.

Emerson, Ralph Waldo. *The Complete Works of Ralph Waldo Emerson*. University ed., 9 vols. New York: Sully and Kleinteich, 1883.

———. *Selections from Ralph Waldo Emerson*, ed. Stephen E. Whicher. Boston: Houghton Mifflin Company, 1957.

Fiedler, Leslie A. *The Return of the Vanishing American*. New York: Stein and Day, 1968.

Flint, F. S. "*Imagisme*." *Poetry: A Magazine of Verse* 1 (March 1913), 198.

Grimes, Larry D. "Walt Whitman's Voice." *Walt Whitman Quarterly Review* 9, no. 3 (Winter 1992), 125–33.

Grimes, William. "On Tape, Scholars Think They Hear Walt Whitman Reading." *The New York Times,* 16 March 1992, sec. B, pp. 1–2.

Hindus, Milton, ed. *Walt Whitman: The Critical Heritage*. London: Routledge and Kegan Paul, 1971.

Hollis, C. Carroll. *Language and Style in Leaves of Grass*. Baton Rouge: Louisiana State University Press, 1983.

Hutchinson, George B. *The Ecstatic Whitman: Literary Shamanism and the Crisis of Union*. Columbus: Ohio State University Press, 1986.

Jaffe, Harold. "Bucke's *Walt Whitman:* A Collaboration." *Walt Whitman Review* 15 (1969), 190–94.

Jarrell, Randall. "Reflections on Wallace Stevens." In *Wallace Stevens: A Critical Anthology,* ed. Irvin Ehrenpreis, pp. 199–211. Middlesex: Penguin, 1972.

Kaplan, Justin. *Walt Whitman: A Life*. New York: Bantam Books, 1980.

Keiser, Albert. *The Indian in American Literature*. New York: Oxford University Press, 1933.

Kramer, Aaron. *The Prophetic Tradition in American Poetry, 1835–1900*. Rutherford: Fairleigh Dickinson University Press, 1968.

Lawrence, D. H. *Studies in Classic American Literature*. Middlesex: Penguin Books, 1961.

Lewis, R. W. B. "The New Adam: Whitman." In *Whitman: A Collection of Critical Essays,* ed. Roy Harvey Pearce, pp. 107–18. Englewood Cliffs, N.J.: Prentice Hall, 1962.

Lindsay, Vachel. *Selected Poems*. New York: Macmillan, 1963.

Longfellow, Samuel, ed. *The Life of Henry Wadsworth Longfellow*. 3 vols. New York: Houghton, Mifflin and Company, 1896.

Martin, Robert K., ed. *The Continuing Presence of Walt Whitman: The Life after the Life*. Iowa City: University of Iowa Press, 1992.

Bibliography

————, ed. *The Homosexual Tradition in American Poetry*. Austin: University of Texas Press, 1979.

Matthiessen, F. O. *American Renaissance: Art and Expression in the Age of Emerson and Whitman*. New York: Oxford University Press, 1941.

Miller, Edwin Haviland, ed. *A Century of Whitman Criticism*. Bloomington: Indiana University Press, 1969.

Miller, James E., Jr. *The American Quest for a Supreme Fiction: Whitman's Legacy in the Personal Epic*. Chicago: University of Chicago Press, 1979.

————. *Walt Whitman's Poetry*. New York: New York University Press, 1968.

Pearce, Roy Harvey. *Savagism and Civilization: A Study of the Indian and the American Mind*. Baltimore: Johns Hopkins Press, 1967.

Perlman, Jim, et al., eds. *Walt Whitman: The Measure of His Song*. Minneapolis: Holy Cow! Press, 1981.

Pound, Ezra. *The Selected Poems of Ezra Pound*. New York: New Directions, 1957.

Rahv, Philip. "Paleface and Redskin." In *Essays on Literature and Politics, 1932–1972,* ed. Arabel J. Porter and Andrew J. Duosin. Boston: Houghton Mifflin Co., 1978.

Rothenberg, Jerome, and George Quasha, eds. *America a Prophecy: A New Reading of American Poetry*. New York: Vintage Books, 1974.

Sandburg, Carl. "Aboriginal Poetry." *Poetry: A Magazine of Verse* 9, no. 5 (February 1917), 253–56.

Sayre, Robert F. *Thoreau and the American Indians*. Princeton, N.J.: Princeton University Press, 1977.

Shively, Charley, ed. *Calamus Lovers: Walt Whitman's Working Class Camerados.* San Francisco: Gay Sunshine Press, 1987.

Simpson, Louis. *At the End of the Open Road*. Middletown, Conn.: Wesleyan University Press, 1963.

————. *The Character of the Poet*. Ann Arbor: University of Michigan Press, 1986.

Stevens, Wallace. *The Collected Poems*. New York: Vintage Books, 1954.

von Schiller, Friedrich. *Naive and Sentimental Poetry,* trans. Julius A. Elias. New York: Friedrick Ungar Publishing Co., 1966.

Waldman, Anne. *Fast Speaking Woman*. San Francisco: City Lights Books, 1975.

Whitman, Walt. *An American Primer*. Facsimile edition, ed. Horace Traubel. Boston: Small, Maynard and Company, 1904.

————. *The Collected Writing of Walt Whitman: The Correspondence,* ed. Edwin Haviland Miller. 6 vols. New York: University of New York Press, 1961–1977.

Bibliography

————.*The Collected Writing of Walt Whitman: Prose,* ed. Floyd Stovall. 2 vols. New York: New York University Press, 1963–64.

————. *The Complete Writings of Walt Whitman,* ed. Richard M. Bucke, Thomas B. Harned and Horace L. Traubel. 9 vols. New York: G. P. Putnam's Sons, 1902.

————. *Leaves of Grass: Comprehensive Reader's Edition,* ed. Harold W. Blodgett and Sculley Bradley. New York: New York University Press, 1965.

————. *Leaves of Grass: A Textual Variorum of the Printed Poems,* ed. Sculley Bradley et al. 3 vols. New York: New York University Press, 1980.

————. *Leaves of Grass.* Facsimile of 1st ed., ed. Richard Bridgman. San Francisco: Chandler Publishing Company, 1968.

————. *Leaves of Grass and Selected Prose,* ed. Lawrence Buell. New York: Modern Library, 1981.

————. *The Uncollected Poetry and Prose of Walt Whitman,* ed. Emory Holloway. 2 vols. New York: Doubleday, Page and Company, 1921.

————. *Whitman's Manuscripts: Leaves of Grass (1860),* ed. Fredson Bowers. Chicago: University of Chicago Press, 1955.

————. *The Works of Walt Whitman,* ed Malcolm Cowley. 2 vols. New York: Funk and Wagnalls, 1968.

Wilentz, Sean. *Chants Democratic: New York City and the Rise of the American Working Class,* 1788–1850. New York: New York University Press, 1984.

Williams, Oscar, ed. *A Little Treasury of American Poetry: The Chief Poets from Colonial Times to the Present Day.* New York: Charles Scribner's Sons, 1948.

Williams, William Carlos. *In the American Grain.* Norfolk, Conn.: New Directions, 1925.

Wordsworth, William. "Preface to *Lyrical Ballads.*" In *The Norton Anthology of English Literature,* vol. II, ed. M. H. Abrams. 5th ed., pp. 157–70. New York: W. W. Norton and Company, 1986.

Wright, George. "The Lyric Present: Simple Present Verbs in English Poems." *Publications of the Modern Language Association* 89 (1974), 563–79.

Young, Philip. "Pocahontas, the Mother of Us All." *Kenyon Review* 24, no. 3 (Summer 1962), 391–415.

II

Neruda and the Latin American Background

Aguirre, Margarita. *Las vidas de Pablo Neruda.* Buenos Aires: Grijalbro, S.A., 1973.

Bibliography

Alazraki, Jaime. *Poética y poesía de Pablo Neruda*. Bloomington: Indiana University Press, 1981.

Alegría, Fernando. "¿Cuál Whitman? Borges, Lorca y Neruda." *Texto crítico* 7, nos. 222–23 (July–December 1981), 3–12.

———. "The Whitman Myth." *Americas,* (February 1954), 10.

———. *Walt Whitman en Hispanoamérica*. Mexico: Colección Studium, 1954.

Alonso, J. M. "Neftalí Ricardo Reyes Invents Pablo Neruda." *Review of the Center for Inter-American Relations* (Winter 1971-Spring 1972), 33–38.

Baines, John M. *Revolution in Peru: Mariátegui and the Myth*. University: University of Alabama Press, 1972.

Bellini, Giuseppe. *Historia de la literatura Hispanoamericana* Madrid: Editorial Castalia, 1985.

Bizzarro, Salvatore. *Pablo Neruda: All Poets the Poet*. Metuchen, N.J.: Scarecrow Press, 1979.

Bloom, Harold, ed. *Pablo Neruda: Modern Critical Views*. New York: Chelsea House Publishers, 1989.

Bly, Robert. "Looking for Dragon Smoke" and "The Three Brains." In *The Seventies* 1 (Spring 1972), 3–8; 61–69.

———, ed. *Neruda and Vallejo: Selected Poems,* trans. Robert Bly et al. Boston: Beacon Press, 1971.

Borges, Jorge Luis. *Inquisiciones*. Buenos Aires: Emecé, 1960.

Brotherston, Gordon. *Latin American Poetry: Origins and Presence*. Cambridge: Cambridge University Press, 1975.

Cardenal, Ernesto. *Homage to the American Indians,* trans. Monique and Carlos Altschul. Baltimore: Johns Hopkins University Press, 1973.

Celaya, Gabriel. "Pablo Neruda, poeta del Tercer Día de la creación." In *Pablo Neruda,* ed. Emir Rodríguez Monegal and Enrico Mario Santi, pp. 15–20. Madrid: Taurus Ediciones, 1985.

Chevigny, Bell Gale, and Gari Laguardia, eds. *Reinventing the Americas: Comparative Studies of Literature of the United States and Spanish America*. Cambridge: Cambridge University Press, 1986.

Darío, Rubén. *Poesías completas*. Madrid: Aguilar, 1968.

de Costa, René. *The Poetry of Pablo Neruda*. Cambridge, Mass.: Harvard University Press, 1979.

Durán, Manuel, and Margery Safir. *Earth Tones: The Poetry of Pablo Neruda*. Bloomington: Indiana University Press, 1981.

Felstiner, John. *Translating Neruda: The Way to Macchu Picchu*. Stanford, Calif.: Stanford University Press, 1980.

Figueroa, Esperanza. "Pablo Neruda en inglés." *Revista Iberoamericana,* nos. 82–83 (enero-junio 1973), 301–47.

Bibliography

Florit, Eugenio, and José Olivio Jiménez, eds. *La poesía Hispanoamericana desde el modernismo.* New York: Meredith Corporation, 1968.

García Lorca, Federico. "Presentación de Pablo Neruda." In *Obras completas.* 14th ed. Madrid: Aguilar, 1968.

García Márquez, Gabriel, and Mario Vargas Llosa. *La novela en América Latina.* Lima: Universidad Nacional de Ingeniera, 1967.

Granzotto, Gianni. *Christopher Columbus,* trans. Stephen Sartelli. Norman, Oklahoma: University of Oklahoma Press, 1987.

Guibert, Rita. *Seven Voices,* trans. Frances Partridge. New York: Alfred A. Knopf, 1973.

Jiménez, José Olivio. *Antología de la poesía Hispanoamericana contemporánea 1914–1970.* Madrid: Editorial Alianza. 1984.

Lévy, I. J. and Juan Loveluck, eds. *Simpósio Pablo Neruda.* University of South Carolina-Las Americas. Long Island City, N.Y.: L.A. Publishing Company, 1975.

Loyola, Hernán. "Pablo Neruda: Itinerario de una poesía." In *Pablo Neruda: Antología esencial,* ed. Hernán Loyola. 3d ed. Buenos Aires: Editorial Losada, S.A., 1978.

Ludmer, Josefina. *Cien años de soledad: Una interpretación.* Buenos Aires: Editorial Tiempo Contemporáneo, 1972.

Martí, José. "Nuestra América." In *Obras completas de Martí,* vol. I. La Havana: Editorial Trópico, 1939.

———. "The Poet Walt Whitman," trans. Arnold Chapman. In *Walt Whitman Abroad,* ed. Gay Wilson Allen. Syracuse, N.Y.: Syracuse University Press, 1955.

Neruda, Pablo. "Algo sobre mi poesía y vida." *Aurora* (Santiago), 1 (julio 1954), 10–21.

———. *Art of Birds,* trans. Jack Schmitt. Austin: University of Texas Press, 1985.

———. *Canto general.* Prologue and chronology by Fernando Alegría. Caracas: Biblioteca Ayacucho, 1981.

———. *Canto general,* trans. Jack Schmitt. Berkeley: University of California Press, 1991.

———. *Canto general.* Barcelona: Seix Barral, S.A., 1983.

———. *Una casa en la arena.* With photographs by Sergio Larrain. Barcelona: Editorial Lumen, 1966.

———. "End of the Party" ("Fin de fiesta," from *Cantos ceremoniales*). Imitation by James Nolan. *New Orleans Review* 14, no. 3 (Fall 1987), 84–89.

———. *Extravagaria,* trans. Alastair Reid. New York: Farrar, Straus and Giroux, 1974.

Bibliography

————. *Fully Empowered,* trans. Alastair Reid. New York: Farrar, Straus and Giroux, 1975.

————. *Incitación al Nixonicidio y alabanza de la revolución Chilena.* Lima: Editorial Causachun, 1973.

————. *Isla Negra: A Notebook,* trans. Alastair Reid. New York: Farrar, Straus and Giroux, 1981.

————. *Memoirs,* trans. Hardie St. Martin. New York: Farrar, Straus and Giroux, 1977.

————. *Obras completas,* 4th ed. 3 vols. Buenos Aires: Editorial Losada, 1973.

————. *Passions and Impressions,* trans. Margaret Sayers Peden. New York: Farrar, Straus and Giroux, 1983.

————. *Residence on Earth,* trans. Donald D. Walsh. New York: New Directions, 1973.

————. *Still Another Day (Aun),* trans. William O'Daly. Port Townsend, Wash.: Copper Canyon Press, 1984.

————. *Stones of the Sky,* trans. James Nolan. Port Townsend, Wash.: Copper Canyon Press, 1987.

Paz, Octavio. *Children of the Mire: Modern Poetry from Romanticism to the Avant-Garde,* trans. Rachel Phillips. Cambridge, Mass.: Harvard University Press, 1974.

————. *The Labyrinth of Solitude: Life and Thought in Mexico,* trans. Lysander Kemp. New York: Grove Press, 1961.

Rodman, Selden. *Tongues of Fallen Angels.* New York: New Directions, 1974.

Reiss, Frank. *The Word and the Stone: Language and Imagery in Neruda's Canto general.* London: Oxford University Press, 1972.

Rimbaud, Arthur. "Lettres dites du 'voyant.'" In *Poesies,* pp. 199–206. Paris: Gallimard, 1973.

Rodríguez Monegal, Emir. *Neruda: El viajero inmóvil.* Caracas: Monte Avila Editores, C.A., 1977.

Sabat Ercasty, Carlos. *Poemas del hombre: Libro del mar.* Montevideo: n.p., 1922.

Salmon, Russell and Julia Lesage. "Stones and Birds: Consistency and Change in Pablo Neruda." *Hispania* 60 (May 1977), 224–40.

Santos Chocano, José. "Panorama lírico (a través de un recital poético." *La Prensa* (Buenos Aires), 12 March 1933.

Sartre, Jean-Paul. *No Exit and Other Plays,* trans. Stuart Gilbert. New York: Vintage Books, 1949.

Silva Castro, Raúl. *Pablo Neruda.* Santiago, Chile: Editorial Universitaria, 1964.

Spitzer, Leo. *La enumeración caótica en la poesía moderna,* trans. Raimundo

Bibliography

Lida. Buenos Aires: Colección de Estudios Estilísticos, 1945.

Teitelboim, Volodia. *Neruda*. Madrid: Ediciones Michay, S.A., 1984.

Vidal, Hernán. *Literatura Hispanoamericana e ideología liberal: Surgimiento y crisis*. Buenos Aires: Ediciones Hispamerica, 1976.

Villegas, Juan. *Estructuras míticas y arquetipos en el Canto general de Neruda*. Barcelona: Editorial Planeta, 1976.

Whitman, Walt. "Pasto de llamas," trans. Pablo Neruda. In *El aviso de escarmentados del año que acaba y escaramiento para el que empieza de 1935*. Madrid: Cruz y Raya, 1935.

Yurkievich, Saúl. *Fundadores de la nueva poesía latinoamericana*. Barcelona: Editorial Ariel, S.A., 1984.

III

American Indian Poetics and the Anthropological Background

Astrov, Margot, ed. *The Winged Serpent: American Indian Prose and Poetry*. Boston: Beacon Books, 1992.

Austin, Mary. *The American Rhythm: Studies and Re-expressions of Amerindian Songs*. New York: Cooper Square Publishers, 1970.

————. "Medicine Songs: Translated from Indian originals." *Everybody's Magazine* 31 (September 1914), 409–18.

Bierhorst, John, ed. *The Sacred Path: Spells, Prayers and Power Songs of the American Indians*. New York: William Morrow and Company, 1983.

Bingham, Hiram. *Lost City of the Incas: The Story of Machu Picchu and Its Builders*. New York: Atheneum, 1973.

Brandon, William, ed. *The Magic World: American Indian Songs and Poems*. New York: William Morrow and Company, 1971.

Brown, Joseph Epes. "The Roots of Renewal." In *Seeing with a Native Eye: Essays on Native American Religion*, ed. Walter Holden Capps, pp. 25–34. New York: Harper and Row, 1976

Campbell, Joseph. *The Flight of the Wild Gander*. South Bend, Ind.: Regnery/Gateway, 1979.

————. *The Hero with a Thousand Faces*. Princeton, N.J.: Princeton University Press, 1968.

————. *The Masks of the Gods: Primitive Mythology*. New York: Viking Press, 1969.

Cardín, Alberto. *Guerreros, chamanes y travestis: indicios de homosexualidad entre los exóticos*. Barcelona: Tusquets Editores, 1984.

Bibliography

Cassirer, Ernst. *An Essay on Man: An Introduction to a Philosophy of Human Culture.* New Haven: Yale University Press, 1944.

Durkheim, Emile, and Marcel Mauss. *Primitive Classification,* trans. Rodney Needham. Chicago: University of Chicago Press, 1963.

Eliade, Mircea. *Cosmos and History: The Myth of the Eternal Return,* trans. Willard Trask. New York: Harper and Row Torchbooks, 1960.

———. *The Sacred and the Profane: The Nature of Religion,* trans. Willard Trask. New York: Harper and Row, 1959.

———. *Shamanism: Archaic Techniques of Ecstasy,* trans. Willard Trask. Princeton, N.J.: Princeton University Press, 1964.

Estrada, Alvaro. *María Sabina: Her Life and Chants,* trans. Henry Munn. Santa Barbara: Ross-Erikson, 1981.

Ferrandiz, Francisco. "Dimensions of Nationalism in a Venezuelan Possession Cult: The Crystallization of an Oral Tradition." *Kroeber Anthropological Society Papers* (University of California at Berkeley), nos. 75–76 (1992), 28–47.

Finnegan, Ruth. *Oral Poetry: Its Nature, Significance and Social Context.* Cambridge: Cambridge University Press, 1977.

Fox, Hugh, ed. *First Fire: Central and South American Indian Poetry.* New York: Anchor Press/Doubleday, 1978.

Graves, Robert. *The White Goddess: A Historical Grammar of Poetic Myth.* New York: Farrar, Straus and Giroux, 1948.

Halifax, Joan. *Shaman: The Wounded Healer.* New York: Crossroads, 1982.

———. *Shamanic Voices: A Survey of Visionary Narratives.* New York: E. P. Dutton, 1979.

Highwater, Jamake. *The Primal Mind: Vision and Reality in Indian America.* New York: Harper and Row, 1981.

Hultkrantz, Ake. *The North American Indian Orpheus Tradition.* Stockholm: Ethnographical Museum of Sweden Monograph Series, 1957.

Kalweit, Holger. *Dreamtime and Inner Space: The World of the Shaman,* trans. Werner Wunsche. Boston: Shambala, 1988.

Kroeber, Karl, ed. *Traditional Literatures of the American Indian: Texts and Interpretations.* Lincoln: University Nebraska Press, 1981.

Laing, Ronald David. *The Politics of Experience.* New York: Parthenon Books, 1967.

Lévi-Strauss, Claude. *The Savage Mind.* Chicago: University of Chicago Press, 1962.

Lincoln, Kenneth. "Native American Literatures." In *Smoothing the Ground: Essays on Native American Oral Tradition,* ed. Brian Swann. Berkeley: University of California Press, 1983.

Bibliography

Liu, James J. Y. *The Art of Chinese Poetry*. Chicago: University of Chicago Press, 1962.

Lommel, Andreas. *Shamanism: The Beginnings of Art,* trans. Michael Bullock. New York: McGraw Hill Book Company, 1967.

Luna, Luis Eduardo. *Vegetalismo: Shamanism among the Mestizo Population of the Peruvian Amazon*. Stockholm Studies in Comparative Religion, no. 27. Stockholm: Acta Universitatis Stockholmienis, n.d.

Métraux, Alfred. *Religions et magies indiennes d'Amérique du Sud*. Paris: Gallimard, 1967.

Momaday, N. Scott. *Angle of Geese and Other Poems*. New York: David R. Godine, 1974.

Mooney, James. *The Ghost-Dance Religion and the Sioux Outbreak of 1890*. Chicago: University of Chicago Press, 1965.

Niatum, Duane, ed. *Harper's Anthology of 20th Century Native American Poetry*. San Francisco: Harper and Row, 1988.

Róheim, Géza. *Magic and Schizophrenia*. New York: International Universities Press, 1955.

Rothenberg, Jerome, ed. *Shaking the Pumpkin: Traditional Poetry of the Indian North Americas*. Albuquerque: University of New Mexico Press, 1991.

——, ed. *Technicians of the Sacred: A Range of Poetries from Africa, America, Asia, Europe and Oceania*. Berkeley: University of California Press, 1985.

Rothenberg, Jerome and Diane, eds. *Symposium of the Whole: A Range of Discourse toward an Ethnopoetics*. Berkeley: University of California Press, 1983.

Sherzer, Joel, and Anthony Woodbury, eds. *Native American Discourse: Poetics and Rhetoric*. Cambridge, Massachusetts: Cambridge University Press, 1987.

Swann, Brian, ed. *Smoothing the Ground: Essays on Native American Oral Tradition*. Berkeley: University of California Press, 1983.

Turner, Victor. *The Ritual Process: Structure and Anti-Structure*. Chicago: Aldine Publishing Company, 1969.

Weatherford, Jack. *Indian Givers: How The Indians of the Americas Transformed the World*. New York: Fawcett Columbine, 1988.

——. *Native Roots: How the Indians Enriched America*. New York: Fawcett Columbine, 1991.

Williams, Walter L. *The Spirit and the Flesh: Sexual Diversity in American Indian Culture*. Boston: Beacon Press, 1986.

Index

Leaves of Grass and *Canto general* are mentioned many times in the text but are indexed sparingly. "Song of Myself" is referenced only when an excerpt of it appears in the text.

Index

Index

Index

Index

Index

Index

Index

Index

Index